Inside the Jury

INSIDE
THE JURY

Reid Hastie
Steven D. Penrod
Nancy Pennington

Harvard University Press
Cambridge, Massachusetts
and London, England
1983

Copyright © 1983 by the President and Fellows
of Harvard College
All rights reserved
Printed in the United States of America
10 9 8 7 6 5 4 3 2 1

This book is printed on acid-free paper,
and its binding materials have
been chosen for strength and durability.

Library of Congress Cataloging in Publication Data
Hastie, Reid.
    Inside the jury.

    Bibliography: p.
    Includes index.
    1. Jury—United States.   I. Penrod, Steven.
II. Pennington, Nancy.   III. Title.
KF8972.H3   1983   347.73′752   83-10694
ISBN 0-674-45525-8   347.307752

To the memory of
Gordon F. Pulsifer
Chief Jury Pool Officer
Middlesex County, Massachusetts

Advisor, Critic, Friend

ACKNOWLEDGMENTS

The research program reported in this volume was long and expensive. It is impossible to thank all of the people and institutions who contributed to its successful completion. Only the major contributors can be listed here, but the authors are also indebted to dozens of supporters who remain unnamed.

Three foundations provided funding for the research: the National Science Foundation, the James Marshall Fund, and the National Institute for Law Enforcement and Criminal Justice. Harvard University and Northwestern University contributed by providing congenial colleagues, excellent facilities, and institutional atmospheres in which hard, protracted intellectual work was possible.

Several people were directly involved in conducting the research. Carol Augenblick, William Cole, Hilary Coons, Joan Dobrof, Jacob Ostrofsky, Steven Rosenblum, Daniel Stefek, and Judith Sykes served as research assistants on the project for six months or longer. Zoe Forbes, Marcia Penrod, and Charlotte Pieters edited and typed portions of the manuscript. Robert Des Maisons and his staff at Harvard Video Services provided technical assistance in creating the videotaped stimulus trial. Myra Klayman drafted the manuscript's figures and displays, which were photographed by CIMA Graphics.

Many members and employees of the Massachusetts court system were generous with their time and advice. Justices Robert Hallisey, David Nelson, and Joseph Mitchell worked directly with the researchers. Chief Justices Walter McLaughlin, Robert Bonin, and James Lynch, Jr., granted approval to allow the research to be carried out in courthouse settings involving citizens called for jury duty. Joseph Romanow and his associates in the office of the Jury Commissioner were constantly supportive, and Gordon Pulsifer and other jury pool officers in Middlesex, Suffolk, and Norfolk counties were helpful in all phases of the research. Attorneys Joseph Travaline and Neil Collechio assisted in planning the research and in creating a realistic stimulus trial.

ACKNOWLEDGMENTS

Literally hundreds of people have provided advice and criticism throughout the project's history. Foremost among these are Eric Davin, Phoebe Ellsworth, David Kenny, Richard Lempert, Judy Ungerer, and Eric Wanner.

Our hope is that both the contributors we have named and the many left unnamed will be able to share in our satisfaction at the publication of the present volume.

CONTENTS

CONTENTS

1

The Right to Trial by Jury

The jury trial is the central element in the American conception of justice. The right to trial by an impartial jury, insulated from influence by oppressive political powers, is one of the oldest and least controversial guarantees in the Constitution. America is distinctive among all nations for the central role accorded the jury trial in its justice system. The more than 300,-000 jury trials a year are of enormous practical and symbolic significance to those who are involved in them and to those who see or hear about them. To the typical American citizen, participation in government is represented by voting and jury service.

Despite the long history of the jury trial and despite its current significance in the legal system, its future is uncertain. Changes in American society have created new demands for justice which may not be met by traditional jury trials. Increases in the volume of civil and criminal trials have clogged the court system and placed unprecedented strains on the ability of the jury system to dispense high quality justice. There have been dramatic increases in the length and complexity of trials. In some jurisdictions, jury selection alone may last as long as a week in a typical criminal case. Although not common, civil and criminal cases lasting months and even years place a burden on the system. On the civil side, advances in science and engineering have created complexities in disputes that challenge the experts in the field and would seem to require an unattainable level of sophistication on the part of jury members. Technological developments are also changing some of the conventions of evidence and procedure at trial and

By Hastie

providing opportunities for public access through media reportage, which has altered the nature of the trial jury.

There have always been disagreement and controversy over the proper place and form of the jury trial. Questions concern the types of disputes that should be submitted to a jury resolution, the standards by which to assess the quality of jury justice, and the optimal form and procedures to be followed by the jury (Kalven, 1955). Surprisingly few guidelines are available from historical and constitutional sources to resolve such basic questions as, "How large should the jury be?" "How much agreement must exist to render a verdict?" "How shall the performance of juries be evaluated?"

The foundation for the right to trial by jury for criminal cases is the constitutional guarantee in the Sixth Amendment, but this guarantee is abstract and contains no reference to the proper size, decision rule, or selection procedure: "In all criminal prosecutions, the accused shall enjoy the right to a speedy and public trial, by an impartial jury of the State and District wherein the crime shall have been committed, which District shall have been previously ascertained by law, and to be informed of the nature and cause of the accusation; to be confronted with the witnesses against him; to have compulsory process for obtaining witnesses in his favor; and to have the assistance of counsel for his defense." As a result, considerable variety in jury procedures exists across states and for criminal and civil trials (Center for Jury Studies, 1981b). The twelve-member, unanimous decision jury is required in both criminal and civil trials in only seven states. Jury size ranges from six members to twelve across jurisdictions, and decision rules range from unanimity, which is required in all states for six-member juries (*Burch v. Louisiana*, 1979), to a two-thirds majority. Thus, the lack of specificity in the constitutional foundation has led to variability and controversy concerning the form of the jury.

History also provides an uncertain foundation for the form of the jury trial (Forsyth, 1852; Holdsworth, 1956; Nemeth, 1981; Pollock & Maitland, 1898). For factors such as size, decision rule, and selection procedures, the historical record reveals enormous diversity across jurisdictions and historical periods. The earliest known juries composed of citizens, in Greece, probably included six members, but at some points in Greek history, such as the trial of Socrates for corrupting the youth of Athens, the total reached as high as 501. The unanimous decision rule that is required in most criminal trials probably originated in a British practice of the fourteenth century, called *afforcement*, which involved starting with a jury of twelve and adding jurors until a majority of at least twelve could agree on a verdict (*Apo-*

daca et al. v. Oregon, 1972, p. 407n2). The use of disinterested citizens to try the facts of a case is a relatively new convention. At the earliest appearances of the jury in Anglo-American practice it was composed of those who were most knowledgeable and even most involved in the matter at dispute. The problem of motivating the jury to perform efficiently and fairly also produced different solutions. For example, in British practice centuries ago it was common to incarcerate the jury without food or water until a verdict had been reached. After the verdict was rendered, the jury members were subject to prosecution if later evidence demonstrated that their verdict was in error. In short, the history of the jury provides few clear guidelines for current procedures and standards.

Uncertainty concerning the proper form and function of trial by jury is reflected in United States Supreme Court decisions. These decisions represent an effort to define the specifics of how a representative and impartial jury should be constituted and how it should behave. However, these decisions exhibit the same uncertainty that surrounds the jury's history. The decisions have been marked by high rates of disagreement among members of the Court and controversy among scholars and legal professionals. The Supreme Court has found that the traditional twelve-member jury size is not a requirement for state criminal or civil trials (*Williams v. Florida,* 1970). The limit on jury size was lowered to six in state criminal trials (*Ballew v. Georgia,* 1978). However, at the federal level twelve members are required in all criminal trial juries (*Thompson v. Utah,* 1898) and six in civil juries (*Colgrove v. Battin,* 1973).

The Supreme Court has decided cases concerned with the proper decision rule, allowing nonunanimous, majority rule verdicts and setting a lower limit on the decision rule quorum requirement for six-person juries by finding that a five-sixths majority is not allowable (*Johnson v. Louisiana,* 1972; *Apodaca et al. v. Oregon,* 1972; *Burch et al. v. Louisiana,* 1979). The Court has also rendered controversial decisions on jury composition, attempting to establish conditions and procedures for representative and impartial jury trials, and on juror competency to try cases involving complex legal or technical matters, even curtailing the right to jury trial in very complex matters (*Swain v. Alabama,* 1965; *Ristaino v. Ross,* 1976; *Witherspoon v. Illinois,* 1968; *Dairy Queen Inc. v. Wood,* 1962; *Beacon Theatres Inc. v. Westover,* 1959; *Ross v. Bernard,* 1970; Sperlich, 1982; Lempert, 1982). However, the Court has extended the right of jury trial to include disputes over relatively small claims and minor criminal offenses, thereby increasing the demand for jury trials to resolve criminal and civil disputes and heightening the public controversy surrounding the jury system (*Duncan v. Louisiana,* 1968; *Baldwin v. New York,* 1970).

3

It is important to examine in more detail the bases of these decisions and controversies. The Supreme Court's analysis of the right to trial by jury is important both because it defines the limits on jury trial procedures in practice and because it contains many insights into the behavior of juries. However, the Court's analysis of jury performance is limited, first, by its heavy reliance on the intuitions and personal experience of the justices; second, by its failure to develop theoretical principles to predict or explain jury behavior; and third, by its lack of rigorous methods to evaluate the empirical accuracy of assertions about jury behavior.

The basic argument that will be advanced in this volume is that the behavioral sciences provide a new and useful source of findings and methods that are relevant to decisions concerning the right to trial by jury. Most of the fundamental questions concerning the proper form and function of the jury can be answered with reference to empirical facts about juror and jury behavior. Even those questions of ethics or values that are essentially undecidable with empirical findings can be sharpened or simplified when related empirical issues are resolved. Our goal in the review that follows in this chapter will be to identify concrete standards or tests from the Court's opinions that provide guidelines for an empirical evaluation of the quality of jury performance.

Form and Function of the Jury

Although constitutional and historical guidelines are of limited use and members of the Court are in considerable disagreement, the record of decided cases yields a systematic set of principles governing the right to trial by jury. On the most general level, the Court has stated that the chief function of the jury is to "safeguard [the citizen] against arbitrary law enforcement" (*Williams v. Florida*, 1970, p. 87). Reinforcing this purpose is the jury's role of preventing oppression by the government and providing the accused "an inestimable safeguard against the corrupt or overzealous prosecutor and against the compliant, biased, or eccentric judge" (*Williams v. Florida*, 1970, p. 100; *Duncan v. Louisiana*, 1968, p. 156).

Two further conditions for a proper jury trial are "the interposition between the accused and his accuser of the common sense judgment of a group of laymen" and "the community participation and shared responsibility that results from the group's determination of guilt or innocence" (*Williams v. Florida*, 1970, p. 100). The requirement for community participation has been amplified to include the need for a representative cross-section of the community in jury decision making (*Swain v. Alabama*, 1965). For example, "meaningful community participation cannot be attained with the exclusion of minorities or other identifiable groups from jury service" (*Ballew v. Georgia*, 1978, p. 236). A related function of the community participation requirement is to free the jury "from outside attempts at intimidation" (*Williams v. Florida*, 1970, p. 100).

Similarly, the "interposition of commonsense judgment" has been explicated to mean the promotion of an effective deliberation process. The jury should be an accurate and reliable fact-finder. Its members must make "critical contributions necessary for the solution of a given problem" and, in particular, must "remember important pieces of evidence or argument" (*Ballew v. Georgia*, 1978, p. 233). Furthermore, "because they have imperfect memories, the forensic process of forcing jurors to defend their conflicting recollections and conclusions flushes out many nuances which otherwise would go overlooked" (*Apodaca et al. v. Oregon*, 1972, p. 386).

Jury deliberation should foster the correct application of common sense to these facts. This includes the "counterbalancing of various biases," to "minimize the potential bigotry of those who might convict on inadequate evidence, or who acquit when evidence of guilt was clear," and to "assure the parties that the jurors before whom they try the case will decide on the basis of the evidence placed before them, and not otherwise" (*Ballew v. Georgia*, 1978, p. 234; *Johnson v. Louisiana*, 1972, p. 398; *Swain v. Alabama*, 1965, p. 219). Deliberation should include "earnest and robust argument" that requires jurors to "fairly weight opposing arguments" (*Apodaca et al. v. Oregon*, 1972, pp. 389, 396).

The results of jury deliberation should be accurate. They should prevent conviction of the innocent, avoid inconsistencies, such as a decision on negligence issues that is inconsistent with a final award in a civil suit, and achieve consistent, rational compromise, such as achieving a consistent pattern of convictions across a number of counts and lesser included offenses in criminal trials. Variation in the verdicts of criminal cases should also be minimized, especially if "the variance amounts to an imbalance to the detriment of one side, the defense" (*Ballew v. Georgia*, 1978, p. 236). The jury's inability to render a "hung," no-verdict result has been interpreted as an indication that an antidefense imbalance was present. Maintaining "the great barricade known as proof beyond a reasonable doubt" is another major feature of jury deliberation. In particular, acquittal jurors should have "the opportunity through full deliberation to temper the opposing faction's degree of certainty of guilt" (*Apodaca et al. v. Oregon*, 1972, pp. 391, 390).

In pursuit of these general goals and purposes of jury trials, the Supreme Court has found two aspects of jury procedure to be crucial: the size of the jury and the decision rule or quorum required to render a verdict. On the issue of jury size, the Court concluded that "the fact that the jury at Common Law was composed of precisely twelve is a historic accident, unnecessary to effect the purposes of the jury system and wholly without significance except to mystics . . . there is no discernible difference between the results reached by the two different sized juries" (*Williams v. Florida,* 1972, p. 102, 101). More recently, the Court concluded that small juries, those with fewer than six members, are less representative, less reliable, and less accurate than large juries (*Ballew v. Georgia,* 1978).

On the appropriate decision rule for juries, the Supreme Court endorsed nonunanimous jury verdicts in state, but not federal, criminal trials when it upheld the conviction of a Louisiana defendant charged with robbery in a state court that allowed such verdicts. The final vote of the Louisiana jury had been nine to three for conviction. The Court found that the lack of jury unanimity alone does not establish reasonable doubt (*Johnson v. Louisiana,* 1972, p. 356). Furthermore, in a case decided at the same time, the Court maintained that there is no reason to assume that the majority of the jury "will deprive a man of his liberty on the basis of prejudice when a minority is presenting a reasonable argument in favor of acquittal" (*Apodaca et al. v. Oregon,* 1972, p. 413).

The Supreme Court most recently has found that a five-sixths verdict in six-member jurys in state criminal trials is unconstitutional (*Burch v. Louisiana,* 1979). Nationally there is near-uniformity in requiring unanimous verdicts from six-person juries in nonpetty criminal matters. The Court further noted that nonunanimous verdicts in small juries would threaten the principle that minimum size of juries is six persons by effectively allowing five or even four jurors to render a verdict.

Our review of the Supreme Court decisions concerned with jury size and decision rule requirements has identified a set of abstract functions that characterize the performance of the proper trial jury. The Court has decided individual cases by applying these principles to the concrete details of particular jury trial procedures. We will now turn our attention to the Court's own reasoning about empirical questions raised in decisions concerning the right to trial by jury. This portion of our review also affords us an opportunity to summarize the views of the Court's members concerning the application of behavioral science findings to address legal policy questions.

Testing the Quality of Jury Performance

Although some justices have cited social science research in their opinions, views on the utility of scientific research to legal policies and procedures are mixed. Justice Blackmun, writing the lead opinion in *Ballew v. Georgia*

(1978), concluded that scientific studies provide "the only basis, besides judicial hunch, for a decision about whether smaller and smaller juries will be able to fulfill the purpose and functions of the Sixth Amendment in deciding these cases" (p. 232n10). However, Justice Powell in his opinion in the same case stated: "I have reservations as to the wisdom as well as the necessity— of Mr. Justice Blackmun's heavy reliance on numerology derived from statistical studies. Moreover, neither the validity nor the methodology employed by the studies cited was subjected to the traditional testing mechanisms of the adversary process. The studies relied on merely represent unexamined findings of persons interested in the jury system" (p. 246).

A systematic tabulation of social science citations in Supreme Court cases in five different years between 1954 and 1974 found the Court to rely increasingly on social science materials (Rosenblum, 1979). However, a detailed analysis of the contents of these citations revealed that although social science sources were cited with increasing frequency, they tended to be cited most heavily in cases of lesser importance, and the citations were used to support peripheral rather than central propositions in the justices' arguments. Nonetheless, the jury trial decisions exhibit a receptivity to social science research on the part of at least some important jurists. Furthermore, the critical review of the adversary system, as exemplified by proceedings in appellate court hearings, provides an excellent forum for the application of social science findings to legal institutions.

In fact, scientific research is relevant not only to concrete issues, such as size, decision rule, and selection, but to most other aspects of trial by jury. Virtually all of the Supreme Court decisions concerned with the jury depend on empirical principles, although the Court has been slow to move beyond speculation and judicial intuition concerning the facts of jury performance (Cohen, 1959; Rosen, 1972; Cook, 1979; Loftus & Monahan, 1980; Ellsworth & Getman, 1982).

A first step toward applying social science methods and findings to issues raised by the right to trial by jury is to derive empirical tests from each of the jury functions identified by the Supreme Court. The Court has already provided an empirical analysis for some of these functions, particularly those concerned with jury composition. In all, five characteristics of jury trials may be used to test jury adequacy: representative cross-section, counter balancing of biases, accurate fact finding, accurate application of the law, and accurate verdicts.

First, the trial jury should be composed of a cross-section of individuals who represent the various types of individuals in the relevant jurisdiction. Assessing the representatives of jury panels or venire rolls typically involves assessing whether or not a cognizable class or distinctive subgroup, identifiable in the larger population of potential jurors, has been systematically excluded from the sample available to serve on jury panels. Enough cases have been considered by appellate courts with reference to the representativeness issue that the definition of cognizable class or identifiable subgroup is almost conventional. The forms of arguments for and against discrimination that threatens representativeness are well established. Typically, the plaintiff in an appeal concerned with jury representativeness tries to demonstrate, using statistical techniques, that a cognizable class, such as a racial subgroup, has been systematically excluded from jury pools or jury panels. Sometimes the plaintiff attempts both to demonstrate that a new type of group, such as individuals holding a certain attitude, qualifies as a cognizable class and that this group has been systematically excluded.

The use of social science methods and data to resolve disputes concerning representativeness, proportionality, and discrimination has a long history in the courts. The first appellate court decision in this country that intensively relied on social research involved survey data of this type, when economic and psychological statistics were cited in a finding upholding a statute limiting women's working hours (*Muller v. Oregon*, 1908). Many courts now consider sophisticated arguments based on survey data (Barksdale, 1957; Baldus & Coles, 1977).

Second, a proper jury should include a variety of viewpoints concerning matters to be decided upon so that there will be a counterbalancing of biases during deliberation. This counterbalancing of viewpoints requires both that differing views be represented and that they be expressed during deliberation in the case.

Courts have been conservative in using social research on the deliberation process to evaluate the quality of jury performance. To some extent this conservatism derives from the lack of extensive empirical research on some of the legally significant aspects of performance and from the large inductive leap that is required to draw conclusions about jury performance from research on other types of group decisions, often studied in artificial laboratory settings. However, empirical results are underutilized in judicial decisions. Even a chain of inferences supporting a generalization from a scientific finding to a practical conclusion may be preferable to a judicial intuition about jury behavior.

Third, the jury should be an accurate and reliable fact-finder. This requires at least three elements: accurate and complete memory for testimonial material; conservative but reasonable inference-making from explicitly stated propositions in testimony; and a fair weighting, particularly with reference to evaluation of credibility, of testimony from various sources and with various implications.

Fourth, the jury should accurately and comprehensively interpret and remember the judge's instructions on the law. The task of correctly "finding" the law parallels the jury's task of finding the facts in a case. The Supreme Court has noted that the standard of proof in criminal cases (beyond reasonable doubt) and presumption of innocence, must be correctly apprehended and maintained by individual jurors (*In re Winship*, 1970; *Estelle v. Williams*, 1976; *Kentucky v. Whorton*, 1979). Substantive instructions concerning the crimes with which a defendant is charged as well as other procedural instructions concerning the presumption of innocence, evaluation of credibility, and reasonable inference should also be included. Although there is considerable variation in the extent to which jurors in state courts are admonished that they must accept the law as given to them in standard instructions by the trial judge, the comprehension and retention of those instructions is critical in the jury decision.

Finally, the jury's verdict should be proper and accurate. At least three aspects of the verdict should be considered with reference to the accuracy standard: there should be little variance in verdicts for a single case, in the hypothetical situation where the same case might be tried repeatedly by similar juries; errors of two types, convicting the innocent and acquitting the guilty, should be minimized; and a few hung juries should occur, particularly in difficult cases, indicating that deliberation processes do not overwhelm all individual doubts.

These five empirical test characteristics are dependent on one another. Varying one procedure in a jury trial, such as selecting a "blue-ribbon" jury of highly educated, highly verbal individuals, might "improve" the performance of that jury over a typical jury in one respect, such as the ability to remember information from testimony. However, the variation cannot be termed desirable, or even permissible, without examining its full impact on all of the critical functional characteristics. A change that produces an improvement in one area might actually lower quality in others, such as the extent to which the jury panel represents the community from which it is drawn, or the extent to which biases are counterbalanced during deliberation.

Each of the characteristics is causally related to other characteristics in the set of functional criteria. For example, increasing the representativeness of a jury panel, at least in a heterogeneous community, tends to increase the variety of viewpoints represented on the panel. Increasing the variety of views, thereby producing a counterbalancing of biases, is likely to affect fact finding. Individuals from a variety of backgrounds are likely to attend to and remember different aspects of the trial evidence, making the jury as a whole remember the total pattern of evidence more completely. A similar

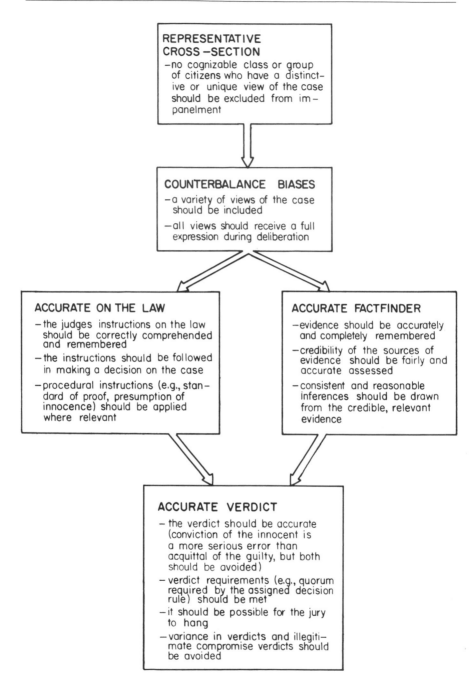

REPRESENTATIVE CROSS-SECTION

—no cognizable class or group of citizens who have a distinctive or unique view of the case should be excluded from impanelment

COUNTERBALANCE BIASES

—a variety of views of the case should be included

—all views should receive a full expression during deliberation

ACCURATE ON THE LAW

—the judges instructions on the law should be correctly comprehended and remembered

—the instructions should be followed in making a decision on the case

—procedural instructions (e.g., standard of proof, presumption of innocence) should be applied where relevant

ACCURATE FACTFINDER

—evidence should be accurately and completely remembered

—credibility of the sources of evidence should be fairly and accurate assessed

—consistent and reasonable inferences should be drawn from the credible, relevant evidence

ACCURATE VERDICT

—the verdict should be accurate (conviction of the innocent is a more serious error than acquittal of the guilty, but both should be avoided)

—verdict requirements (e.g., quorum required by the assigned decision rule) should be met

—it should be possible for the jury to hang

—variance in verdicts and illegitimate compromise verdicts should be avoided

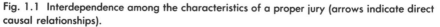

Fig. 1.1 Interdependence among the characteristics of a proper jury (arrows indicate direct causal relationships).

argument can be made for the generation of reasonable inferences and the evaluation of witness credibility. A variety of viewpoints expressed during deliberation may also improve the individual juror's application of the beyond reasonable doubt standard of proof. Finally, all of these factors taken together are likely to affect the jury's verdict (Fig. 1.1).

Two forms of test can be applied to compare types of juries or to evaluate a single type of jury with reference to the functional characteristics we have identified. The first kind of test compares a jury with a population standard. The test question is: Does the jury deviate significantly from the population mode of jury performance? Tests for jury representativeness are of this type. An ideal population mode is defined with reference to the characteristics of members of a population of potentially eligible jurors. Statistical tests are then performed to determine whether or not jurors called to serve, or actually impaneled, differ from the population mode with reference to identifiable characteristics.

On a few occasions, appellate courts have considered a similar form of test for the adequacy of jury performance. For example, a jury that convicts with a greater probability than a modal jury from a jurisdiction may be ruled improper. This reasoning occurred in a California Supreme Court case where the petitioner contended that death-qualified juries, sitting on capital cases, were not impartial in deciding the defendant's guilt or innocence. The decision noted, "The concept of a neutral jury is intimately related to the Constitutional doctrine regarding the representative cross-section of the community," and "For present purposes it is assumed that a Constitutionally neutral jury is one which is drawn from a pool of persons eligible to serve in a noncapital criminal trial" (*Hovey v. Superior Court of Alameda County*, 1980, p. 1312, n. 54). Thus, the test for "diffused impartiality," or neutrality, was defined as a comparison between a population standard (jury drawn from pool of persons eligible) and a test case (death-qualified jury).

A similar form of test was applied in a federal court hearing also concerned with death-qualified juries. Here the court defined a "functional equivalency" test under which "the necessary showing is that the difference in make-up of such a jury, as compared to a jury selected without regard to attitudes towards capital punishment for the determination of guilt, results in the functional difference in the operation of that jury" (*Grigsby v. Mabry*, 1980, p. 1388n23).

The second form of test for performance quality postulates an ideal standard or ideal scale against which jury performance can be measured. For example, if one type of jury is less accurate at recalling information from trial testimony during deliberation than another, the less accurate jury can be deemed less desirable than the more accurate jury. Or if two juries have equally complete and accurate recall during deliberation, the jury that recalls information equitably from both sides of the case, such as recalling testimony by prosecution and defense witnesses with equal correctness, can be deemed more desirable than a jury that differentially recalls information from the sides of a case.

Tests of this form, called ideal standard evaluations, have not been applied by legal authorities. However, such tests may be useful in evaluating jury performance for at least four of the jury's functional attributes. First, a test for the counterbalancing of biases should favor, as more proper, a jury that exhibits greater heterogeneity of viewpoints and permits full expression of different viewpoints over a jury that is more homogeneous.

Second, the same test of accuracy and equitability of recall of information from testimony can be extended to drawing inferences from testimony on both sides of a case or to weighting witness credibility from both sides of a case. An even more powerful test can be developed if the assumption is made that legal experts can render preferred or even optimal conceptualizations of case materials. With such an expert standard, it is possible to evaluate the acceptability of inferences drawn by jurors in jury deliberation. If a jury deliberation includes many departures from the expert-defined standard and these departures are not corrected during deliberation, the jury can be classified as improper.

Third, the accuracy of representation and interpretation of the judge's instructions on the law can be evaluated with reference to expert or scholarly analyses of the trial judge's instructions. A jury whose discussion departs far from an acceptable interpretation of the law in the eyes of experts can be deemed less proper than a jury that adheres closely to the experts' interpretations.

Fourth, for some cases expert opinion, such as the opinions of an appeals court, identify improper verdicts for a case or perhaps even indicate proper verdicts. This verdict evaluation can be used as a standard, and juries that depart from the standard can be deemed improper.

Legal authorities have been reluctant to accept evaluations of quality based on comparisons to a rational or expert standard, and there are no precedents for such an evaluation in the Supreme Court's analysis of the right to trial by jury. Rather, the population mode, which is essentially a representativeness standard, has been applied to evaluate all attributes of quality. The preference for population standard tests over ideal standard tests derives from the difficulty of defining a rational or expert test standard and then implementing comparisons between the standard and test jury performances. But there are conditions under which the rational or expert standard test should be attempted. Several results from the jury decision-making study reported in this volume are evaluated by such a test.

In summary, the jury trial is an important institution, whose form and place in the American justice system are controversial. Constitutional and historical precedents do not provide clear principles with which to evaluate the acceptability of jury performance. While some of the Supreme Court's analyses of the right to trial by jury have articulated and reviewed empirical tests of jury performance, this view is not acceptable to all jurists. Yet many functional attributes of jury performance are directly relevant to empirical tests of quality and adequacy. A major task in the design of the present empirical study has been the development of methods to measure these characteristics of jury performance.

Empirical evidence, particularly studies of individual and group decision processes, is critically and perhaps uniquely relevant to an evaluation of the right to trial by jury. The study of jury decision making reported in this volume addresses many questions, both implicit and explicit, in the Supreme Court's analysis of the right to trial by jury. The experimental method employs an extremely realistic but highly controlled simulation of the jury decision task. The study was carried out in actual courthouses with the assistance of court personnel and using citizens called to jury duty as experimental subjects.

The present study focuses on the effects of varying the jury decision rule on jury performance. Decision rule was selected for study because less is known about its effects than about the effects of variations in size or impanelment procedures and several Supreme Court decisions have been concerned with this issue.

Another focus of the study is the juror's behavior during deliberation, a subject that has been neglected in scientific research on jury performance. Several of the critical functions of the jury that have been identified in Supreme Court decisions involve a consideration of events occurring during deliberation. Our review of legal analyses of the right to trial by jury produced eight attributes of jury performance that are relevant to the quality or permissibility of various jury procedures: counterbalancing of viewpoints in discussion of evidence, accuracy as a factfinder, thoroughness or robustness of deliberation, application of the standard of proof, accuracy and completeness of recapitulation and application of the judge's instructions on the law, accuracy of verdicts compared to a standard provided by experts, variance in verdicts across juries for a single stimulus case, and frequency of deadlocked juries.

The study also deals with the influence of individual differences in background, which exist before jury service, on juror behavior. A large folklore of legal hypotheses concerns itself with the relationship between individual characteristics, such as demography, personality, and attitude, and the juror's verdict preference, confidence, or influence during deliberation. The present study provides the most thorough analysis to date of individual differences in juror behavior.

The final goal of the study is to develop a theoretical framework within which to view juror and jury behavior. Such a theory, grounded firmly on systematic empirical research, can reduce the dependence of legal policy makers on the vagaries of intuition and personal experience.

2

The Psychology of Juror and Jury Decision Making

The dominant theoretical paradigm in experimental psychology is the human information processing approach (Newell & Simon, 1972; Estes, 1978; Anderson, 1980). This approach is based on a metaphor of information flow and transformation from the environment, through mental processing stages within the organism, and back into the publicly observable world in the form of responses. Juror decision making can be analyzed within the information processing approach by describing the trial as a psychological stimulus, identifying the processing demands of the juror's decision task, and outlining the sequence of cognitive processes performed by the juror.

The Trial as Psychological Stimulus

The trial produces "data," or information input, that the jurors have to utilize in their decision-making task. For criminal trials, this information can be divided into nine different conceptual units, which usually occur in court in a certain order (Fig. 2.1). First comes the indictment, a statement of the charge against the defendant, naming the crime that he or she is accused of by the government. This is generally read by an officer of the court, and a copy is sent into the jury deliberation room. Next, the defendant's plea, the response to the indictment, is entered. This may vary from pleading not guilty, to pleading guilty to a lesser charge, to pleading guilty as charged. In

By Hastie and Pennington

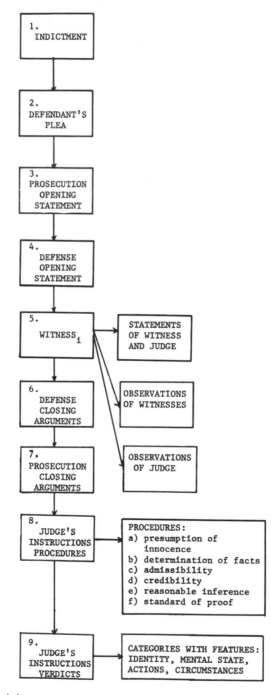

Fig. 2.1 The trial data.

the case of a guilty plea, the juror usually has no decision making in which to engage.

The prosecution's case, which is presented first, may begin with an opening statement by the prosecuting attorney. This statement is a general outline of what the prosecution intends to prove. Next, the defense may present an opening statement. This statement usually summarizes the evidence that will be used in denying the prosecution allegations. This statement is frequently presented after the witnesses for the prosecution and before the witnesses for the defense, if any, are heard.

The major part of the trial is the testimony given by the various witnesses. This is usually a series of prosecution witnesses followed by defense witnesses. The testimony of a single witness typically does not describe events in the sequence in which they originally occurred. In addition to statements made by the witnesses, there are questions posed by the attorney who called the witnesses, questions by the opposing attorney, objections to testimony by the attorneys, and decisions rendered by the judge.

After the presentation of evidence by the witnesses, closing arguments are made by the defense and prosecuting attorneys, in that order. These arguments are a summary of the case presented by each side, and they usually include statements outlining the inferences the attorney would like the jurors to draw from the evidence.

Finally, the judge instructs the jurors in two areas. First, the judge informs the jurors what their task consists of during deliberation and what procedures they should employ in reaching a verdict. The procedures defined by the judge generally include the instruction that the juror is to regard the defendant as innocent until proven otherwise; that the burden of proof is on the prosecution; that the juror's task is to determine the facts on the basis of credible evidence; that certain information may be regarded as evidence, such as direct testimony of witnesses, charts and exhibits, observations of the witnesses, and reasonable inferences drawn from the testimony; that other information may not be regarded as evidence, such as statements and questions posed by the attorneys, or race and background of defendant; how to assess the credibility of testimony, such as each witness' opportunity to observe, possible bias, character, and contradictions in testimony; what constitutes a reasonable inference as opposed to unwarranted speculation; and what is the meaning and application of the standard of proof, namely beyond a resonable doubt, in assessing the truth of allegations. The second portion of the judge's instructions defines for the jurors a complete set of possible verdicts, of which they must choose one. Each verdict may be seen as a category which has criterial features that must be brought into correspondence with the identity, intent, and actions of the accused.

These nine input items constitute all of the data that the juror has to work with coming from external sources, namely the trial itself. However, other types of knowledge are used in the juror's task whose source is internal. The juror uses "factual" knowledge of the social and physical world that appears relevant to the case. Factual knowledge includes the juror's beliefs, although these beliefs are not necessarily true, such as beliefs about the effects of a certain weapon, motives and behavior, eyewitness memory, alcohol and its effects on motor coordination, or opinions about social customs among ethnic groups. Another type of information that is not part of the trial data is the "strategic" knowledge that the juror employs in the decision process. This knowledge comprises information-processing strategies that determine how the data is organized and combined to form a mental "product" that can be transformed into a decision.

Information-Processing Demands

The juror's predeliberation task can be broken down into seven component information-processing components according to an analysis developed by Pennington and Hastie (1981a). However, this analysis of an ideal juror's performance is psychologically unrealistic in at least two ways. First, it suggests that the juror's decision-making tasks are performed in a certain order, that most tasks are performed after the judge has instructed the jury, and that they are completed before social influence processes begin in deliberation. These temporal specifications are almost certainly false in a typical courtroom setting. Second, few jurors are likely to complete all of the processing tasks prescribed for a typical legal trial. Thus, the set of seven perception, memory, inference, and decision processes describe a far more orderly and thorough judgment machine than the juror in a typical jury box. However, they provide a useful perspective from which to view juror and jury decision making both theoretically and in practice (Fig. 2.2).

The first task component in juror decision making is encoding trial contents. The ideal juror is characterized as a relatively passive record-keeper during the trial who encodes the events of the trial verbatim. The representation of the juror as a tape recorder corresponds to an underlying assumption of the legal system that jurors suspend judgment and evaluation until all the evidence has been presented and until after they have been instructed at the end of the trial how to evaluate and what to judge. Actual juror performance may deviate from this ideal through mechanisms of selective attention, forgetting, inferential embellishment, and reorganization. There is always extensive cognitive activity by the perceiver in compre-

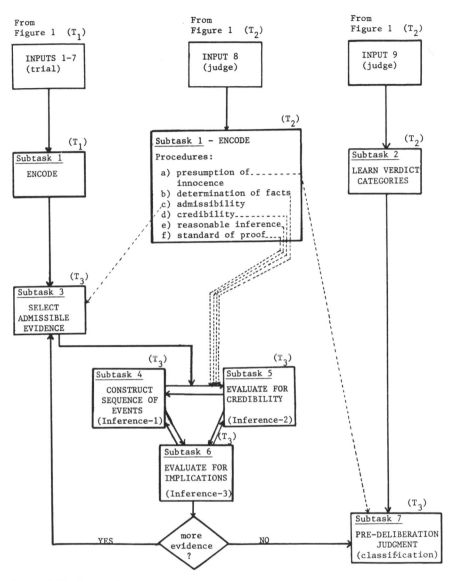

From
Figure 1 (T₁)

INPUTS 1-7
(trial)

From
Figure 1 (T₂)

INPUT 8
(judge)

From
Figure 1 (T₂)

INPUT 9
(judge)

(T₁)

Subtask 1

ENCODE

(T₂)

Subtask 1 - ENCODE

Procedures:

a) presumption of
   innocence
b) determination of facts
c) admissibility
d) credibility
e) reasonable inference
f) standard of proof

(T₂)

Subtask 2

LEARN VERDICT
CATEGORIES

(T₃)

Subtask 3

SELECT
ADMISSIBLE
EVIDENCE

(T₃)

Subtask 4

CONSTRUCT
SEQUENCE OF
EVENTS
(Inference-1)

(T₃)

Subtask 5

EVALUATE FOR
CREDIBILITY

(Inference-2)

(T₃)

Subtask 6

EVALUATE FOR
IMPLICATIONS

(Inference-3)

more
evidence
?

YES

NO

(T₃)

Subtask 7

PRE-DELIBERATION
JUDGMENT
(classification)

Fig. 2.2 The juror task.

hension and memory tasks (Crowder, 1976; Bransford, 1979; Kintsch, 1974; Tulving, 1974).

The second task component in the model is establishing judgment categories. At the conclusion of a trial it is assumed that the juror has a fairly accurate recording of events during the trial. The task at this time is for the juror to establish judgement categories based on the judge's instructions about substantive statutory issues, such as the elements of crimes in an indictment. Each verdict may be thought of as a category defined by a list of criterial features specifying the identity, mental state, circumstances, and actions that bear on the verdict choice (Kaplan, 1978; Saks & Hastie, 1978). The complexity of this set of concepts is illustrated by elaborate verdict categogories for a murder trial (Fig. 2.3). The complete representation of the verdict categories is a difficult task. The comprehension and memory problems are further complicated by the interference from erroneous descriptions of verdict categories presented in television, movies, popular fiction, newspapers, and other public media. The task requires that the juror set aside preconceptions of the verdict categories that are in conflict with the judge's instructions. Jurors are specifically instructed to do this by the judge.

The third component of the decision task is selecting evidence. Jurors are instructed that certain trial input is not to be regarded as evidence in reaching a decision; that is, it is to be excluded from consideration. In a criminal trial this includes the fact that the defendant was indicted, the attorneys' opening statements and closing arguments, the attorneys' behavior and questions, the judge's behavior, the judge's mention of any facts in the case, and items of evidence declared inadmissible by the judge.

The juror must now construct a plausible sequence of events. Using only information that has been selected, the juror must determine what happened at the time of the alleged crime. This is represented by the combined processes of construction, inference, and credibility evaluation. Construction involves the fitting of information into a coherent story or even more than one story. The companion process to construction is evaluation. Each item of information must be evaluated in two respects, for its credibility and for its implications. The juror has received guidelines regarding these evaluations in the judge's instructions on credibility and reasonable inference. Frequently the evaluations cannot be carried out on the item of information in isolation but require contextual or related information as well. It is for this reason that construction and evaluation are seen as interwoven.

The construction component task is to make a story of what happened with respect to the defendant, the crime he or she is accused of committing, and the possible events surrounding the crime. Each evidence item is checked against the story for admissibility. If selected, it is compared to the story and evaluated for credibility and for implications within each context that refers to it. The results of this analysis are then inserted into the story and finally reevaluated for their credibility and implications. At the end of this procedure, the next evidence item is retrieved and the processes are repeated (Pennington & Hastie, 1981a; Pennington, 1981).

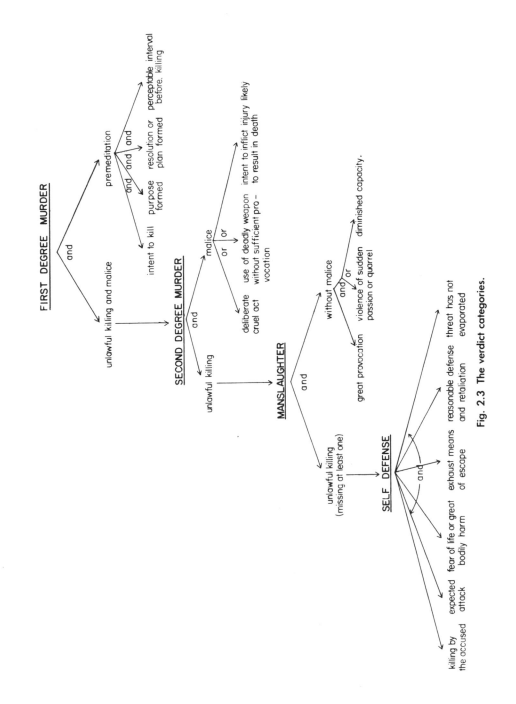

FIRST DEGREE MURDER

and — premeditation
- and — purpose formed
- and — resolution or plan formed
- and — perceptable interval before. killing

and — intent to kill

unlawful killing and malice

SECOND DEGREE MURDER

and — malice
- or — deliberate cruel act
- or — use of deadly weapon without sufficient pro-vocation
- or — intent to inflict injury likely to result in death

unlawful killing

MANSLAUGHTER

and — without malice
- and — great provocation
- or — violence of sudden passion or quarrel
- or — diminished capacity.

unlawful killing (missing at least one)

SELF DEFENSE

and —
- killing by the accused
- expected attack
- fear of life or great bodily harm
- exhaust means of escape
- reasonable defense and retaliation
- threat has not evaporated

Fig. 2.3 The verdict categories.

At the end of the construction and evaluation tasks, the juror has determined the facts of the case by constructing alternative versions of the story, evaluating their credibility, and drawing inferences with respect to the identity, intentions, and actions of the participants. Now the juror must consider this story construction in relation to the verdict categories to select a verdict. The processes in this decision component take the form of a category classification task. The juror evaluates the fit of the case, represented as the final output of the story construction stage, into each of the possible verdict categories presented in the judge's charge to the jury. This evaluation for goodness-of-fit can be characterized as a feature matching test in which each feature of the verdict category is compared to attributes of the case story structure. If the fit to one of the verdict categories is good, the juror will finish with a decision that the case fits the category to the degree specified by the relevant standard of proof, namely beyond a reasonable doubt.

The Story Model

The idealized information-processing task analysis is closely related to a model of the juror's actual cognitive processing called the Story Model (Pennington, 1981). The Story Model has three processing stages. First, the story construction stage specifies the processing during which evidence is comprehended and organized into one or more plausible accounts describing "what happened" at the time of events testified to during the trial. The model postulates that general knowledge about the structure of human purposive action sequences, characterized as an abstract episode schema, serves to organize events according to the causal and intentional relations between them as constructed by the juror. Second is the verdict-category establishment stage, which involves the representation of each verdict alternative as a category with defining features and a decision rule specifying their appropriate combination. Third, the story classification stage specifies that the juror's decision takes the form of a classification in which the best match between story features and verdict category features is determined. Application of standard-of-proof and presumption-of-innocence procedures are central in this stage.

This model retains the basic features of the ideal juror analysis but acknowledges that the ideal assumption that there is no important constructive and inferential processing during trial comprehension is unrealistic from a psychological point of view. In the Story Model it is proposed that stories organize information in ways that help the juror perform the three interpretive operations proposed in the ideal juror analysis: by locating the

central actions around which the point of the story will be drawn (story construction), by creating an interpretive context for the actions at the center of the story through inferences about the relationships among elements in the story (evaluation for implications), and by evaluating the interpretations against social frames to determine the degree of internal consistency and descriptive adequacy of completeness (evaluation for credibility). The Story Model addresses a problem identified as significant by legal and psychological experts on evidence (e.g. Wigmore, 1937; Schum, 1977) by providing a plausible psychological account of the linkages between events in each unique legal case which must be specified before inferences about guilt may be made.

Empirical support is provided for the Story Model in an interview study of juror decision processes (Pennington, 1981). Citizens sampled from trial court jury pools watched realistic filmed trials and then talked aloud as they reviewed the evidence in reaching an individual verdict decision. The unconstrained talk-aloud period was followed by a systematic interview that probed the subjects' memories and inferences relevant to their verdicts. The interview protocols were found to exhibit story structures that can be characterized as causal event chains having a hierarchical episode structure. Central stories for subjects choosing different verdicts also vary in both content and structure, and these differences correspond to specific legally required features of the subjects' chosen verdict categories. And verdict category structure and story classification rules do not vary systematically by verdict group.

The stories jurors tell are thus related to the verdicts they choose, and the causal relations between events referenced by trial evidence are central in the juror's representation of the decision-relevant evidence base. Variability in verdict computation, or verdict category representation and classification rules, cannot account for variability in verdict choice.

The Story Model provides a complete psychological account of cognitive processing in juror decision making, and it receives support from jury research, political science analysis, jurors' accounts of their experiences during trials, and other work (Colasanto & Sanders, 1978; Bennett, 1978, 1979; Chaberski, 1973; Kennebeck, 1973; Timothy, 1974; Pennington & Hastie, 1980; Pennington & Hastie, 1981b; Kuhn, Pennington, & Leadbeater, 1983). Alternative models for juror decision making have been proposed based on a variety of mathematical formulations (Poisson process models: Thomas & Hogue, 1976; Kerr, 1978; information integration theory: Anderson, 1959; Ostrom, Werner, & Saks, 1978; Kaplan & Schersching, 1980; Bayes' theorem: Schum, 1977; Schum & Martin, 1982; Grofman, 1981). But none of them include the full range of juror decision task components, and they have not been applied to realistically complete juror decision tasks.

The Jury's Task

As in the case of the individual juror's processing task, the analysis of the jury task demands is simplified, idealized, and speculative. It includes the major component tasks that have been cited by legal analysts, observed by social scientists, or reported by journalists. Virtually all models of jury decision making assume that individual jurors have reached initial predeliberation verdict decisions at the start of deliberation. Thus, the input at the beginning of the jury task is a set of jurors with verdict preferences. Each juror may be presumed to have completed all of the preliminary information-processing subtasks identified in the analysis of the juror's task before beginning the six component tasks in the jury decision task (Fig. 2.4).

Most juries begin with a discussion of an agenda for deliberation or voting. Typically the jury returns to these plans periodically over the course of deliberation. Selection of a foreman is the first task addressed by many juries. However, in some courts, as in Massachusetts, the foreman is appointed by the trial judge before deliberation begins. The other major issues addressed concern the focus of discussion (as on evidence or verdicts, or on a specific verdict alternative or pair of alternatives) and the timing of events (such as taking a vote sooner or later, or terminating discussion for a lunch break).

The second task is to review the evidence and instructions. This subtask is the center of the deliberation process. It includes the exchange of information and opinions pertinent to the decision.

The third task is to identify juror verdict preferences. The jury has several mechanisms whereby to make known to all its members the distribution of verdict preferences. These mechanisms include public statements during deliberation as well as open or secret polling procedures.

The fourth task is to check whether a verdict rendering quorum has been reached. The results of polls and personal tabulations are frequently compared to the verdict-rendering quorum size that was set by the judge's instructions on decision rule. Typically, in criminal trials the jury foreman periodically announces the results of each poll to determine if the jury is unanimous in its preference for a verdict category. When the necessary quorum is reached, deliberation is usually terminated, and the jury returns to the courtroom to make the verdict public.

The fifth task is to assess progress toward consensus. Periodically the jury reviews its progress toward group consensus. When it is apparent that continued discussion and polling are unlikely to produce increased consensus, the jury may declare itself deadlocked and unable to render a verdict. In practice this decision is usually made when no changes in individual verdict

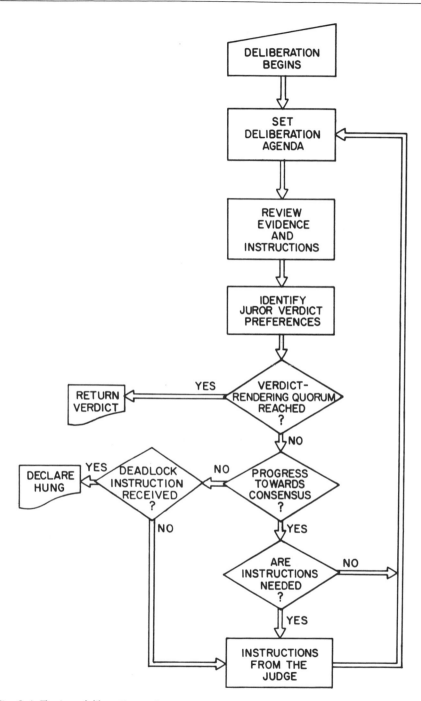

Fig. 2.4 The jury deliberation task.

preferences are observed across several polls. If the jury informs the trial judge that it is deadlocked, or if the judge infers from prolonged deliberation or requests for further instructions that deadlocking is likely to occur, the judge reads the jury a "dynamite charge" instruction which encourages the jurors to try once more to resolve their differences. Usually such an instruction is given only once. If a jury returns to the court deadlocked a second time, it is usually declared hung and dismissed.

The sixth task is to request additional instructions. The jury is instructed that if progress toward a verdict is impeded by disagreement or confusion concerning the law or the evidence in the case, further instructions may be requested from the trial judge. Typically the jury votes on the matter of requesting instructions and makes the request in writing. Most judges are responsive to questions concerning substantive instructions and attempt to amplify or re-express their earlier instructions on the law.

Social Science Models

Social scientists have developed many explicit models for jury decision making, but these approaches rarely provide a complete analysis of behavior in actual legal decision-making tasks (Pennington & Hastie, 1981a; Penrod & Hastie, 1979). For the most part these models are unrealistically simple or provide analyses of limited subtasks within the larger legal judgment task.

Typically the simplicity or incompleteness of the social science models is deliberate. Many of the particular model applications were developed to demonstrate the extendability of theoretical formulations or to serve as examples of the direction in which useful developments might proceed. For example, the major models proposed by social scientists for jury decision making do not attempt to model events during deliberation. Three classes of models—Social Decision Schemes, probabilistic models, and Bayesian models—were designed to predict final verdict distributions of juries from initial verdict distributions of jurors (Davis, 1973; Davis et al., 1975; Walbert, 1971; Saks & Ostrom, 1975; Gelfand & Solomon, 1973, 1974, 1975, 1977; Grofman, 1976). Empirical evaluations of these models have often used data aggregated over hundreds of different cases and case types; thus the models portray a population of cases represented by the sample rather than individual or group decision behavior.

A fourth class of models is defined by the use of mathematical principles to characterize individual juror verdict-preference changes during deliberation (Klevorick & Rothschild, 1979; Penrod & Hastie, 1980; Kerr, 1981; Stasser & Davis, 1981). These models propose precise verdict-to-verdict transition rules as well as principles as to when the transition rules are to be applied.

Our favored approach to modeling jury behavior is to model all major trial events using a computer program simulation. This theoretical medium provides powerful representational capabilities so that principles from a diverse sample of models and empirical generalizations can be combined. The computer simulation approach, which requires precision from the theoretician, provides deductive power to derive implications from a system of assumptions. The approach also provides enough flexibility to model a wide range of jury or jury-like tasks in natural or artificial settings. A model of the jury decision process, implemented in the form of a computer program, will be presented in Chapter 9 of the present volume.

Jury Performance

A sizable literature of behavioral science research on jury decision-making processes already exists. Conclusions concerning jury behavior come from three sources: postdeliberation interviews with actual jurors, observations by other nonjuror participants in the trial, and systematic observations of mock juries. These results identify the major determinants of verdicts, deliberation time, information pooling, and election to the role of foreman. The following review is a summary of these findings.

A result obtained in virtually all research on small decision-making groups is that larger factions, within a group, exert more influence on the group's decision than do smaller factions. For example, a postdeliberation survey of jurors in 225 criminal cases concluded that "the jury in roughly nine out of ten cases decides in the direction of the initial majority" (Kalven & Zeisel, 1966, p. 488).

A survey of trial judges found that 5.6 percent of trials resulted in deadlocked juries when unanimous verdicts were required, and the rate dropped to 3.1 percent when majority verdicts were allowed. Based on the jurors' retrospective reports, hung juries occurred only when a substantial minority faction existed at the start of deliberation, even though a minority of one might hang the jury at the end of deliberation, which occurred in twelve of the forty-eight hung juries studied.

Deliberation time increases with case complexity and with strictness of decision rule (Saks, 1977). Nonverdict-rendering juries take approximately three times as long to deliberate as verdict-rendering juries (Kalven & Zeisel, 1966).

Analyses of the contents of mock jury deliberations have conluded that jurors perform their task in a conscientious manner (James, 1959, 1967;

Kessler, 1973). Over 80 percent of the mock jurors' discussion was judged relevant to their decisions, and most of their discussion was of "high quality" in the eyes of attorneys, law students, and social scientist observers. Jury size and decision rule factors did not affect the content of deliberation (Saks, 1977).

Four polling procedures have been observed in jury deliberations: the written secret ballot; the public show of hands; the verbal go-around; and the verbal expression of dissent only. The verbal go-around and written secret ballot procedures were most common in one study, accounting for approximately 70 percent of the polls (Hawkins, 1960). Juries that took an early poll in deliberation tended to render a verdict more quickly. Furthermore, the use of written secret ballot procedures was associated with the occurrence of jury deadlocking.

Individuals involved in group discussions participate at sharply different rates, with a few individuals dominating discussion (Stephan & Mischler, 1952; Steiner, 1972). For example, three of twelve jurors typically produce more than half of the communications in deliberation (Strodtbeck, James, & Hawkins, 1957). Furthermore, variability in speaking rates increases as group size increases. In six-member juries approximately 5 percent of the jurors fail to participate at all, whereas more than 20 percent of the mock jurors in twelve-member juries are silent (Kessler, 1973; Saks, 1977). Faction size within the jury also affects faction members' participation rates (Hawkins, 1962). As factions grow, they account for an increasing amount of the total discussion, although the probability that individual jurors will speak drops as their faction grows.

Juror sex and occupational status are correlated with participation rates. Males speak more than females, and higher socioeconomic status jurors participate at a higher rate than lower status jurors (Strodtbeck & Mann, 1956; Simon, 1967; Strodtbeck, James, & Hawkins, 1957; James, 1959; Hawkins, 1960). Physical location at the rectangular jury table also affects participation rates, with jurors seated at the ends and middle participating at higher rates than corner or flank jurors (Strodtbeck & Hook, 1961).

The role of foreman is the only explicitly defined differentiation among members of the jury. When the foreman is elected by the jury, juror sex, social status, and seat location are correlated with election to the foreman role. Males, higher classes, and end seating are overrepresented in the role. Once selected, foremen participate in deliberation at a rate two to three times that of other jurors (Hawkins, 1960; Simon, 1967; Strodtbeck & Hook, 1961; Strodtbeck, James, & Hawkins, 1957). However, the correlations between sex, education, occupation, seat selection, foreman status, and other factors make it impossible to identify the unique causal contribution of each of these factors to participation rates or to other behavioral measures.

Jury Decision Rule

There are several empirical studies of the effects of varying structural and procedural conditions of the jury decision task. Detailed summaries of the experiments and surveys concerned with jury decision rule and size will be presented because of their direct relevance to the original empirical research reported in this volume.

Juries required to reach unanimous decisions were found likelier to hang, having a 5.6 percent rate, than were majority rule juries, with a 3.1 percent rate (Kalven & Zeisel, 1966). However, these differential hung jury rates are not necessarily related exclusively to the decision rule because the two sets of data were collected from different jurisdictions, and many factors in addition to decision rule may have varied.

In an experiment on mock juries using college students, the jurors were presented with a 45-minute tape recording of a rape case and allowed to deliberate for a maximum of thirty minutes (Davis, et al., 1975). The jury size was six-person versus twelve-person, and the decision rule was unanimous versus two-thirds majority. The effects of the decision rule were small. Verdict distributions were not affected, and a two-thirds majority decision rule provided the best characterization of both unanimous and majority rule jury performance. One weakness in the method of this study that probably accounts for the lack of a relationship between decision rule and verdict distributions was the strong defense bias of the rape case materials. Only 22 percent of the individual jurors voted to convict on a postdeliberation ballot, and no jury voted for conviction. The decision rule did affect two measures of performance. Unanimous juries took longer to reach a verdict, and more polls were taken during a deliberation.

Another experiment, which used a more realistic videotaped version of the rape case, obtained a substantial rate of convictions by juries. It compared the effects of decision rule on unanimous and two-thirds majority mock juries that were presented with no explicit definition of the beyond-reasonable-doubt standard of proof, a "lax" definition, or a "stringent" definition (Kerr et al., 1976). Unanimous juries had longer deliberation times and took more polls than majority rule juries. A five-sixths majority decision rule provided a good characterization of jury performance for both decision rules. Although verdict distributions were not sharply affected by the decision rule manipulation, unanimous rule juries were more likely than majority rule juries to deadlock. Jurors in majority rule juries were less satisfied with their jury verdicts, and minority faction members were especially likely to believe that they had not had opportunity to express all their arguments concerning the case. Marginally higher hung jury rates also occurred in unanimous as compared to five-sixths majority rule juries (Bray, 1974).

Two mock-jury studies using college students and jurors who had recently served in Franklin County, Ohio, varied jury size between six persons and twelve persons and decision rule between unanimous and two-thirds majority (Saks, 1977). In one experiment the jurors read a ten-page transcript of a robbery case, and in the other they viewed a one-hour videotaped burglary case. Again unanimous juries took longer to reach verdicts and were likelier to deadlock before rendering a verdict than majority juries. Moreover, majority rule jurors communicated with one another more frequently than unanimous rule jurors, and majority rule jurors recalled more arguments raised during deliberation than did unanimous rule jurors.

Two other studies examined unanimous and two-thirds majority rules in six-person mock juries (Nemeth, 1977). College students in one study read a short written summary of a murder trial and deliberated for a maximum of two hours. Predeliberation ballots were used to produce four-to-two initial faction splits either weighted toward or against acquittal in every mock jury. There were no effects of decision rule on conviction rates, but deadlocked juries were only observed under unanimous decision rules. Direct measures of total deliberation time did not show decision rule effects. However, there was a difference in functional deliberation time, defined as the point at which arguments for one verdict outweigh arguments for the other verdict to such an extent that a reversal of group opinion is practically precluded. Majority juries reached this critical point more rapidly than unanimous juries. The only decision rule effect on the quality of deliberation was that unanimous jury members found deliberation less comfortable and dominated by majority faction influence in contrast to majority rule jurors. Unanimous rule jurors also believed that their jury's verdict was correct with greater confidence than did majority rule jurors. The other study covering seven trials was too small in size and had too much across-case variability in deliberation to be sensitive to decision rule effects, but it at least showed no sharp deviations from jury performance in the first, more artificial experiment.

When these two studies were analyzed for male-female differences in deliberation behavior and minority faction influence, the results were equivocal. Male jurors appeared to dominate deliberation by offering more suggestions, opinions, and information than females, but this difference was clear only in the more artificial experiment (Nemeth, Endicott, & Wachtler, 1977). Minority faction influence was also an extremely delicate phenomenon and did not manifest itself at a high enough rate in either study to yield a definite characterization (Nemeth, 1976; 1977).

Other research on decision rule requirements has found a minority faction influence (Hans, 1978). Six-person mock juries, recruited from adults in a Toronto science museum, listened to a fifteen-minute audiotaped robbery case and then deliberated to unanimous or five-sixths majority verdicts. Minority faction members played a more active role in deliberation under unanimous than under majority rule conditions. The increased participation rates for minority faction members in unanimous rule juries took the form of within-faction discussion rather than between-faction persuasive attempts. This conclusion was confirmed when law student observers were asked to rate the performance of the juries. The observers perceived minority faction members in unanimous rule juries as being significantly more influential and more active than minority faction members in majority rule juries. However, there were no differences in the perceived quality of the complete deliberation, although interobserver agreement on ratings of quality was fairly low (Hans, personal communication). Thus, the unreliability of rated quality may have obscured true decision rule differences. Verdict differences between decision rules were also not consistent, although there were slightly more hung juries in the unanimous rule condition.

An exceptionally realistic mock-jury experiment used actual jurors from Queens County courts in New York (Padawer-Singer, 1977; Padawer-Singer, Singer, & Singer, 1977). Juror volunteers were shown a three-hour videotaped reenactment of a murder trial and then asked to deliberate in six-person or twelve-person juries under unanimous or two-thirds majority decision rules. Hung juries were again more likely to appear in unanimous decision conditions than under majority rule instructions.

College student subjects in a study at West Virginia University listened to a fifteen-minute audiotaped summary of a murder trial and then deliberated in twelve-member juries for up to two hours (Foss, 1981). Fourteen juries were instructed to deliberate to a unanimous consensus and fourteen to a ten-out-of-twelve majority quorum. Unanimous rule juries were more likely to deadlock than were majority rule juries; 6/14 versus 0/14 hung juries, respectively. Unanimous juries also required more time to complete deliberation. As shown by the changes in disagreement among jurors across the course of deliberation jurors converged on their final verdict more quickly in majority rule juries as compared to unanimous juries. That is, the rate of convergence was faster, an effect that occurred in addition to the shorter total deliberation time to reach a verdict.

Another study used actual jurors viewing a thirty-minute videotaped reenactment of a murder trial in mock juries of varying size, namely six and twelve persons, and decision rule, namely unanimity and five-sixths majority (Buckhout et al., 1977). Although the experiment was cut off before a sizable sample had accumulated, decision rule appeared to affect the verdict distribution for the juries. The hung jury rate was exceptionally high under the unanimity rule, with only three experimental juries rendering verdicts, while only one jury hung under the majority decision rule.

One last study had student mock juries deliberate on two criminal cases presented in a short audiotaped summary format (Friedman & Shaver, 1975). Neither the decision rule, unanimous and nonunanimous, nor the jury size, six and twelve persons, had any consistent effect on verdicts, deliberation time, or perceptions of deliberation. However, jurors' postdeliberation perceptions of the motivations of trial participants, such as defendants and victims, were affected by the decision rule.

There are only two studies of decision rule effects on civil case verdicts. In one study, citizens sampled from jury pools were presented with an audiotaped automobile accident tort case (Broeder, 1958). Twelve-person mock-juries assigned unanimous and three-fourths majority decision rules did not differ in liability decisions or in the amount of damages awarded to the plaintiff. Similar no-difference results were obtained in a study of college student mock-jurors presented with different civil case materials (Bray & Struckman-Johnson, 1977).

In summary, decision rules have four clear effects. First, hung or deadlocked final decision states are more common in unanimous than in majority decision conditions. The exception is civil trial juries, where decision rule has no apparent effect on verdict patterns. Second, unanimous rule juries tend to take more time and more polls compared to majority rule juries before rendering a verdict. Although this difference frequently does not reach levels of statistical significance, it must be taken into consideration in any conceptualization of decision rule effects. Third, overall satisfaction is higher in unanimous rule than in majority rule conditions. The lower satisfaction ratings for majority rule juries are produced by holdout jurors, who never join the verdict-rendering majority faction. Such jurors do not exist at the end of verdict-rendering deliberation under a unanimous rule. Related measures, such as each juror's belief that all case-relevant arguments have been fully explored and that deliberation has been thorough, reveal similar decision rule differences. Fourth, minority faction members participate with greater frequency and are perceived as more influential in unanimous as compared to majority rule juries.

Jury Size

Research on the effects of panel size on jury performance indicates that the use of six-member juries does not result in significant differences in either trial outcome or deliberation quality. Critics have argued that methodological flaws make any conclusions from these studies tentative at best (Zeisel & Diamond, 1974; Lempert, 1975; Saks, 1977; Grofman, 1980). For example, several archival studies are frequently cited as showing no differences between six- and twelve-person jury performance; however, all these studies were correlational, and alternate interpretations in each study undermine the conclusion that jury size does not causally influence jury performance. Moreover, since opportunities for data collection were limited by the existing legislation governing jury size, only civil juries could be examined.

Verdict distributions were studied for 128 six- and twelve-member juries in the state of Washington (Bermant & Coppock, 1973). Cases were limited to those involving the Workmen's Compensation Act during a one-year period following the enactment of a statute providing for six-member nonunanimous juries at the Superior Court level except in cases where one party expressly demanded a twelve-member panel. There were no significant differences in the distribution of verdicts for plaintiff and defendant. However, these results may have been confounded by the fact that attorneys were free to select jury size at the beginning of trial proceedings.

A similar study in the New Jersey courts, in addition to examining verdict distributions, collected data as to the type of case involved and the amount of damages requested and received (Institute of Judicial Administration, 1972). Six-person juries made more efficient use of trial time and jurors without affecting conduct or trial outcome. Although a number of differences between six- and twelve-member juries were reported, these were attributed to differences in the types of cases selected by lawyers to be tried by different-sized juries and not to jury size per se. Lawyers tend to prefer larger panels in more complex cases involving greater sums of money. For example, whereas six-member juries were used in 77 percent of the automobile negligence cases sampled, they comprised a mere 15.4 percent of the juries in malpractice suits. Similarly, significantly greater use was made of six-member juries in bifurcated trials, namely trials in which liability and damages are decided separately. Typically, lawyers reserved the option to have a twelve-member panel rule on damages. Three specific differences in performance between six- and twelve-member juries were observed: an increased proportion of nonunanimous verdicts in twelve-member juries (45.0 percent versus 20.2 percent), a tripling of damage awards in cases tried by twelve-member juries, and a doubling of trial time in cases tried by twelve-member juries. All of these factors may be attributable to differences in case complexity. Although deliberation time tended to be 33 percent shorter in six-member panels, this difference disappeared in cases where the damages awarded exceeded $10,000.

The bias introduced by attorneys' systematic selection of different sized juries was eliminated in a study of six- and twelve-member juries in Michigan courts over two six-month periods, before and after compulsory use of a six-member civil jury was introduced (Mills, 1973). There were no significant differences in verdicts or in the amounts of damages awarded. Although a significant difference was found in the amounts of damages awarded as a proportion of damages sought, this difference appeared only in automobile negligence cases. These results cannot be attributed to the size change, since the change from twelve- to six-member juries was accompanied by two other procedural changes which allowed for discovery of insurance policy limits and the creation of a mediation board. Either of these changes may have led to a greater number of settlements for certain types of cases.

A survey of jury performance in 180 civil cases in Maine, New Hampshire, Massachusetts, and Rhode Island also precluded the possibility of attorney bias (Beiser & Varrin, 1975). As compared to twelve-person juries, six-person juries were quicker to reach a verdict (median deliberation time was 2.5 hours versus 3.2 hours), less likely to find for the plaintiff (47.5 versus 76.9 percent), and less generous in the amounts awarded for damages (median award was $5100 lower). Although a differential in the amount of damages persisted even when the magnitude of the amount sought was taken into consideration, other factors, such as economic inflation and the high variance in awards, may also explain the observed difference.

Experimental studies too have revealed few significant differences between six- and twelve-person juries. There were no significant differences in either verdict distribution or the number of votes taken in one study of six- and twelve-member panels, although the fact that no jury voted to convict the defendant limited the usefulness of these findings (Davis et al., 1975). Another study failed to uncover significant differences due to size effects (Buckhout et al., 1977). In still another study deliberation time decreased in six-member juries, but the average contribution by individual jurors was the same in juries of both sizes (Friedman & Shaver, 1975). Twelve-member juries were found to be more likely to hang than were six-member juries, which failed to have any hung juries (Padawer-Singer, Singer, & Singer, 1977). In 23.9 percent of the six-member juries studied, five or six jurors had similar predeliberation opinions on the case. In these juries, deliberation time was very brief (77 minutes versus 155 minutes), which suggested that six-member panels are likely to start deliberation with undifferentiated verdict preferences.

Several effects of jury size replicate research on nonjury small groups (Saks, 1975). Large juries as a group recalled more trial evidence than small juries, were likelier to include divergent viewpoints and thus less popular views, and produced more discussion in deliberation.

In a frequently cited study of jury size a videotaped reenactment of an automobile negligence case was presented to sixteen student mock-juries assigned to either six- or twelve-member panels (Kessler, 1973). Deliberations were recorded on audiotape, and the juries were observed through one-way mirrors. In accordance with Michigan law, a five-sixths majority was required to render a verdict. Jurors on six-member panels were more likely to participate in discussion: 95 percent of jurors on six-member panels contributed to discussion, as compared to only 75 percent on twelve-member panels. However, this study had four major flaws (Diamond, 1974; Zeisel & Diamond, 1974; Saks, 1977). The sample size was too small. The stimulus case was heavily weighted in favor of the defendant and not a single conviction was reported. The major conclusion was partly an artifact of the way participation was measured: because there are fewer people in a six-person jury, even with an equal rate of participation each juror will use up a greater proportion of the total deliberation time. And in six of the twelve-member juries and four of the six-member juries, predeliberation questionnaires showed that a verdict-rendering quorum had been reached before deliberation commenced.

In a study at the University of Georgia student mock-jurors were randomly assigned to six- and twelve-member juries (Valenti & Downing, 1975). Half of the juries in each group heard an audiotaped case in which the apparent guilt of the defendant was high; the other half heard a case in which the defendant's apparent guilt was low. Deliberations were audiotaped, and visual observations were made through two-way mirrors. Jury size was found to have no effect on verdict distribution in cases where the apparent guilt of the defendant was low, but in cases where apparent guilt was high, six-member juries were more likely to vote for conviction. However, when hung juries were assigned verdicts, based on the majority faction preference, all effects on verdicts due to jury size vanished. Six-member jury deliberations were short and unlikely to deadlock, and members of six-person juries rated twelve-member juries as more thorough in comparison to six-member juries. These effects were particularly pronounced in six-member, high apparent guilt juries. Unfortunately, random assignment of juries to experimental condition does not necessarily equalize pre-experimental group differences. Subjects assigned to the six-member, high apparent guilt condition were more likely to be conviction-prone before deliberation. When statistical adjustments are made to account for this predeliberation difference, all of the major experimental findings wash out (Saks, 1977; Grofman, 1976).

In summary, methodological flaws in the research designed to detect jury size effects render any conclusions tentative. A few tentative conclusions are warranted. Six-person juries reach verdicts more quickly than twelve-person juries. Recall of evidence during deliberation is likely to be more complete in larger juries. And, the variety of viewpoints represented on a twelve-person jury is likely to be greater than on a six-person jury.

A thorough review of research on jury decision making yields a large catalogue of empirical generalizations. However, events occurring during deliberation, including communication among jurors, are still poorly understood. Theoretical analyses of jury decision making are also uninformative on the topic of deliberation processes. The study of jury performance that is reported in this book is the most extensive analysis of behavior during jury deliberation that has been conducted to date. It concludes with a general and empirically validated theoretical model of jury decision making.

We have presented conceptualizations of the juror and jury decision tasks based on current psychological theory. The juror task analyses concentrated on the comprehension and inference processes involved in: constructing a credible narrative by integrating trial testimony and arguments with general world knowledge, establishing the verdict categories as presented in the trial judge's charge, and classifying the story into the best-fitting verdict category. The Story Model of juror decision making will be cited frequently in our discussions of results that are relevant to individual juror behavior.

Less is known about jury decision processes and our conceptual analysis is closer to a loosely structured description of deliberation events than to a tightly-knit predictive model. These events include: agenda setting, discussion, expression of verdict preferences, assessment of current faction sizes, deadlocking, and requesting additional instructions from the trial judge. One major goal of the present research is to develop this model by establishing well-defined relationships among these subprocesses (see Chapter 9).

After presenting our own conceptual framework, we noted that most traditional social science models for juror and jury decision making are of limited use in understanding actual jury performance including the full chain of subtasks we have identified. Finally, we presented an outline of empirical results from past research on jury performance. We concluded that there are still large gaps in our knowledge, particularly on the nature of events occurring during jury deliberation. We are now ready to introduce our own research program to study jury decision making.

3

The Study of Jury
Decision Making

The present study of jury decision making was designed to examine a major unexplored area: events during deliberation. Unlike most other research in social science, which is designed to extend the generality of theory, this study was planned primarily to obtain valid empirical knowledge about the performance of actual juries. However, it did not adopt the tactic of observing jurors in actual courtroom trials. Rather, because of laws prohibiting the direct scrutiny of actual juries and because of the important advantages of scientific experimental methods, the subjects chosen for study were mock juries, composed of prospective jurors deliberating to a verdict on filmed trial materials in a courtroom setting.

The Simulation Method

The word "simulation" is applied to several types of methods. These methods include simulation games (such as war games, diplomacy games, and business games), role playing, psychotherapy techniques, computer models of complex natural systems, and experimental simulation research paradigms. The experimental simulation paradigm was used in the present jury study. Over one thousand citizens called for jury duty in state trial courts were asked to view a three-hour filmed reenactment of a murder trial. After viewing the trial twelve jurors retired to a jury room to deliberate to a verdict on the case as if they were actual impaneled jurors.

By Hastie

This method is called a jury simulation or a mock jury experiment.

The central concept of the experimental simulation method is that the researcher selects subjects, designs a research task, and measures factors that systematically mimic, often on a miniature scale, the characteristics of a natural setting to which conclusions will be generalized. For example, an engineer or architect may construct a small model of a bridge or a building to use in experiments to test a new design principle. Similarly the mock jury is designed to imitate many aspects of a real jury, while control over the conditions in which the mock jury operates is retained by the experimenter.

Two major methodological concerns face a researcher when designing a study, namely internal validity and external validity. Internal validity refers to the degree to which changes in the measured dependent variables can be attributed to the manipulated independent variables. External validity refers to the degree to which the findings or results of research in one setting, such as a laboratory experiment, can be generalized to another setting, such as an actual courtroom. Threats to internal validity generally arise when factors other than the independent variables may be the causes of observed changes in the dependent variables. Threats to external validity arise when differences between the two settings—the research setting and the target setting—are such that effects found in the research setting do not hold in the target setting.

There is a tension between the concerns of internal and external validity. The more control one has over an experimental environment, the more one can ensure that all variables other than the dependent variable are held constant, thereby decreasing or eliminating the possibility that these extraneous or confounding variables have a causal role in producing the observed effects. This means increased confidence in the internal validity of experimental findings. However, experimental control usually comes at the cost of increased artificiality of the research environment. This means decreased external validity or generalizability of any observed cause-and-effect relationships. In the other direction, the closer an experimental environment is to a real world setting, the more likely that any experimental result will be valid in the real world situation. But by drawing the complexities of the real world into an experiment, one usually sacrifices the control and simplicity of design that increase internal validity. For example, one field study identified a correlational relationship between the race of a defendant and the severity of sentence for interracial crimes (Bullock, 1961). However, it would be difficult to conclude with any confidence that the race of the defendant alone caused the differences in sentencing. Any one of a number of other factors that may not have been measured and which certainly were not controlled could have contributed to the observed difference in sentencing. Indeed, subsequent research showed that the observed differences may have been attributable to the prior criminal history of the defendants rather than to racial factors (Green, 1964; Hagan, 1974).

Yet carefully controlled research has been carried out in settings whose artificiality also renders useful practical generalizations untenable. Probably the only practical approach to studying the effects of such long-term causal contexts as media exposure, educational programs, and legal sanctions is through the use of relatively uncontrolled, nonexperimental, longitudinal methods (Cook & Campbell, 1979; Glass, 1968; Eron, 1982).

In jury research, field studies may be even more difficult to execute than in other areas of social research. Because of legal and ethical restrictions, a jury researcher can seldom, if ever, systematically manipulate the conditions under which an actual jury operates, such as jury size or decision rule, and can never directly observe many events of major interest, such as the content of jury deliberations (Katz, 1972). As a result, most jury research has used the mock-jury simulation method.

The main advantages of studying mock juries as opposed to real juries derive from the high internal validity of the controlled experiment. One of the most serious threats to internal validity is the possibility that the apparent cause in a cause-and-effect relationship is not the true cause (Suppes, 1970). To be confident that a particular cause is actually producing an observed effect, it is desirable to hold all conditions besides the independent or causal variable constant. Thus, for example, to study the effect of the defendant's race on sentencing would require making sure that all variables other than race were the same in each group of cases. This is not possible in a natural setting, where each trial is different, each defendant is different, and a large set of variables besides race may differentiate two groups of cases which have been divided into categories by race. In a simulation, these potentially confounding variables may be controlled.

Social scientists often substitute statistical control for experimental control of confounding factors. Under some conditions statistical modeling methods can provide statistical control that allows a researcher to make causal inferences (Kenny, 1979; Cook & Campbell, 1979). In some cases, particularly where policy analysis is involved, statistical control may be more appropriate than experimental control (Fairley & Mosteller, 1977). However, experimental or converging experimental and nonexperimental analyses are always preferable to statistical control alone in scientific research (Campbell & Stanley, 1963).

Extraneous differences in a real trial, such as the facts of the case or the characteristics of the defendant, are not the only possible sources of confounding of a relationship. Differences in the personal characteristics of members of a real jury can also confound a relationship. Here the advantage of a jury simulation is that the same stimulus trial may be shown to many sets of experimental juries. The performance of multiple replications removes the potentially confounding effect of individual differences, such as social class or gender. The method also permits study of a distribution of juror behavior, making it statistically possible to assess the replicability of observed differences.

The experimental control in a jury simulation which allows for increased confidence in observed effects also allows for systematic evaluation of an independent variable far beyond what could be done in a natural setting. One can ask mock jurors questions that the legal system would not usually ask real jurors. Mock jurors may be asked demographic questions, attitude questions, and questions concerning their feelings toward jury deliberation and verdicts or their assessments of other jurors. In addition to flexibility in the choice of measures, the jury simulation allows for observation of the mock jury's reactions to the trial and juror behavior during deliberations.

While methodological and practical reasons thus compel use of the simulation method for extensive jury research, the jury simulation entails drawbacks in the area of external validity. The seriousness of these drawbacks depends on the questions to be answered by the simulation and the way it is carried out. One problem has to do with the subject population. The vast majority of jury simulations have used students as mock jurors; only 12.5 percent have used subjects from an actual jury pool (Bray & Kerr, 1982). But the use of student subjects is questionable. (Foss, 1976). Because students differ as a group from actual jurors in terms of age, education, income, and ideology, students' behavior differs systematically from the behavior of real jurors (Simon & Mahan, 1971; Miller et al., 1975; Bray & Kerr, 1982; Colasanto & Sanders, 1976, 1978). Students tend to be less likely to vote for conviction than typical jurors. Younger jurors and jurors with less jury experience are apt to show leniency, which may explain the leniency bias found among students (Sealy & Cornish, 1973a). Since age and trial experience distinguish students from actual jurors, these two factors create a problem for generalizing from student mock jurors to real jurors. In general, evidence suggests that differences between students and real jurors pose a threat to the external validity of many conclusions from jury simulations that use only student subjects.

Another important problem of simulation is the method of presenting the mock trial, including its format (written transcript, audiotaped summary, videotaped trial proceeding), location (classroom, psychological laboratory, courtroom), and procedural elements (*voir dire*, opening statements, testimony, closing arguments, judge's instructions, deliberation). The most common method in jury simulations is to use a written fact summary of a trial and present it in an experimental laboratory simulation (Bray & Kerr, 1982). This unrealistic method of presentation eliminates the information available to the mock jurors through the trial participants' gestures and expressions. Furthermore, the written summary dramatically truncates the facts and circumstances of the case. These simplifications may cause the experimental independent variables to be unnaturally salient, thereby amplifying their effects (Miller & Fontes, 1979). Mock jurors in highly simplified simulations in fact experience an "extreme lack of involvement." Because of this, the findings in such simulations "may well be due to decisions being made impulsively without a thorough consideration of the evidence" (Foss, 1976). That is, typically unimportant nonevidentiary factors may play a larger role in simulation juries than they would in actual juries.

Still another important issue for jury simulations is the difference between the consequences of real jury and mock jury decisions. A real jury decides the fate of an actual defendant; a mock jury usually knows that its decision will have no such impact. Comparison of the verdicts of "alternate" jurors (subjects from the jury pool who observed as a group in the gallery of a courtroom) with real jurors in ten cases, revealed a greater tendency toward conviction among the alternate juries (Zeisel & Diamond, 1978). In contrast, comparison of two groups of student jurors, half of whom were told they were actually deciding a student discipline case and half of whom were told they were mock jurors, found the mock juries more lenient (Wilson & Donnerstein, 1977). A similar study found no verdict differences between mock juries and real juries (Kerr, Nerenz, & Herrick, 1979). For the present, the conflicting results of experiments studying the effects of decision consequences on jury verdicts preclude the statement of any summary conclusions concerning the effects of this factor.

Another problem concerns the unrealistic nature of most jury simulations that have been attempted. Given practical constraints, such as the impossibility of exactly replicating a live trial many times, the minimum requirements for a realistic jury simulation are subjects who approximate actual jurors in terms of demographic characteristics and attitudes, information and presentation conditions that closely approximate the actual courtroom trial, and conduct of deliberations so that mock juries are studied as group decision-making entities.

An obstacle to the practical application of laboratory-based findings is that the major goal of psychological researchers is to evaluate abstract theories and hypotheses concerning human behavior. When research is primarily concerned with theoretical issues, it is sensible to choose or create research settings to maximize the exploration of theoretrical issues with little or no consideration of their application to important natural settings (Pennington & Hastie, 1981; Winkler & Murphy, 1974; Ellsworth, 1977).

However, the present study of jury decision making had a primary goal of understanding the performance of actual juries, and major experimental design and procedure questions were decided with this goal in mind.

The major independent variable in the experiment, verdict decision rule, was selected because of its interest to contemporary courts and legislatures. The subjects were members of the major trial court jury pools in Massachusetts. A filmed reenactment of a typical felony trial was produced with the assistance of practicing trial attorneys and a Superior Court judge. The case materials were based on an actual murder trial transcript, and all essential testimony, argumentation, and instructions were preserved. Legal experts and jurors rated the film as extremely realistic.

Mock jury behavior appeared to approach the performance of actual juries. The most frequently chosen verdict of mock juries in the research was second degree murder, which matched the actual jury verdict, and the median mock-jury deliberation time of 138 minutes was within 10 minutes of the duration of the actual deliberation. All experimental procedures were carried out on working days in courtrooms and jury rooms in Massachusetts courthouses. During deliberation the researchers were not present, and a single observation camera was placed out of the line of sight of jurors seated in the jury room, although jurors were fully informed at the time that observations were being made. Deliberation was unbounded in time but with a practical limit of around one week. The longest experimental jury deliberated for four consecutive days before rendering a verdict. Standard deliberation procedures, such as the option of asking for further instructions from the trial judge and the presentation of a special instruction to continue deliberation after reaching an initial deadlock ("dynamite charge"), were included in the research.

Most of the experimental jurors had served on actual juries before participating in the research, and they gave the simulation extremely high ratings for realism and seriousness. When the experimental jurors were asked to rate the realism of the stimulus trial film and the seriousness of their deliberation, the average rating was over 8.5 on a 10-point scale. A vast majority of the experimental jurors believed that their verdict matched the actual trial verdict. A final evaluation of the seriousness and realism of the experimental mock juries was provided by a tabulation of jurors' oral references to the experimenters, to the experimental nature of the task, or to any other aspect of their role as research subjects. Less than 2 percent of all remarks fell into this category, and these remarks typically occurred only at the beginning and end of deliberation.

Although the study used a simulation method that was very realistic, the method departed from an actual jury experience in some respects. First, the procedure was conducted by researchers, not court officers. Second, an unrealistically brief *voir dire* procedure was employed to eliminate jurors who would probably not have been seated if the two participating attorneys had tried the case before an actual jury.

Third, the impact of the trial in a videotaped medium may be subtly different from that of a live trial. For example, comparison of live and videotaped modes of presentation of the same civil cases has shown that although presentation mode does not affect jury decision, there is a significant improvement in accuracy of jurors' memory for testimony when presented on videotape rather than live (Miller, 1975; Miller et al., 1975). However, jurors are slightly more accurate at detecting deliberate lying by witnesses in live as compared to video- or audiotaped modes (Miller & Fontes, 1979). A study comparing live, videotaped, audiotaped, and written formats to present a civil trial, also seemed to show no impact of mode of presentation on verdict decisions, but nevertheless revealed significant effects on juror evaluations of the credibility of certain witnesses (Farmer et al., 1975; 1977).

Fourth, the mock trial was shorter than a comparable live trial. The enactment was three hours long, whereas the trial on which it was based filled three working court days. The difference in lengths was due to the elimination of recesses, of pauses for bench conferences, of time spent waiting for witnesses to appear, and of repetitions in testimony, questioning, and instructions. Fifth, immediately after the case had been presented, the experimental jurors had to complete a one-item questionnaire to ascertain their predeliberation verdict preferences.

Sixth, the mock jurors were aware that observers were recording their behavior during deliberation, which may have had an important effect on their behavior. For example, perhaps the knowledge that they were under scrutiny induced experimental jurors to be on their best behavior. Thus, estimates of the rates at which jurors openly expressed antidefendant prejudices, encouraged discussion of inadmissible evidence, or urged fellow jurors to reach a compromise verdict may have been low.

Seventh, experimental jurors were aware that their verdicts would not affect a real defendant's fate. Although experimental jurors went so far as to discuss the effects of their verdict on the defendant and his family, the gravity of their deliberations did not match the quality of an actual murder trial. The clearest sign of this occurred at the end of the deliberation when a verdict was rendered. Experimental jurors typically greeted the end of their task with feelings of relief and pleasure, while a typical postconviction murder juror is a study in dejection and solemnity. The significance of this factor for the generality of the study's results is hard to assess. At a minimum, it sharply limits any conclusions about the emotional climate of deliberation. Yet emotional involvement in the experimental task was very high, and it seems that other characteristics of jury performance, including the nature of the verdicts reached, would not necessarily be disturbed by this difference.

The method in the present jury simulation study had considerable similarity to the actual criminal jury trials to which its conclusions are to be generalized. The major limitations on generalizing from this experiment to actual trials concern the jurors' violations of the judge's instructions on testimony admissibility and compromise verdicts, the overt expressions of ad hominem prejudice or bias, and the emotional quality of deliberation behavior.

Given the realistic jury simulation method, another problem is created by the need, when testing the effects of an independent variable, to hold all the facts and content of the mock trial constant except for the levels of the manipulated independent variable. For this reason only one case is usually used in a jury simulation; the same case is presented to many mock juries under varying experimental conditions. The problem this raises for external validity has to do with whether effects found using a single case will also appear in similar cases. This question cannot definitely be answered without repeating the experiment using different cases.

In the end, the evaluation of external validity involves the basic question: What is the relation between the results of the simulation and the operation of the naturally occurring phenomenon? There are four possible answers to this fundamental question. The first possibility is that the results of the simulation exactly match the real phenomenon. The second possibility is that the pattern of the effects is ordinally the same in the real world and in the simulation but that exact quantitative levels of measured variables do not match. For example, other mock jury experiments have found that unanimous juries deliberate longer before reaching verdicts than nonunanimous juries (Saks, 1977). This ordinal relationship may hold for actual juries under the different decision rules, but it is not likely that specific quantitative values will also hold. The third possibility is that the simulation produces an effect not present in the real setting or that the simulation fails to include an effect that is present in the real setting. For example, one problem in detecting the impact of variation in jury size on the quality of the jury's performance is that even very important differences in performance may be too slight to detect using a realistically complex mock-jury method with a limited number of juries (Lempert, 1975). The final possibility is for an effect found in one direction in the simulation to be found in the opposite direction in the real case. This last possibility is the most disturbing, in that it suggests that totally different processes operate in the simulation and in the situation it attempts to simulate.

Improper generalization is probably the major error in social science research (Meehl, 1977). It is never possible to say with absolute certainty exactly what relationship holds between a simulation and the natural phenomenon to which it refers. This problem of inductive reasoning from one case to another has been an enigma to philosophical and scientific analysis for centuries (Goodman, 1965; Cohen & Nagel, 1934). Modern statistical theory provides only limited solutions that apply chiefly to projections across time, and even these cases have been considered within a dense network of restrictive assumptions (Hacking, 1965).

A systematic approach to the problem of induction can begin by assuming that the existence of a phenomenon, such as a cause-effect relationship, in one setting is a prima facie case for its generality. Then the projectability of the result can be systematically evaluated by examining each conceptual dimension along which variation occurs from one setting to the other. In studies of jury decision making the dimensions where differences occur include subject, as between college sophomore and citizen juror, setting, as between laboratory and courtroom, stimulus material, as between audiotaped trial summary and full courtroom trial proceeding, and task, as between completion of a questionnaire and deliberation as a jury (Davis, Bray, & Holt, 1977; Gerbasi, Zuckerman, & Reis, 1977; Pennington & Hastie, 1981a).

The present experimental procedures were carefully designed to match actual trial conditions closely on the major dimensions along which generalization would depend. Whenever the experimental method departs from actual trial procedures in a manner that might threaten generalization from the experiment to actual trials, this limitation will be noted in our discussion of results obtained in the experiment.

Experimental Procedure

Experimental subjects in the mock jury study were recruited from the Superior Court jury pools in three counties in Massachusetts. At the beginning of each one-month sitting, the study was described to the jury pool by a judge and one of the researchers. A printed volunteer form was passed out, and names of potential mock jurors were collected. Generally the volunteer rate ranged between 75 percent and 85 percent of the jury pool.

Later in the sitting, when a mock-jury was to begin, the chief jury pool officer called a panel of sixteen to twenty volunteers. These volunteers were taken to a small hearing room and subjected to an informal *voir dire* conducted by the experimenter. During this *voir dire* jurors were excluded who were law enforcement agents or had members of their immediate families so employed, had recently been the victims of a violent crime, had heard

Table 3.1. Characteristics of participants in the mock-jury study and the jury pool.

Characteristic	Mock-juries (%)	Jury pool (%)
Male	56	66
Married	69	58
Occupation		
White collar	44	46
Blue collar	13	23
Housewife	11	6
Student	1	2
Retired	5	6
Unemployed	4	3
Other	22	20
Total	100	100

from other jurors about the experimental procedure or the details of a previous experimental session, or had been excused from jury duty for the following day. As soon as thirteen mock-jurors—twelve actual and one alternate—had been selected in the *voir dire*, the remainder were excused and asked to return to the jury pool to participate in the study at a later date.

The sampling procedure was designed to insure that the experimental mock juries would be composed of a representative cross-section of the population of citizens eligible for jury duty. The volunteers who participated in the study differed somewhat from jurors in the entire jury pool (Table 3.1). The proportion of female jurors who participated in the research was slightly higher than the proportion in the original pool. Married jurors participated in the research at a slightly higher rate than unmarried jurors in comparison with the relevant proportions in the pool. The distribution of occupations in the pool and in the sample of participants were similar, although blue-collar workers were underrepresented in the sample.

Following the *voir dire* selection, the mock jurors were taken to a vacant courtroom or jury room to view a videotaped reenactment of an actual trial. At this point the mock jurors were instructed that the trial was a reenactment of a real case and that the reenactment included all of the important evidence, details, and testimony presented during the original trial. They were told to refer to the reenactment itself during deliberation. Finally, they were informed that they would be asked, after watching the trial, to deliberate to a verdict, and that they would be observed during the deliberation. At this point the experimenter selected a foreman, usually choosing a juror who had previously served in that role. If none of the participants had previously served as a foreman, the experimenter selected a foreman at random by seat number, according to the procedure used in Massachusetts Superior Court trials.

The Trial

The stimulus trial was based on a complete transcript of a murder trial obtained with the cooperation of the Massachusetts Superior Court. The case was selected wth two criteria in mind: that it be typical of serious felony cases, and that it be sufficiently complex to afford a variety of plausible verdict preferences. The transcript was edited and the names and other details changed to conceal the identities of the original participants.

The reenactment was performed by university faculty, professional actors, a police officer, a Superior Court judge, and two attorneys. Each actor was given a summary of the case highlighting his or her testimony. The participating judge and attorneys were provided with unabridged copies of the actual judge's instructions, selections of relevant testimony, and the actual attorneys' opening and closing arguments as they were originally presented.

The reenactment was composed of spontaneous improvisations closely following the original case. The judge and attorneys acted in their usual courtroom manner, creating the mundane atmosphere of a real trial. The four-hour filmed trial was edited and condensed into three one-hour segments.

The trial opened with the clerk's reading of the indictment charging Frank C. Johnson with the murder of Alan Caldwell on the night of May 9, 1976. Next, the prosecutor's opening statement outlined the state's case. A police officer patrolling his beat had been attracted by a loud exchange of words between two men standing in front of Gleason's Grill. As he moved closer, he saw the victim, Caldwell, strike the defendant, Johnson, and the defendant retaliate by drawing a knife and stabbing downward, in an overhand thrust, into the chest of the first man. The officer interceded, disarmed Johnson, and requested help over a police callbox telephone. A second officer arrived and took Johnson to the station house. The first policeman remained at Gleason's bar until Caldwell's body was removed by an ambulance.

The first witness, the first police officer, took the stand and testified to the facts outlined in the prosecution's opening statement. On cross-examination the defense pressed the witness to establish details of the setting and the fight, eliciting the comment that in several years of prior acquaintance the defendant had behaved as a "quiet, law-abiding citizen." An effort to obtain a comment on the victim's "reputation for peacefulness" was cut off by an objection from the prosecutor.

The second witness, the police officer who took Johnson to the station house, testified to events at that time. He mentioned a conversation in the police cruiser, before Johnson had been apprised of his legal protections against self-incrimination ("Miranda rights"), in which Johnson remarked: "You know me, I don't cause any trouble. The man pulled a razor on me, so I stuck him." Following an objection by the defense, this testimony was stricken from the record and the jury was instructed to disregard it. On cross-examination the defense attorney established that the second policeman had known Johnson for years and that Johnson had not been in trouble before.

The third prosecution witness, the medical examiner who performed an autopsy on Caldwell, testified concerning the condition of the body, its personal effects, and the causes of death. He noted that a closed straight razor was found in the left rear pants pocket. Caldwell had been drinking heavily before his death, and the blood alcohol level of 0.32 percent would indicate he was intoxicated. When pressed by the defense, the witness stated that his examination of the stab wounds could not reveal the exact direction of the knife thrust, whether downward from above or upward from below. However, considerable force would have been required to cause the wounds.

The final prosecution witness was the owner and bartender from Gleason's Grill. He testified that on the afternoon before the fatal fight Caldwell and Johnson had engaged in a verbal quarrel. The quarrel ended with Caldwell threatening Johnson with a straight razor, at which point Johnson left the bar. Later that day, in the early evening, Johnson and one of his friends returned to the bar. A few hours later Caldwell entered the bar, and shortly afterward he and Johnson stepped outside together. The bartender looked out the bar window and caught a glimpse of the fight. On cross-examination, the defense established that a large neon sign blocked most of the view through the bar's window. The defense's effort to elicit comments on Johnson's reputation for peacefulness was blocked by objections from the prosecution.

At this point the defense case began with an opening statement suggesting that self-defense was the motive for Johnson's actions during the fight. The first defense witness, the friend who accompanied Johnson to the bar on the night of the fight, testified that he and Johnson attempted to avoid an encounter with Caldwell that night. He noted that Caldwell entered the bar after their arrival and initiated the conversation that led to Johnson's departure with Caldwell. The witness also claimed that he was able to observe the fight through the bar's door and that he saw Caldwell strike the first blow and follow up by drawing a straight razor. The defense also established that Johnson often carried his knife to use when fishing. An effort to elicit testimony concerning Caldwell's reputation for violence was cut off by prosecution objections. Cross-examination emphasized how difficult it would have been for the witness to see details of the fight through the narrow barroom door. Redirect examination established that Caldwell was a big man, 6'2" tall and weighing over 200 pounds.

The second defense witness, a barmaid from Gleason's Grill, confirmed the bartender's account of events inside the bar on the evening in question. She also testified that a car was parked in the street outside the bar, located where it would have obstructed the beat police officer's view of the fight. Again, the defense efforts to bring in testimony concerning Caldwell's reputation for violence were blocked by prosecution objections.

The final defense witness, Frank Johnson, the defendant, testified about his personal background and then described the events on the day of the killing. His description of the quarrel in the afternoon credited Caldwell with losing his temper and threatening him with the straight razor after Caldwell misunderstood an exchange between the defendant and a woman customer in the bar. He left the bar to avoid trouble and spent the afternoon and early evening with his wife and six children. A friend, the first defense witness, stopped by his house at 9:00 P.M., and the two of them went out for a drink at Gleason's Grill. Caldwell entered the bar after Johnson and invited him to step outside for a conversation. Once outside, Caldwell became hostile, threatened to kill Johnson, and finally punched him in the face. As Johnson stumbled away after the blow, he saw Caldwell draw a straight razor. Johnson drew his fishing knife from his pocket, and Caldwell ran onto it as he attacked Johnson. Johnson concluded his direct testimony by noting that he carried his fishing knife by habit, to keep it out of the reach of his children, and that he was in poor health, suffering from asthma. Cross-examination focused on the knife, Johnson's reasons for carrying it, and on the details of the fight. Johnson did not deviate from his original account.

The defense's closing argument outlined an interpretation of the testimony that would support a verdict of not guilty because Johnson acted in self-defense. The prosecution argued for first degree murder.

After the closing arguments, the judge began his instructions to the jury, noting that they, as the "sole judges of the truth," performed an important service both for the parties involved in the case and for the community at large, and that in so doing, they should put aside all prejudices and conscientiously seek the truth. He informed them that in order to arrive at a lawful verdict, they must determine what actually happened from the evidence presented during the trial, including both testimony and exhibits, and must establish the component elements of the crime charged according to the law as he presented it.

The judge suggested that in the task of reconciling conflicting testimony, they should consider certain factors that might bear on the credibility of a particular witness' testimony: the opportunity of a witness to observe and recall events and details, the potential biases a witness might have that would alter what was perceived, the contradictions or degree of consistency in a witness' account of the facts, and the character or personal characteristics that might affect the integrity of a witness. He then instructed the jury on the legal elements that must be established in determining the degree of the defendant's guilt and the possible verdicts they could render. Murder in the first degree was defined as a deliberately premeditated killing with malice aforethought. Murder in the second degree was defined as a killing with malice but without premeditation. Manslaughter was defined as a killing without malice, as when a person, in the heat of passion or in sudden combat, inflicts a fatal wound upon another. A verdict of not guilty by reason of self-defense derives from the right to protect oneself and pertains to a killing only when three circumstances exist: there is a reasonable expectation of suffering great bodily harm, all reasonable means of avoiding or escaping from the confrontation once it is apparent have been exhausted, and the means of defense is reasonable given the threat.

The judge also instructed the jury that, according to law, every defendant comes to trial with the presumption of innocence and that it was the state's burden to prove each of the elements of the crime charged beyond a reasonable doubt. He specified that the jurors were obligated to find the defendant guilty of the most serious crime of which he was guilty. He also reminded the jurors that, in making their decision, it would be improper for them to compromise on some unlawful, irrational basis.

At the conclusion of the charge, the judge instructed the jurors on the decision rule governing the number of jurors who must agree on a verdict in order for it to be properly rendered. At this point changes were introduced in the instructions from the actual trial to create three different experimental conditions. One-third of the juries were given a unanimous decision rule, whereby all twelve jurors were required to agree on a verdict; one-third were given a majority decision rule whereby ten of the twelve jurors were required to agree on a verdict; and one-third were given a majority decision rule whereby eight of the twelve jurors were required to agree on a verdict. Juries assigned to the unanimous, or twelve-out-oftwelve, decision rule were told: "Under the law of this state a verdict by unanimous agreement of all jurors is a proper verdict, so that when all twelve of the jurors agree on a verdict, that is the verdict to be returned." Similar instructions were given, with appropriate variations, to subjects assigned to the ten-out-of-twelve and eight-out-of-twelve deliberation rules.

The Deliberation

Immediately before the start of deliberation, the jurors filled out a questionnaire asking which verdict they would choose if they had to decide the case at that time, how certain they were of their choice, and which verdict they would select as a second choice. Responses to this questionnaire were used by the experimenters to determine jurors' membership in predeliberation verdict-favoring factions.

The decision rule assignments were made according to a random schedule that equalized the number of juries run by each experimenter in each decision rule treatment and balanced these factors across the fifteen-month period when experimental data were collected, from December 1976 through March 1978.

Twelve jurors were taken to an adjoining deliberation room where they were seated around a table with the foreman at one end. The table was arranged with ballot pads and pencils for each juror, photographs of the exhibits and of the street diagram used in the trial, and a copy of the indictment, just as in an actual trial. A small television camera was positioned in one corner of the room out of the direct sight of the jurors. They were instructed that a recording would be made of their activities during deliberation.

The experimenter reminded the jurors of their decision rule and gave them instructions. They were provided ballot pads for the option of secret ballots, but they could vote in any manner of their choice, if they chose to do so at all. They would be given a lunch break and excused at the end of the day but would have to return until they finished their deliberations. If they needed further instructions on points of law, the foreman could put the jury's question in writing and give it to the experimenter, who would remain in an adjoining room throughout the deliberation. In the event that jurors asked for further instructions, the experimenter would replay those requested portions of the judge's instructions on a television monitor. Similarly, if the foreman declared the jury deadlocked, the experimenter would present a videotaped charge from the judge, encouraging them to try once more to agree on a verdict (*Commonwealth v. Tuey*, 1851; *Commonwealth v. Rodriguez*, 1973; *Allen v. U.S.*, 1896; *Yale Law Journal*, 1968). Jurors would then resume deliberation until they rendered a verdict, or until they could not reach a verdict a second time, in which case they were declared a hung jury.

Immediately following deliberation, jurors were given a postdeliberation questionnaire to be completed individually without discussion. Jurors were instructed how to complete the questionnaire, and the experimenter stayed in the room to answer any questions and to ensure that jurors did not communicate with one another before the questionnaire was completed. The responses to this questionnaire provided five types of information: jurors' opinions about the character and quality of the videotaped trial and the mock deliberation experience, sociometric ratings of every other juror, personal and demographic background, recall of factual information contained in the trial, and postdeliberation opinions on pivotal issues in the trial.

For the first kind of information, a few questions were asked to obtain the jurors' reactions to the videotaped trial itself. For example, jurors were asked how difficult the case had been for them to decide personally and how realistic they had found the reenactment. Other questions asked specifically about the deliberation process. For example, they were asked how confident they were that the jury had reached a just verdict, how thoroughly they had considered all the evidence, and how seriously they had treated the case.

The second set of questions allowed jurors to rate themselves and every other juror on two dimensions. The first dimension concerned how influential and persuasive each juror had been in contributing to the group's decision. The second dimension concerned how open-minded and reasonable each one had been in considering opposing opinions. This rating task was aided by providing each juror with an individualized seating diagram that identified the respondent's seat in relation to the seats of every other juror.

The third set of the questions dealt with the jurors' previous jury experiences and their personal backgrounds. They were asked how many cases they had served on and how many of those were criminal cases. They also were asked for information about their political views, educational background, age, marital status, and family income.

The fourth set of questions assessed the jurors' ability to remember information contained in the trial contents and in the judge's instructions to the jury. First, jurors were asked to recall particular facts that could be viewed as important evidence relevant to major issues in the trial. For example, jurors were asked to recall the alcohol content of the decedent's blood, the location and nature of the stab wound, the distance from which a key witness had viewed the fight, and the order in which the two men had arrived at the bar that night. Second, jurors were to provide definitions of the verdict categories as specified in the judge's instructions to the jury, as well as definitions of some critical procedures the jurors had been instructed to employ, such as the criteria of reasonable doubt, of what constitutes evidence, and of reasonable inference.

In the final section of the questionnaire the jurors were asked to state their opinions about nine key issues in the trial. These nine issues were selected with the assistance of legal experts to represent the pivotal issues in the trial, opinions which would form the basis for discriminating between the four verdict choices available to the juror. These issues included why the defendant was carrying a weapon, why the defendant returned to the bar, who started the conversation and the ensuing fight, whether the victim had displayed his weapon, whether the key prosecution witness could see the fight, whether the defendant had tried to avoid combat, and how the killing occurred. The questions assessed the degree of agreement within a given jury on these important issues after they had agreed on a verdict. If the jurors had been convinced that the resulting verdict was indeed "correct" or "just," then the jury should also show internal consistency of opinion about the critical underlying issues. In contrast, if there was no internal consistency, it would imply that a high degree of superficial persuasion or coercion was involved in coming to verdict agreement. The questions also assessed the degree to which jurors and juries agreed on these critical issues in relation to the verdict they had decided on. In other words, they indicated if the jury was basing its decision on the same criteria as those deemed appropriate by legal experts.

When all questionnaires were completed, the experimenter debriefed the jurors by explaining to them the general purpose of the research and answering any questions. The experimenter then thanked the jurors for their participation and implored them not to discuss the experiment, the case, or their verdict with other jurors in the pool.

Summarizing the Deliberation

One distinctive characteristic of the present study, in contrast to most research on jury decision making, was that it aimed to measure a considerable amount of behavior during deliberation. An observational coding scheme was designed to summarize the videotaped deliberations along dimensions cited by legal and social science experts on jury performance: relative participation rates of jurors, voting patterns of the jury, extent to which the jury reviewed the evidence in the case, and accuracy with which the jury applied the law from the judge's charge to the evidence. Other observational classification schemes have been developed to study events that occur during social interaction, many of them designed to classify verbal and nonverbal behavior in psychotherapy or self-analytic groups as well as other types of groups (Russell & Stiles, 1979; Kiesler, 1973; Bales, 1950; 1970; Bales & Cohen, 1979; Schutz, 1958). But to apply them to the jury study would have incurred a great loss of precision and task-relevant specificity (Hackman & Morris, 1975).

The study's classification scheme was designed to capture the major events that were relevant to the jury's explicit information-processing task. The heart of the scheme was a system to code verbal references to evidence, the law, and statements of the relationships between the evidence and the law.

Each jury deliberation was coded by one of two coders, working directly with the videotapes, who scored each "utterrance" into four kinds of categories. Category one identified each speaker by seat number (1 to 12). Categories two and three identified the content of each utterance with reference to the trial facts (evidence or testimony) and the legal issues (judge's instructions) that should be central to the jury's task of rendering a verdict. Category four indicated the type of each remark. Remarks were classified as conveying information (assertion), asking for information (question), or urging the group to take action as in a vote (direction). Special codes were used to indicate events such as balloting, requests for further instructions from the court, and declarations of deadlocking. For a given event in deliberation, the speakers, the facts, the legal issues, and the remark types identified the verbal activity, discussion, or procedural activity, such as receiving further instructions from the trial judge, that was occurring. Thus, the basic unit for an analysis of deliberation content was the four-variable, speaker-fact-issue-type entry. At the start an attempt was also made to note the target of each speaking event, the juror or jurors to whom the remark was addressed, but coding this information from the videotaped recordings proved unreliable.

Defining the event was the most difficult problem in the development of an adequate coding scheme. Most between-coder disagreement (coder unreliability) arose from differences in event definition. The first condition of an event was that it be an utterance with more content than a simple exclamation or expression of assent or dissent. Remarks such as "yes," "uh-huh," and "goodness" were not counted. The remaining constraints on a coded event derived from the nature of the information specified by the fact, issue, and type codes. The basic rule was that whenever new fact, issue, or type information occurred, it signaled the start of a new event. This rule was qualified to allow for expanding a single event into a more complex multiple event code without starting a new event. Multiple events occurred when a speaker interrupted another speaker and repeated the original remark; when more than one fact, issue, or type code applied to a remark; or when fact and issue codes were applicable to a remark but no semantic connection was explicitly stated by the speaker.

The fact category, for which there were 43 classification codes, was used to summarize speaking references to the trial evidence and testimony. There were three classes of fact codes: specific, undisputed testimonial assertions, such as, "The victim pulled a razor on the defendant in the afternoon," or, "The defendant spent the evening with his family at home"; clusters of facts concerned with a specific event, such as all references to the fight during which the decedent was stabbed, including the location of the fight, presence of witnesses to the fight, and lighting or noise during the fight; and key facts concerned with matters that were the focus of the dispute between the prosecution and defense cases. Most of these facts were associated with conflicting testimony from prosecution and defense witnesses, and all of them were cited as points of dispute in the prosecution and defense closing arguments. For example, the defendant's testimony that the victim drew a razor during the fatal fight was called into question by the medical examiner's testimony that a closed razor was found in the dead man's left rear pocket. References to drawing or not drawing the razor comprised one of the key fact code topics. These points of dispute were given key fact status in the coding scheme because verdict decisions were expected to depend on the resolution of the ambiguities present in each item. Legal experts supported the use of the distinction and suggested that a sensitive measure of the quality of deliberation might be the ratio of key fact discussion to total fact discussion.

Several other types of discussion content were indexed by fact codes. References to the legal system concerning the conventions of trial procedure, the role of the juror, the disposition of the case, and laws not directly relevant to the jury's immediate decision were noted, as were anecdotes, analogies, and other references to personal experience. The relevance or nonrelevance of each event to *Commonwealth v. Johnson* was indicated in a type category code. Comments on the experimental procedures, the videotaping of the trial, and the research were also noted. A "zero code" was entered whenever remarks did not include fact category content, as when discussion centered on purely legal issues or on the procedures to follow in deliberation.

The issue category, for which there were 39 classification codes, was based on material presented in the trial judge's instructions to the jury. Specific legal categories included the substantive verdict definitions for each crime, such as premeditation, malice, or reasonable defense, and procedural conditions, such as the reasonable doubt standard of proof, reasonable inference, and the admissibility of evidence. The trial judge's instructions concerning witness credibility were also noted, such as the witness' opportunity to observe and remember, personal bias, contradiction or inconsistency, and integrity. Again, as for the fact codes, a zero code indicated that no legal issues were cited in a remark.

The type categories, for which there were 18 classification codes, indicated the apparent function of a remark (Austin, 1962; Grice, 1968, 1975; Searle, 1967, 1969, 1975). Three major types of speech were distinguished on the basis of their function: statements (conveying information), questions (requesting information), and directions (suggesting that the jury take an action). Although these performative types do not correspond directly to philosophers' and linguists' typologies, they clearly distinguish among functionally important events during jury deliberation (Katz, 1977).

Statement codes were used whenever the speaker expressed a point of view on an issue ("I think that it was first degree murder") or communicated information (answering a question or summarizing testimony content). Whenever a statement was in error, explicitly contradicting the content of trial testimony or the judge's instructions, a separate statement-in-error code was used. Questions and other requests for information ("What verdict do you favor?" "Did the defendant say that he left the bar first?") were coded in the question category. Coders were instructed to infer the intention of the speaker and to attempt to separate genuine requests for information from rhetorical questions that functioned as statements ("How can you possibly think that there was premeditation?"). These inferences depended on subtle cues, such as the general context of discussion, the speaker's tone of voice, and the nature of the responses elicited from listeners. The third type code, direction codes, was used to indicate jurors' suggestions or directions to other jurors to take an action. Typical directions included imperative remarks ("Let's discuss the definition of second degree murder," "I think that we should take a vote now").

Type codes could also indicate that the content of an entry was irrelevant to the jury task ("My car wouldn't start today and so I took the subway to the courthouse"). Finally, whenever more than four jurors spoke at once, an "outburst code" indicated that it was impossible to code the specific remarks by individual jurors. The outburst code was used on the assumption that remarks made in such confusion would not be of major significance in determining the outcome of deliberation, and, in any case, it was virtually impossible for the coders to capture specific remarks during an outburst. Nonspeaking events were also indicated with type codes, including balloting procedures, requests for instructions from the court, presentation of additional instructions, and instructions to a deadlocked jury.

Two general standards, reliability and validity, are applied to evaluate measurement techniques such as the deliberation coding method. Validity concerns how well the method measures the target phenomenon. The jury study addressed this issue in three ways: by using measures that had high plausibility or face validity as measures of the target, by using measures that had been used by other researchers to measure the same target, and by using multiple measures that converged on a target phenomenon (Garner, Hake, & Eriksen, 1956).

The reliability of a method has to do with how much nonsystematic, random error it introduces into the measurements. Both validity and reliability are necessary conditions for an adequate measurement instrument. However, reliability has precedence, at least procedurally, in that the assessment of reliability is fairly straightforward and is a necessary preliminary to the assessment of validity (Cronback, Gleser, Nanda, & Rajaratnam, 1972). The concept of reliability is closely associated with the notion that measurements should be repeatable. If measurement operations are applied to the same unchanging entity twice, the conclusions should match. This indicates that the measurement operations are free from nonsystematic, random error.

Two evaluations were made of the reliability of the jury coding scheme. Two coders, one male and one female, college graduates in their early twenties, coded all of the experimental jury deliberation videotapes. In addition, one coded samples of the deliberation twice, separated by an interval of several months, to assess the repeatability of coding within coders. The same samples of videotaped deliberation were also coded by other coders independently, to assess the repeatability between coders. Six deliberations were selected for this purpose, two from each decision rule condition, and three 20-minute segments from each selected deliberation were coded by each test coder. In short, eighteen samples were selected to represent the full variety of the deliberation tapes.

A statistic to indicate coding repeatability for nominal coding systems, called a Kappa was used to assess reliability within and between coders (Cohen, 1960, 1968). The mean Kappa for the eighteen samples evaluating within-coder reliability was acceptably high (+.84 for coder A, +.89 for coder B). Between-coder agreement was somewhat lower (+.57), but when compared to the maximum Kappa that could have been achieved for these applications (+.65), it seemed reasonably high.

In a typical 20-minute sample comparison of 162 events identified by coder A, there was agreement on 135 events. Eighty-three percent of coder A's events were matched by an event in coder B's results. This means that 27 events noted by coder A, or 17 percent, did not appear in coder B's results. Moreover, 85 of coder A's total sample of events, or 52 percent, were coded identically by coder B, showing exact agreement on speaker, fact, issue, and type codes. There was also substantial agreement on all of the similar-but-not-identical events, where only one variable code disagreed or the codes were semantically close in meaning.

Although this high level of intercoder reliability achieved for the fine grain level deliberation coding system is important, even more important is a high degree of reliability obtained for the dependent variables (Mitchell, 1979). Correlation coefficients across the eighteen 20-minute reliability check samples between the two coders for six quantitative dependent variables—namely number of events coded, facts coded, issues coded, different facts coded, different issues coded, and fact-issue pairings—ranged in magnitude from +.78 to +.93. An adequately high degree of intercoder reliability was achieved at the dependent variable level of analysis.

The deliberation events for each jury and the questionnaires for each juror produced four major data files: by jury, by juror, by time, and by movement between factions. The major categories of the 100-150 independent and dependent variables contained in each of these files were: experimental conditions; demographic, sociometric, and general attitudinal background indices; verdict preferences; coalition behavior; volume, quality, extent, and integratedness of deliberation activity; and trial recall and opinion measures. Statistical analyses were performed using these variables as summaries of the practically and theoretically important aspects of jury performance.

In summary, the advantages of the simulation method are its control of the experimental task conditions and manipulated variables, its power to "repeat" the task under virtually identical conditions for independent samples of subjects, and its opportunity to observe and measure behavior that would not be accessible in actual trial settings. The major weakness of the simulation method involves threats to the generalizability of results obtained with it. In the present study care was taken to ensure that the simulation was as realistic as possible to allow the application of results to actual jury trials. Checks on the realism of the method confirm its realistic nature and support the conclusion that results will generalize to actual juries.

4

Products of
Jury Deliberation

The major products of deliberation are the jury verdicts and individual jurors' intellectual and evaluative reactions to the stimulus trial and the experience of deliberation. These products are the focus of legal discussions of the right to trial by jury, and they have been almost the sole characteristic of performance that has been captured in theoretical analyses of jury decision making.

Verdicts

The modal verdict, second degree murder, was reached by thirteen juries in each decision rule condition (Table 4.1). There was a shift from the favorite predeliberation juror verdict preference of manslaughter to the final modal jury verdict of second degree murder. This shift was unexpected, and it could be the result of several processes of small group dynamics. For example, the shift might be a "polarization effect," such that the group verdict is more extreme on the conviction side of an acquittal-conviction continuum (Myers & Lamm, 1976); it might be a "harshness shift," such that groups are more callous to the consequences for the defendant than are individuals; or it could be a "shift to accuracy," such that the second-degree murder verdict is the most appropriate verdict for the particular case. However, in view of the initial distribution of juror preferences, the shift can be best understood as the natural resolution of social forces in the jury.

By Hastie

Table 4.1. Pre- and postdeliberation verdicts and deliberation times.

Jury verdicts	Decision rule		
	12/12	10/12	8/12
Postdeliberation			
First degree murder	0	5	1
Second degree murder	13	13	13
Manslaughter	7	5	8
Not guilty	0	0	0
Hung	3	0	1
Predeliberation preferences			
First degree murder	21%	28%	17%
Second degree murder	24%	23%	26%
Manslaughter	30%	29%	33%
Not guilty	12%	05%	11%
Undecided	13%	15%	13%
Holdout jurors at end of deliberation			
in verdict-rendering juries (averaged)	0.00	1.61	2.89
Deliberation time (averaged in minutes)[a]	138	103	75

$F(2,63) = 6.56$
$p < .003$
$MS_e = 3096$

a. See Appendix for statistical analysis procedures.

At first glance, the decision rule has no large or statistically reliable effects on the jury's verdict. On closer scrutiny, the data on decision rule have two notable characteristics: the relatively large number of hung juries under the unanimous decision rule, and the relatively large number of first-degree murder verdicts under the ten-out-of-twelve rule. The high frequency of hung juries under the unanimous rule must be labeled a trend because in absolute terms the effect is small (three hung under unanimity rule versus zero and one under majority rules). However, this trend probably reflects a true effect of decision rules. Several other experiments and at least one survey have observed higher hung-jury rates under the unanimous rule (Kalven & Zeisel, 1966). Furthermore, on common sense and theoretical grounds, it is difficult to doubt that deadlocking would occur more frequently under increasingly strict consensus requirements in almost any group task.

The relatively high frequency of first-degree murder verdicts in the ten-out-of-twelve condition is the other distinctive feature of the verdicts. Even slight biases in the jury decision, especially biases that might oppose the defendant, have great practical importance. For no apparent reason jurors randomly assigned to deliberate under the ten-out-of-twelve rule were likelier to prefer the first-degree murder verdict before deliberation started (an average of 3.3 per jury under the ten-out-of-twelve rule versus 2.4 and 2.3 per jury under other decision rules). This phenomenon, called sampling variability, can occur in real world juries when the distribution of initial verdict choices of the chosen jurors does not resemble the distribution of the population of potential jurors.

Statistical examination of the frequencies of first-degree murder verdicts in all sixty-nine experimental juries classified as unanimous or majority rule (ten-out-of-twelve combined with eight-out-of-twelve) gives a probability of obtaining results that are as extreme or more extreme in the direction of more first-degree murder verdicts in majority rule juries than were actually obtained in the study. The Fisher exact probability statistic indicates that this probability is .08, which supports the conclusion that first-degree murder verdicts are more likely to occur in majority rule juries (Mosteller & Rourke, 1973). However, this test does not distinguish between the contribution of sampling variability at the start of deliberation and decision rule effects during deliberation.

The appearance of first-degree murder verdicts only in majority rule juries is probably more than merely an accident of juror verdict preference sampling. Among juries that started deliberation with relatively large first-degree murder verdict-favoring factions (containing four, five, or six jurors), five such factions are found in twelve-out-of-twelve juries, ten such factions in ten-out-of-twelve juries, and one such faction in eight-out-of-twelve. This difference in the appearance of large first-degree murder factions reflects the sampling variation effect. However, the fate of these juries is different in the three decision rule conditions: none of them render first-degree murder verdicts in the twelve-out-of-twelve condition (0/5); four of them end with a first-degree murder verdict in the ten-out-of-twelve condition (4/10); and the single jury in the eight-out-of-twelve condition reaches a second-degree murder verdict (0/1).

A statistical analysis can be made to evaluate decision rule effects beyond the initial verdict distribution sampling effect. The sixteen juries that started deliberation with at least four jurors in favor of first degree murder allow comparison of the frequencies of first-degree murder verdicts in unanimous and majority rule juries (unanimous versus ten-out-of-twelve and eight-out-of-twelve). There are five such juries in the unanimous deliberation rule condition and no first-degree murder verdicts, while there are eleven such juries in majority rule conditions and four first-degree murder verdicts. Here the Fisher exact probability is .18, which is substantial enough to imply that first-degree murder verdicts in the stimulus case are associated with majority rule deliberation processes.

A similar conclusion can be drawn from juries with smaller first-degree murder factions, comprising two or three jurors. None of the twelve such juries rendered first-degree murder verdicts under the unanimous decision rule (0/12), one of the ten ten-out-of-twelve juries (1/10) ended with first degree murder, and one of the fifteen eight-out-of-twelve juries (1/15) found the defendant guilty of first degree murder. Again, the only first-degree murder jury verdicts occurred in the majority rule experimental conditions. In addition, while less frequent, these verdicts were not restricted to juries whose initial faction for first degree murder was large.

Sampling variability may have an advantage in determining final verdicts under less strict majority decision rule conditions. This possibility is reinforced by the fact that the first degree verdict for the stimulus case is virtually untenable in the eyes of legal experts. No experienced trial judge or attorney out of a sample of over twenty found the first degree verdict acceptable. Thus, a first-degree murder verdict is indicative of a failure of the deliberation process. Another indication that initial verdict preferences dominate final verdicts to a greater degree under less strict decision rules is the fact that majority rule deliberations are shorter and less thorough than unanimity rule deliberations, and jury verdicts are more closely related to initial juror verdict preferences in majority rule conditions. Thus, majority rule deliberations as contrasted with unanimous deliberations exert less of a moderating or damping influence on exceptional initial inclinations of individual jurors.

Deviations from the second-degree murder verdict for the stimulus case are a cause for concern, because this verdict is the "correct" one on a number of grounds. First, the jury in the actual trial on which the case was based returned a verdict of second degree murder. Second, the legal experts who viewed the case consistently selected the second-degree murder verdict. Third, second degree murder is the modal verdict for the experimental juries. However, the issue of the correctness of the final verdict cannot be resolved in absolute terms, for there are no ideal rational or empirical criteria for accuracy in jury decisions. At a minimum, each jury's evaluations of witness credibility, reasonable inferences from the testimony, and reconstruction and interpretations of the judge's summary of the law must be considered in order thoroughly to assess verdict correctness. For example, in the stimulus case, if a jury decided that all testimony from defense witnesses was false, a verdict of first degree murder could be acceptable. Yet, such an interpretation of the evidence would be very unconventional. For the most part, the exceptional, nonsecond-degree murder verdicts were associated with jurors' errors of comprehension and memory for testimony or the judge's instructions.

In short, juries under the three decision rule conditions are equally likely to reach the second-degree murder verdict that is the proper verdict. However, there is a trend to reach first-degree murder verdicts under the majority rule conditions. Moreover, all three hung juries under the unanimous rule would have rendered improper, nonsecond-degree murder verdicts if the largest faction had prevailed. Although these trends reach only marginal statistical levels of significance, they provide some evidence for differential "improper" conviction rates across decision rules for the stimulus trial.

Predicting the Final Verdict

The major focus of all theoretical models of jury performance has been on predicting the jury's final verdict from information about the jurors' personal characteristics or from the distribution of verdict preferences at the start of deliberation. Predictions from five types of models can be compared to the performance of the mock juries: voting rule models, belief continuum models, choice agenda models, bellwether prediction rules, and discussion valence models (Table 4.2).

Table 4.2. Rules to predict jury verdicts.

	Correct predictions (%)			
Prediction rule	Overall	12/12	10/12	8/12
Plurality rule. Verdict category receiving greatest number of initial ballots is predicted jury verdict. If no plurality exists, predict a hung jury.	43	43	39	48
Unweighted average rule. Jurors' initial ballots are averaged with not guilty (NG) scaled as 4 points, manslaughter (MS) 3 points, second degree murder (M2) 2 points, and first degree murder (M1) 1 point. Classification rule:	59	43	70	63

Average	*Predicted verdict*
0–1.50 points	M1
1.51–2.50 points	M2
2.51–3.50 points	MS
3.51–4.00 points	NG

Table 4.2. (*Cont.*)

Prediction rule	Correct predictions (%)			
	Overall	12/12	10/12	8/12
Weighted average rule.[a] Jurors' initial ballots are averaged using the weighting rule determined from a linear regression model:	75	65	83	78

$$Y = -.12 \times \text{(votes for M1)}$$
$$-.03 \times \text{(votes for M2)}$$
$$+.10 \times \text{(votes for MS)}$$
$$+.14 \times \text{(votes for NG)}$$
$$+2.0.$$

Classification rule:

Weighted average	Predicted verdict
0–1.50 points	M1
1.51–2.50 points	M2
2.51–3.50 points	MS
3.51–4.00 points	NG

Social choice theory agenda rules. Based on initial verdict preference, each juror votes for the alternative set that includes the most preferred verdict. Each vote outcome is decided by majority rule; if there is no clear majority, no prediction is made. After each vote, losing jurors shift preferences to the nearest verdict category that has not been eliminated in earlier votes.

First Vote Second Vote Third Vote

Agenda #1

M1 ······ M1 ······ M1	64	65	65	61
M2 ······ M2 ······ M2				
MS				
NG ······ MS ······ MS				
NG ······ NG				

Agenda #2

M1 ······ M1 ······ M1	65	70	65	61
M1 ······ M2 ······ M2				
M2 ······ M2				
MS ······ MS ······ MS				
NG ······ NG				

Table 4.2. (*Cont.*)

	Correct predictions (%)			
Prediction rule	Overall	12/12	10/12	8/12
Agenda #3	51	52	48	52
MS ······ MS				
M2				
M1 ...... M2 ······ M2				
NG M1 ······ M1 ...... M1				
NG NG ...... NG				
Bellwether juror rule. First juror to shift verdict preferences from initial vote will move to a verdict category that is the final jury verdict.	45	40	52	41
Hoffman discussion content valence rule. The difference between the number of remarks made for and against each verdict category or its elements is the verdict's valence index.				
Prediction Rule #1. First verdict to "lead" with highest valence index will be the jury's verdict (hung juries excluded).	48	52	39	52
Prediction rule #2. First verdict to reach or exceed a valence index value of 5 will be the jury's verdict (hung juries excluded).	40	35	52	32
Juries in which final verdict has highest valence index at end of deliberation	78	85	78	73
Juries in which final verdict has highest valence index at any point during deliberation	81	90	83	73
Mean time at which winner first had highest valence index	—	83 min	63 min	48 min

a. Initially undecided jurors are excluded, but the additive constant (2.0) may reflect their influence. M1, M2, MS, and NG denote the verdicts for first degree murder, second degree murder, manslaughter, and not guilty.

Combinatorial voting rule models assume that the relationship between the predeliberation distribution of juror verdict preferences and the final jury verdict can be stated as a simple election rule, such as "majority wins" or "two-thirds majority wins, otherwise hung." For example, postdeliberation interviews with jurors from 225 trials to reconstruct first-ballot verdict distributions found that "the jury in roughly nine out of ten cases decides in the direction of the initial majority," implying that a "majority wins" election rule described the jury decision process (Kalven & Zeisel, 1966, p. 488). Presumably this study dealt with convict-acquit verdict decisions, but the majority rule applies as well to multiple verdict alternative cases. One application to results from the present experiment lumps all convictions together and predicts conviction verdicts for all but three of the mock juries. The precise majority prediction rule is: ignore initially undecided jurors; total the numbers of jurors voting for first degree murder, second degree murder, and manslaughter; compare the number for conviction to the number for not guilty; and then predict the final verdict from the winner. Since no jury returned a verdict of not guilty, the rule is very successful. However, as it does not predict hung outcomes and predicts not guilty in three juries, it misses in six out of sixty-nine juries, for a 91 percent accuracy rate when guilty versus not guilty outcomes are the only consideration.

However, it is possible to go beyond the majority rule and attempt to predict final verdicts from the most popular initial verdict, again, ignoring initially undecided jurors. This plurality rule has an overall accuracy of 43 percent, or slightly higher under the eight-out-of-twelve decision rule. The logic of the plurality rule is close to the faction size principle for social influence, which predicts that the larger the most popular faction is, the likelier it is to prevail. This prediction is supported by the mock jury results, for when the most popular initial faction (plurality) has 8 or more members, it prevails 100 percent of the time; 7 members, 75 percent; 6 members, 57 percent; 5 members, 47 percent; 4 members, 33 percent; and 3 members, 25 percent. However, the shift from the modal juror verdict preference of manslaughter to the modal jury verdict of second degree murder is problematic for majority or plurality rules.

Probably the most sophisticated voting rule models for consensus-seeking groups are Social Decision Schemes (Davis, 1973; 1980). In the past these models have been applied only to two-alternative jury decisions, with a third possibility, "hung," for the group product. Social Decision Schemes are typically defined by presenting a matrix with individual verdict preference distributions at the start of deliberation as a row index (such as 12 versus 0 votes for guilt, 11 versus 1 votes, etc.) and final jury verdicts as a column index (such as guilty, not guilty, hung). Thus, the cells of the matrix represent every possible initial deliberation-final verdict combination. A

Table 4.3. Transition matrices for twelve-member juries with three verdict alternatives.

Initial distributions of verdict preferences (guilty, not guilty)	Majority			Proportionality			Two-thirds majority		
	Guilty	Not guilty	Hung	Guilty	Not guilty	Hung	Guilty	Not guilty	Hung
12, 0	1.00	.00	.00	1.00	.00	.00	1.00	.00	.00
11, 1	1.00	.00	.00	.92	.08	.00	1.00	.00	.00
10, 2	1.00	.00	.00	.83	.17	.00	1.00	.00	.00
9, 3	1.00	.00	.00	.75	.25	.00	1.00	.00	.00
8, 4	1.00	.00	.00	.67	.33	.00	1.00	.00	.00
7, 5	1.00	.00	.00	.58	.42	.00	.00	.00	1.00
6, 6	.00	.00	1.00	.50	.50	.00	.00	.00	1.00
5, 7	.00	1.00	.00	.42	.58	.00	.00	.00	1.00
4, 8	.00	1.00	.00	.33	.67	.00	.00	1.00	.00
3, 9	.00	1.00	.00	.25	.75	.00	.00	1.00	.00
2,10	.00	1.00	.00	.17	.83	.00	.00	1.00	.00
1,11	.00	1.00	.00	.08	.92	.00	.00	1.00	.00
0,12	.00	1.00	.00	.00	1.00	.00	.00	1.00	.00

Social Decision Scheme is then defined by a pattern of probability values assigned to the cells in the matrix.

Transition matrices for three Social Decision Scheme models can be defined for three example group decision principles (Table 4.3). The first principle is a simple "majority wins, otherwise hung" rule. The second principle is a proportional probability rule model, where the proportion of initial verdict preferences directly predicts the proportion of juries across many cases rendering each final verdict. The third principle is a "two-thirds majority, otherwise hung" rule. Each entry in a matrix indicates the probability that a jury with a certain initial juror verdict preference distribution will render a particular verdict. For example, consider each model's prediction for juries that begin deliberation with five jurors voting guilty and seven jurors voting not guilty. The first model predicts the verdict will be not guilty with a probability of 1.00; the second model predicts .42 of the juries will reach guilty verdicts and .58 not guilty verdicts; and the third model predicts all juries will hang with a probability of 1.00.

The Social Decision Scheme representation has been applied to empirical results in two ways. In the model-testing approach the matrix of probabilities is specified before jury performance data are examined and then the matrix is compared using statistical tests of overall goodness-of-fit to evaluate its validity. Typically several alternate Social Decision Scheme matrices are defined *a priori* and a competitive goodness-of-fit testing procedure is used to select the best-fitting matrix. For example, Davis and his colleagues (Davis et al., 1975) tried thirteen alternative Social Decision Schemes for data from a mock jury study and concluded that the best-fitting model assigned probabilities to the matrix in accord with a 2/3 majority rule (if 2/3 of the initial preferences favor a verdict, predict that verdict for the jury; otherwise, predict a hung jury). The second application of Social Decision Schemes, which is labeled model-fitting, involves starting with a summary of the data as probability entries in the standard matrix (Kerr, Stasser, & Davis, 1979). Then an *a posteriori* Social Decision Scheme model is induced by searching for a parsimonious summary of the structure of the matrix.

The plurality rule and the majority rule can easily be treated as Social Decision Scheme models. The plurality rule predicts victory for the largest faction, otherwise hung. An alternative form of this Social Decision Scheme would predict victory for the largest faction, otherwise the probability of victory matches the proportion of committed jurors in the largest factions ignoring undecided jurors and small faction members. For example, this scheme would predict a .50 chance of victory for both manslaughter and second degree murder from an initial distribution of one first-degree murder vote, four second-degree murder votes, four manslaughter votes, two not-guilty votes, and one undecided juror. The same logic could be extended to yield a strictly proportional model in which each final verdict's probability is defined as the proportion of initial votes for each verdict. Proportion-based rules are frequently proposed within Social Decision Scheme applications, although tests of their validity require considerably more data than is available in the present mock jury study. Enough groups must be studied to allow the researcher to estimate empirically all probabilities in the matrix.

A second approach to the verdict prediction problem begins by representing individual and jury verdicts as locations along a unidimensional subjective belief continuum, such as convictability, probability of guilt, or seriousness of the defendant's offense. For example, the juror verdict alternatives in the mock jury study can be ordered from least to most serious: not guilty, manslaughter, second degree murder, first degree murder. One can go a step beyond this ordinal scale and apply modern psychological scaling methods to establish quantitative interval scale values for verdict seriousness that provide both ordinal and between-verdict distance information (Thurstone, 1927; Coombs, 1967). For simplicity, an equal-spacing interval rule was used which arbitrarily assigns first degree murder a value of 1; second degree murder, 2; manslaughter, 3; not guilty, 4. (Alternate analyses using interval scaled values based on college students' ratings produce similar results.)

One plausible prediction rule is an unweighted average, or center-of-gravity, rule that predicts the jury verdict from the average predeliberation preference on the verdict seriousness continuum. There are two parts to the prediction procedure: first a calculation procedure that estimates the average verdict for each jury, and then a classification procedure that assigns each estimate to a predicted final verdict category. For example, in a jury with no initial votes for first degree murder, six votes for second degree murder, three votes for manslaughter, one vote for not guilty, and two undecided jurors, the jury average would be 2.5 ($[0 \times 1] + [6 \times 2] + [3 \times 3] + [1 \times 4]$)/10). The classification procedure used for the mock jury study is: if the jury average is less than or equal to 1.5, predict first degree murder; if the jury average is greater than 1.5 but less than or equal to 2.5, predict second degree murder; if the jury average is greater than 2.5 but less than or equal to 3.5, predict manslaughter; if the jury average is greater than 3.5, predict not guilty. The example jury would be classified in the second-degree murder verdict category. The accuracy rate of this rule for the sixty-nine experimental juries is 59 percent.

A slightly more sophisticated version of the averaging model is an unequal weight-averaging model in which different initial verdict preferences receive different weights to maximize predictive accuracy. Several processes for deliberation could produce unequal weights. For example, jurors favoring particular verdicts, such as relatively extreme verdicts, might also be more persuasive during deliberation, or simply more talkative, or more stubborn. An illustrative weighted-average prediction rule was derived from a statistical regression analysis (Mosteller & Tukey, 1977). The weighting rule obtained in this analysis implies that initial votes for second degree murder are relatively uninformative as predictors of the final verdict, being weighted only −.03. This prediction rule includes an additive constant which might be interpreted as the final verdict prediction for a jury with all members undecided initially. This constant was estimated to be 2.0, suggesting that undecided jurors would eventually favor a second-degree murder verdict. This rule has fairly high predictive utility, and it classifies 75 percent of the experimental juries correctly.

The relatively large weights assigned to more extreme verdicts in the unequal weight prediction rule (−.12 to first degree murder verdicts and +.14 to not guilty verdicts) are consistant with a polarization effect; a tendency for individual judgments to shift during group discussion to become more extreme with reference to the midpoint of the relevant decision continuum. Thus, in a laboratory experiment focusing on mock jurors' judgments on a guilty-not guilty continuum, individual opinion shifts occurred such that members of juries that were predominantly not guilty before discussion were more extreme in their final not-guilty ratings, and the opposite shift occurred for juries initially voting guilty (Myers & Kaplan, 1976). The over-all shift from a modal verdict preference of manslaughter to second degree murder, for both jury verdicts and individual postdeliberation ratings in the present study, is consistent with the polarization shift interpretation.

Recently economists and political scientists have applied game theory and other economic developments to nonmarket decision making (Black, 1958; Farquharson, 1969; Fishburn, 1973; Arrow, 1963; Brams, 1975). The earliest contributors to this analysis of social choice were French social philosophers concerned with the establishment of political voting procedures that would maximize social welfare or, at a minimum, would not violate principles of consistency in social preference (deBorda, 1781; deCondorcet, 1785).

Social choice models have not been extensively applied to the jury decision task, although some prescriptive, normative analyses are closely related, as are the combinatorial voting models (Smoke & Zajonc, 1962; Friedman, 1972; Grofman, 1981). Agenda influence models are one especially promising development of social choice theory (Plott & Levine, 1978). Whenever a series of votes is used to express individual preferences among three or more alternatives, such as political candidates, policy actions, or verdicts, it is possible to influence the outcome of the votes by choice of voting scheme (majority, unanimity, preference ranking); addition or removal of alternatives from the choice set; deliberate misrepresentation of voters' preferences (insincere voting); or variation in the order or agenda in which alternatives are voted upon (Grofman, 1976).

An agenda is a series of partitions that groups alternatives into sets to be decided among by voting. For example, consider a jury that is attempting to decide between not guilty and guilty verdicts in the stimulus case, where the set of guilty verdicts includes manslaughter, second-degree murder, and first-degree murder alternatives. Following the first not guilty versus guilty decision, the jury might attempt to decide between manslaughter and murder, and finally between murder in the second and first degrees. The series can end at any point if a decision favors an alternative set containing only one verdict: not guilty on the first decision or manslaughter on the second decision. This example is not the only agenda decision tree that can be defined for the four alternative verdicts. Alternatively the agenda might pit the most serious verdict (first degree murder) against the others or start with a split between murder (first and second degree) and nonmurder (manslaughter and not guilty). In fact, fifteen distinct agenda trees are possible for a four-verdict alternative case.

Social choice theories predict the effects of varying the agenda structure on group choice for various distributions of individual preferences within the group (Plott & Levine, 1978). Three individual decision rules are postulated, one of which describes each voter. The sincere voting rule holds that a voter deciding between two sets of alternatives will vote for the set that includes the most-preferred alternative. The avoid-the-worst rule prescribes that, given a choice between two sets, the voter will vote against the set that includes the least-preferred alternative. The average value rule holds that the voter will choose the set of alternatives with the highest average value across all of its members. Assuming that the majority wins at any vote, predictions can be made as to which agendas favor which alternatives under various distributions of individual preferences.

A possible application is the use of agenda models to predict final verdicts from initial vote distributions in the present study. For this purpose, five simplifying assumptions are made. Verdict alternatives are treated as vote alternatives in the agenda. Only two-way voting decisions are considered in the agendas, such as a choice of not guilty or manslaughter versus second or first degree murder, or of not guilty versus manslaughter or second degree murder. A majority wins, or otherwise deadlocked rule will determine winners at each decision point. After a vote is taken, jurors who voted for the losing set will change preferences to prefer the nearest alternative along the not guilty, manslaughter, second-degree murder, first-degree murder continuum, and initially undecided jurors will be ignored in determining the outcome. Finally, the individual juror will vote according to the sincere voting hypothesis. Given these assumptions, the general concept of a voting agenda, and the distribution of initial individual verdict preferences, it is possible to determine whether or not a specific agenda decision tree is consistent with a jury's behavior. That is, given these hypotheses about voting processes and an initial juror preference distribution, each agenda tree structure uniquely predicts either a final verdict choice or undecided. The predicted verdict can be compared to the mock jury's verdict; if they match, the agenda tree is consistent with the result. (The next step in a thorough evaluation of the agenda model approach would be to examine the pattern of formal balloting during deliberation, so as to evaluate the consistency between the sequence of votes in each agenda decision tree and the sequence of formal decisions by the jury.)

The performances of three agenda structures are compared to results from the study of jury decisions (Table 4.2). The first structure starts with a murder versus not murder decision, namely first or second degree murder versus manslaughter or not guilty, followed by a decision between the pair of verdict alternatives in the winning set, namely between first and second degree murder or between manslaughter and not guilty. The second structure is an intuitively plausible sequence that begins with a guilty versus not guilty decision; then murder versus manslaughter; and finally first degree versus second degree murder. The ordering of decisions seems quite plausible in that more serious charges are considered only if lesser charges are rejected. However, the appearance of conservativism ("reluctance to consider serious charges") is superficial, and the agenda gives an advantage to more serious verdicts under most distributions of verdict preferences. For example, it correctly predicts that there will be no not-guilty verdicts but allows three first-degree murder verdicts under nonunanimous decision rules. In the third agenda structure sets of alternatives are constructed by ignoring any sensible ordering according to the harsh-lenient continuum. For example, first degree murder, second degree murder, and not guilty are grouped together as a set and pitted against manslaughter in the first decision. This anomalous structure is considerably less successful than the first two intuitively more plausible agendas.

Even this simplified application of the most successful agenda model (#2) can yield a 65 percent accuracy rate. Furthermore, it would probably be more reasonable to assume that each jury might adopt one of several possible agendas. Thus, rather than selecting a single most consistent agenda across many juries, the analysis could identify the best-fitting agenda for each jury separately. The examples presented here also ignore the complexities of considering characterizations of the alternatives that are partitioned to produce decision sets in the agenda structures. Most cases can be structured according to a multitude of evidentiary and legal issues. The use of special verdict interrogatories in many actual cases is an acknowledgment of the importance of the jury's decision agenda, and the contents of interrogatories suggest that the representation based solely on verdicts is simplified and perhaps invalid.

Actual balloting during deliberation includes many examples of deliberate or incidental agenda setting. The most common instances occur when not guilty versus guilty (manslaughter, second degree murder, first degree murder) ballots are suggested and taken. First degree murder versus lesser verdicts (second degree murder, manslaughter, not guilty) is also a common starting agenda. Many jurors understand the power of these simple agenda-setting strategies. Jurors in weaker factions defined with reference to these example agendas often resist balloting by arguing for alternative agendas or to defer voting.

The existence of majority rule juries, multiple verdict alternative trials, and special verdicts, especially if taken together, virtually guarantees that agenda structure can affect jury decisions (Levine & Plott, 1977). The differential success of the simple family of agenda models presented here is evidence for the significance of agenda structure. Furthermore, agenda models have potential as devices to predict final jury verdicts from initial verdict juror preferences.

Bellwether juror prediction rules hypothesize that the first juror to shift from verdict preference to verdict preference has special significance as a predictor of the final jury verdict (Hawkins, 1960). In two-verdict alternative cases one study of college-student mock juries found that the first shift predicted the final verdict in 81 percent of the juries (Kerr, 1981).

The same rule of thumb was applied to the data from the present mock jury study. Predict accuracy is higher if the behavior of initially undecided jurors is ignored, with final jury verdicts predicted correctly in 45 percent of the juries. If the predictive standard is relaxed, requiring only that the first shift is in the direction of the final verdict along the harsh-lenient verdict continuum, accuracy increases to 63 percent.

Behavioral scientists studying managerial decision making have used the contents of discussion at the beginning of a meeting to project to the conclusions reached in the meeting. In a study of group problem-solving discussions, the numbers of remarks made for and against possible solutions to the problems were coded (Hoffman, 1979). A valence index was constructed by subtracting the total number of remarks against a solution from the total number of remarks for the solution. The first solution that had a valance index greater than 15 was declared the winner and predicted to be the group's final choice. This prediction was correct in approximately two-thirds of the experimental groups.

This principle can be applied to jury decisions but with modifications to fit the jury's task. The earliest empirical research on the valence model was conducted on leaderless college students in three- or four-member groups who attempted to solve a production-team management problem (Hoffman & Maier, 1964). Their task differed from the jury decision task in important ways: the groups were small and discussed without an appointed leader; solution categories, analogous to verdict categories, were not provided in the problem statement; discussions were relatively brief, presumably lasting about forty minutes; the problem statement was short and available during discussion so that case-specific memory limits were not a critical determinant of performance; and discussion was not likely to be organized as a debate among competing factions, as it often is in jury deliberations.

A problem-specific coding scheme allowed observers to identify and tabulate remarks for and against each solution to the managerial production problems (Hoffman, 1979). One positive valence point was counted for each statement that described a solution, noted the positive benefits of a solution, indicated agreement with descriptions or justifications, urged other group members to accept a solution, or requested more information about a solution. Negative points were counted for critical remarks of the same types: rejection; justification of rejection; disagreement; urging others to reject; or, questions implying doubt. In the present study a parallel series of codes was set up for the mock juries within the general deliberation content coding scheme. In essence the codes substituted verdicts and verdict elements for problem solutions and counted agreements and disagreements with statements, questions, and advocacy of verdict alternatives.

Because the jury codes tended to include fewer types of statements than the discussion codes, valence indices were not as large as those obtained by Hoffman. Thus, the prediction rule declaring the first solution to reach a valence index of 15 the winner, had to be modified. Several absolute threshold rules were tried, such as calling the first valence index to reach 5 the winner, as well as relative thresholds, such as calling the first valence index to lead (the second place index) by 5 the winner. All these rules performed at comparable levels of accuracy. For example, the first verdict to lead rule was 38 percent accurate; the first verdict to lead by 5 rule was 35 percent accurate; and the first to reach a valence index of 5 rule was 40 percent accurate.

Although the valence index prediction rule is not impressively accurate, the verdict valence is clearly associated with the final verdict choice. The verdict with the largest valence index matched the jury verdict in 81 percent of the verdict-rendering juries. Thus, valence is correlated with verdict although the early valence index is a poor predictor of verdict. One explanation is that the jury task—namely story construction, verdict category establishment, and classification of story into verdict category—implies that discussion of verdict alternatives will tend to follow the jury's review of the evidence. Thus, verdict valence will not matter until the jury turns to the classification subtask. A tabulation of the average minute at which the final winning verdict first had the largest valence index was consistent with the view that the valence index does not favor the winner until well after the half-way point in deliberation for the average jury.

A conceptual problem also arises when a simple version of the valence model is applied to the jury task. In this application the valence model predictions may be primarily a reflection of the faction size effect that is the basis of the plurality rule Social Decision Scheme. Or discussion valence may cause solution choice rather than being an effect of an underlying true cause which might be faction size. However, it is impossible to distinguish among the alternate causal models that could relate valence, faction size, and verdict. Fluctuations in faction size and in the valence index across deliberation shows that the two variables tended to track one another's movements. Thus, the two variables were correlated within deliberation. However, there was no systematic tendency for shifts in one index to precede shifts in the other, and there was no support for either a simple "valence causes faction size" interpretation or the reverse.

At a minimum, the simple valence index model does not add predictive power to the plurality Social Decision Scheme in the mock jury study. It is still possible that a more elaborate form of the valence model could improve on the plurality model, perhaps by identifying juries in which reversals are likely to occur. However, the current form of the valence model may not be appropriate for consensus-seeking discussion groups in which the decision task is composed of conceptually distinct but functionally necessary subtasks. For example, it is not sensible to speak of "effective deliberation time" in a jury task where the verdict classification subtask depends on the previous completion of the story construction and verdict establishment subtasks. Finally, there is no empirical analysis that demonstrates that discussion valence exerts a causal influence on group solution adoption.

The practical predictive usefulness of these five types of psychological models can be determined by two comparative standards: actuarial base rates of verdicts for similar cases in typical courts and judgmental accuracy of legal experts. On the first standard, most criminal cases that go to jury trials are decided against the defendant. A survey of trial judges produced an estimated conviction rate of 63 percent, and current statistics from the Massachusetts courts where the mock jury study was conducted put the rate at 85 percent to 90 percent (Kalven & Zeisel, 1966). If the base rate for conviction is 85 percent, a predictor who simply guessed conviction for every case would be correct 85 percent of the time. The majority rule for prediction could improve on this to yield a 91 percent correct rate for the guilty-not guilty prediction when jurors' predeliberation verdict preferences are known. Given the high base rate of convictions that occur in typical jury trials, only an exceptionally powerful predictive rule could be of much use in making guilty-not guilty predictions (Meehl & Rosen, 1955). However, to give the theory-based prediction rules due credit, the prediction of specific verdicts in complex, multiple verdict cases would be an impressive accomplishment. The predictive rules are doubtless all superior to simple actuarial rules.

The second evaluative comparison is between the predictive powers of the theoretrical device and the predictions of expert observers. The mock jury study did not include the collection of data on expert predictions for the stimulus case, experimental juries, or other actual jury trials. These experts would prersumably be very accurate in predicting trial outcomes if given a summary of evidence or observations of the trial itself. However, they would probably not be impressively accurate at predicting individual jurors' initial verdict preferences when given the personal background of each juror, or the jury verdicts when given juror backgrounds or even intial verdict preferences (Penrod, 1979).

In short, present theory-based prediction rules are of limited utility. Major limits on their application stem from the unavailability of information required to generate predictions, such as predeliberation verdict preferences and first vote shifts. A better approach to the practical and theoretical prediction problems would be to develop a model of the entire jury trial process from initial jury pool composition to final verdict rendering.

Final Faction Patterns

Although the jury verdict distributions were virtually indistinguishable for the three types of mock juries, final juror consensus patterns varied dramatically. At the end of deliberation, verdict-rendering juries under the unanimous rule included no jurors who dissented from the jury verdict, while ten-out-of-twelve juries included an average of 1.6 dissenters, and eight-out-of-twelve juries included an average of 2.8 dissenters. The postdeliberation questionnaires, where jurors could privately note that they rejected the jury verdict even though they had supported it publicly, confirms this impression: there was an average of 0.9 dissenters per unanimous jury, 2.4 per ten-out-of-twelve jury, and 4.3 per eight-out-of-twelve jury (hung juries were excluded).

The lower rates of final consensus in nonunanimous juries are reflected in lower ratings of satisfaction with deliberation, lower juror agreement with the final jury verdict, lower ratings of the quality of other jurors' performance, and other measures of perceived adequacy of jury decision processes. These products are not as important in practical terms as jury verdicts. Nonetheless, satisfaction with the jury decision process is a critical attribute of the jury as an institution in American society. Public belief that jury decisions provide thorough, humane, and fair resolutions to important disputes is one of the major justifications for the jury institution. The conclusion that individual jurors are less satisfied with their verdicts under nonunanimous rules than unanimous rules is an important consideration in assessing the social value of alternative forms of jury trials.

Deliberation Time

The mean deliberation times for the mock juries showed a clear effect of decision rule, such that the stricter the rule, the longer the deliberation, with twelve-out-of-twelve being the strictest (Table 4.4). This result has been obtained in every experiment that involved variations in decision rule quorum requirements. Moreover, hung juries required almost twice as much deliberation time as verdict-rendering juries, again replicating the results of previous studies.

Table 4.4. Perceptions of the deliberation, verdict, other jurors, evidence, and instructions.

	Decision rule			
	12/12	10/12	8/12	
Pressure to change opinions[a]				
Majority	3.01	2.76	2.75	$F(1,785) = 0.81$,
Holdout	3.28	3.75	2.47	$p < .37$, $MSe = 6.02$
	$F(2,785) = 2.78$, $p < .06$, $MSe = 6.02$			
Decision difficulty[a]				
Majority	5.04	4.83	4.55	$F(1,785) = 2.79$,
Holdout	4.71	6.19	4.26	$p < .48$, $MSe = 5.76$
	$F(2,785) = 8.12$, $p < .0003$, $MSe = 5.76$			
Thoroughness of deliberation[a]				
Majority	8.29	8.05	7.99	$F(1,785) = 11.68$,
Holdout	7.86	6.94	7.22	$p < .0007$, $MSe = 2.30$
	$F(2,785) = 3.73$, $p < .20$, $MSe = 2.30$			
Seriousness of deliberation[a]				
Majority	8.27	7.93	7.92	$F(1,785) = 1.39$,
Holdout	8.29	7.67	7.38	$p < .23$, $MSe = 2.15$
	$F(2,785) = 2.28$, $p < .10$, $MSe = 2.15$			
Agreement with verdict[a]				
Majority	8.06	8.28	8.00	$F(1,785) = 211.99$,
Holdout	4.43	3.64	4.08	$p < .00001$, $MSe = 3.53$
	$F(2,785) = 0.27$, $p < .76$, $MSe = 3.53$			
Confidence in verdict[a]				
Majority	7.81	8.03	7.78	$F(1,785) = 161.32$,
Holdout	3.43	4.53	5.09	$p < .00001$, $MSe = 3.48$
	$F(2,785) = 2.32$, $p < .10$, $MSe = 3.48$			
Agreement among jurors on nine key issues (100 = perfect agreement)				
Majority	86	87	82	$F(1,785) = 15.96$,
Holdout	70	76	79	$p < .0001$, $MSe = 290$
	$F(2,785) = 0.62$, $p < .54$, $MSe = 290$			
Persuasiveness[b]				
Self	3.46	3.29	3.20	$F(2,613) = 42.22$,
Other	3.12	2.98	2.98	$p < .00001$, $MSe = .64$
	$F(2,613) = 3.91$, $p < .02$, $MSe = 1.1$			
Ingroup	2.77	3.09	3.05	$F(1,468) = 36.92$,
Outgroup	2.17	2.63	2.84	$p < .00001$, $MSe = .53$
	$F(2,468) = 5.27$, $p < .005$, $MSe = 1.20$			
Open-mindedness[b]				
Self	4.41	4.20	4.00	$F(2,664) = 122.84$,
Other	3.85	3.66	3.72	$p < .00001$, $MSe = .57$
	$F(2,664) = 13.56$, $p < .00001$, $MSe = .63$			

Table 4.4. (*Cont.*)

	Decision rule			
	12/12	10/12	8/12	
Ingroup	3.68	3.79	3.81	$F(1,478) = 80.72$,
Outgroup	2.84	3.08	3.48	$p < .00001$, $MSe = .57$
	$F(2,478) = 5.36$, $p < .005$, $MSe = 1.41$			
Juror memory for facts from testimony[c]	.59	.61	.60	$F(1,825) = 399.15$, $p < .00001$, $MSe = .03$
Juror memory for judge's instructions[c]	.45	.42	.46	
	$F(2,825)= 0.73$, $p < .48$, $MSe = .07$			
Jury memory for facts from testimony[c]	.93	.92	.93	
Jury memory for judge's instructions[c]	.81	.81	.85	

a. Scale ranges from 0 to 9.
b. Scale ranges from 0 to 5.
c. Proportion correct (1.00 = perfect memory).

Postdeliberation Impressions and Memories

One frequently cited benefit of the jury trial system is the increased respect accorded to legal institutions by citizens who have served. An effort was made to assess the jurors' attitudes toward the experience of deliberating in the mock jury and their memory of decision-relevant trial information. In the questionnaire administered following deliberation, jurors rated the quality of the deliberation in terms such as thoroughness and seriousness, the quality of the verdict in terms of their agreement on it, and the characters of other jurors in terms such as persuasiveness and open-mindedness. They also completed a test of memory for information from the trial testimony and from the judge's instructions (Table 4.4).

The questionnaire data were separated into ratings by majority faction jurors, who were usually in verdict-rendering factions, and holdout jurors, who did not agree with the final jury verdict. It is difficult to interpret the responses of the holdout jurors because under some conditions, most notably the twelve-out-of-twelve decision rule, all holdout jurors were members of hung juries. Thus, the ratings of majority faction jurors are emphasized in this summary.

Jurors' global impressions of the character of deliberation suggest that behavior in unanimous rule juries is more thorough and grave than in majority rule juries. Two measures of the quality of deliberation were the perceived difficulty in reaching a group decision and the perceived pressure to change one's opinion, each of which showed consistent decreases across decision rules. Unanimous rule majority-faction jurors felt more pressure to change their opinion from other jurors, and they also felt that the group decision-making process was more difficult than did members of nonunanimous juries. Holdout jurors, under unanimous decision rules, felt considerably more pressure to change their opinions than majority jurors or jurors in the eight-out-of-twelve decision rule condition. Unanimity rule jurors also rated the perceived thoroughness of deliberation and the seriousness of jurors in their juries as higher than did jurors in the nonunanimous conditions.

Individual jurors' agreement with the jury verdict was indexed with three measures of consistency of the jurors' attitudes concerning the verdict at the finish of deliberation. Jurors were asked to rate their confidence that their jury verdict was a proper or correct verdict. This rating did not vary systematically with decision rule for members of majority factions, although majority faction jurors were more confident than holdout jurors that their jury had rendered a proper decision. If the jury as a whole is taken as the unit of analysis, nonunanimous juries, where there are more holdout jurors, show an overall lowered confidence in the jury's verdict. Jurors were also asked to rate the extent to which they agreed with their jury's verdict. These ratings exhibited the same pattern as the ratings of confidence that the jury verdict was correct.

A final measure of group decision consistency was based on jurors' ratings of their beliefs on nine verdict-relevant issues within the trial. For example, jurors were asked to rate whether they believed that the victim had run onto the knife held by the defendant or had been stabbed in a violent attacking action by the defendant. This issue and eight other key issues were rated by legal experts as central to the discrimination between verdict categories in this case. The extent to which the members of each jury gave similar patterns of ratings across these nine issues was taken to reflect the extent to which jurors' conclusions about the overall pattern in the case were consistent with one another. This average interjuror agreement on the nine issues showed a slight decrease across decision rules from unanimous to eight-out-of-twelve. However, the big difference was between majority rule jurors and holdout jurors. Holdout jurors showed considerably less agreement with the overall jury on key decision issues than did majority rule jurors. Again, considering that there are more holdout jurors in nonunanimous decision rule conditions, the overall verdict-relevant agreement in a jury is clearly lower in the nonunanimous conditions.

Another important product of a jury trial concerns the interpersonal per-

ceptions of persuasiveness and open-mindedness that develop during deliberation. Each juror was asked to rate every other juror's apparent persuasiveness and open-mindedness. One clear effect is the tendency to rate one's
own persuasive influence and open-mindedness as higher than average ratings for other jurors. This egoistic tendency was apparent in all decision-
rule conditions. Jurors had more positive impressions of all participants in
deliberation in unanimous rule juries as compared to majority rule juries.
Ratings on persuasiveness and open-mindedness were separated according
to assignment to members of the rater's own verdict faction (ingroup persuasiveness) or to all other faction members (outgroup persuasiveness). To
assure generality, in- and out-group classifications were calculated at three
separate points during deliberation, based on initial ballot verdicts, mid-de-
liberation factions, and on final factions. These three calculations yielded
very similar rating patterns and they are collapsed together in the statistics.
Nonverdict rendering or hung juries are not included in the analysis.

The ingroup-outgroup comparison paralleled the self-other comparison;
ingroup members were given higher ratings on persuasiveness and open-
mindedness than outgroup members. A decline in all ratings occurred between unanimous and majority rule juries, such that majority rule jury
members rated either ingroup or outgroup members as less persuasive and
less open-minded than unanimous rule jurors. As a result, self and ingroup
members were given higher ratings on persuasiveness and open-mindedness
compared to all others or to outgroup members across decision rules. In addition, all ratings showed a clear tendency to drop across decision rules.
This suggests that jurors leave nonunanimous deliberations with a relatively
low impression of their own and other jurors' persuasiveness and open-
mindedness.

Individual postdeliberation memory for information from the trial testimony and memory for information in the trial judge's instructions was not
related to decision rule conditions or to majority or holdout status. Although it is difficult to draw any conclusions about absolute levels of memory, jurors seemed to perform remarkably poorly on this test. Memory on
the eight fact items tested appeared to run at a rate of about 60 percent accuracy for information directly stated in testimony, such as recall of the
items that the medical examiner testified were found in the decedent's
pockets. Performance on the judge's instruction memory questions were
even lower, less than 30 percent accurate on questions about material
stated directly in the judge's final charge, such as the elements of the legal
definition of second degree murder. It is also difficult to make a direct comparison between accuracy of memory for testimony and memory for the
judge's instructions. However, memory appears to be more accurate for testimonial matters than for information in the judge's charge. This impression

is strongly supported by analysis of the errors made in discussion during deliberation.

A more meaningful examination of memory in the jury decision task is provided by group memory data (Hartwick, Sheppard, & Davis, 1982). Memory accuracy was calculated by crediting each jury with recall of information if any member of that jury had recalled that information. This composite of individual jurors' recollections interprets jury performance to reflect the best possible performance of all its members taken together. The picture of jury memory provided by the composite memory index is considerably more positive than the average juror recall statistics. Jury memory averages over 90 percent correct for evidentiary material and over 80 percent for information from the judge's instructions. There is no systematic variation with decision rule.

Specific types of information were forgotten by jurors. The major sources of error on the evidence concerned the knife wound, where somewhat technical material was embedded in complex testimony from the medical examiner, and a verbal exchange between the defendant and a police detective after his arrest, where some information was stricken from the evidence on an instruction from the trial judge. In this last circumstance poor memory is actually a sign that the jurors were behaving according to the court's instruction. The failures to recall information from the judge's final jury instruction were more disturbing. Most errors of recall concerned definitions of the verdict categories of manslaughter and not guilty by reason of self-defense. In fact, the modal performance for over 75 percent of the juries on each of these items was less than perfect: approximately one-half of the elements or conditions were recalled for each verdict by the most accurate juror out of twelve.

In summary, expert views of the stimulus trial, the verdict of the actual jury in the original trial, and the modal verdict for the mock juries all declared the second degree-murder verdict the most proper or correct verdict for the case. Juries from all three decision rules were equally likely (13 out of 23 juries in each condition) to reach the second-degree murder verdict. There was some variation in the fates of juries that did not reach this verdict across decision rules. In particular, there was an elevated rate of first-degree murder verdicts under the ten-out-of-twelve majority decision rule and of hung juries under the unanimous decision rule.

The task of predicting the final jury verdict, given information about the initial verdict distribution, early voting behavior, or early contents of discussion, was used to compare alternate models for jury decision making. The weighted averaging prediction rule, based on a regression analysis, and the social choice model using an agenda decision-making rule are the winners with reference to proportions of accurate predictions. However, all of the models are of some value conceptually in helping to understand jury decision making. However, none of the models appears to be extremely useful in practical prediction situations.

With reference to the group products of jury decision making, two decision-rule effects were expected. First, the stricter the decision-rule quorum requirement, the longer it took for deliberation to meet that quorum requirement. Second, in nonunanimous juries deliberation usually ended with substantial numbers of holdout jurors who subscribed to a minority, non-verdict-rendering point of view. Postdeliberation ratings of the quality of deliberation by individual jurors provided the first substantial sign that the nonunanimous decision rules might not be desirable. In general, jurors deliberating under nonunanimous (ten-out-of-twelve, eight-out-of-twelve) decision rules viewed deliberation as less thorough and less serious, and jury members, regardless of whether there were any holdout faction members, were less apt to agree on the verdict and on the issues underlying the verdict under the nonunanimous decision rules than in the unanimous decision rule condition. Furthermore, jurors had a relatively negative view of their fellow jurors' open-mindedness and persuasiveness under the less strict decision rules.

Individual and group-composite memory measures yielded negative evaluations of the jury decision-making process. Juries operating under all three decision rules performed poorly on the memory tests. In particular, individual juror recall of information from the trial judge's instructions was disturbingly poor.

5

Contents of
Jury Deliberation

The Supreme Court's evaluation of jury performance raised issues about the content of discussion during deliberation, such as the thoroughness of the decision process and the extent to which unpopular viewpoints were represented. Social psychological analyses have raised similar issues regarding information pooling and the bases of social influence. One of the distinctive characteristics of the present mock jury study is the use of a detailed, case-specific coding method to capture the major events occurring during deliberation. The few other studies that have attempted to deal with deliberation content reported only excerpts or partial content (Simon, 1967; Saks, 1976). The present study goes further and examines the complete pattern of communication as well as the context in which it occurs, including balloting, instructions from the trial judge, and other procedures.

The overall deliberation content under each decision rule is reflected in the three variables in each coded speaking entry identified in the analysis of videotaped deliberations. This content was analyzed in terms of the total volume of deliberation (speaking entries only) that included references to trial testimony, and in terms of the proportion of speaking entries relative to the total speaking entries for the entire deliberation that comprised each subcategory figure. Summaries were also made of the discussion of legal issues raised in the judge's instructions, and the jurors' remarks were broken down functionally into pragmatic types.

By Hastie

Table 5.1. Discussion of trial evidence.

Trial evidence	Decision rule			$F(2,63)$ p value	
	12/12	10/12	8/12	MSe	
Non-key testimony					
Mean number of entries	344.6	272.1	193.9	4.92	.01
(Proportion of total	(.26)	(.26)	(.28)	20,181	
discussion)					
Key factual material	270.9	215.4	147.0	4.16	.02
	(.21)	(.21)	(.21)	17,407	
General aspects of legal					
system	18.1	15.2	10.0	4.01	.02
	(.01)	(.01)	(.01)	87	
Voting procedures	20.2	18.3	16.1	2.96	.06
	(.02)	(.02)	(.02)	26	
Personal anecdotal material	18.3	17.3	7.9	3.63	.03
	(.01)	(.02)	(.01)	182	
Experimental realism	14.7	16.5	7.0	3.25	.04
	(.01)	(.02)	(.01)	130	
Total trial evidence	686.9	555.1	382.3	5.22	.009
	(.53)	(.53)	(.54)	131,475	
Total speaking entries	1306.4	1041.3	702.3	5.81	.005
				304,472	
Different evidence entries	37.3	37.2	34.4	6.06	.004
(Proportion of 43 possible	(.87)	(.87)	(.80)	10	
entries)					
Different key evidence entries	13.3	13.3	12.0	5.79	.005
(Proportion of 15 possible	(.89)	(.89)	(.80)	2.1	
entries)					

References to Testimony

Decision rule shows a simple effect across all categories of testimony discussion (Table 5.1) such that larger volumes of discussion are associated with stricter rules. The explanation for this pattern is that speaking occurs at a fairly constant rate during deliberation and the decision rule requirement determines the length of deliberation. Thus, unanimous decision rule juries take the longest to reach a verdict, and volume of speaking in any of the coded fact categories is highest under this decision rule.

All of these decision rule effects vanish when the proportions of speaking events are calculated. Statistical tests calculated to assess the reliability of decision rule differences on proportion measures revealed only two significant effects, and these small differences are probably not replicable. The constancy of these proportion measures across decision rules is remarkable.

Comparisons of specific content categories within juries are of limited generality in that they depend on the nature of the particular case materials and the structure of the experimental coding scheme. For the stimulus case, about 53 percent of the remarks made during deliberation included references to information presented in the trial testimony. These remarks did not focus more sharply on the fifteen key factual testimony categories defined by the experimenter than on the twenty-eight non-key categories. Remarks on aspects of the legal system (such as case disposition or juror duties), voting procedures, personal matters, and the experimental nature of the mock jury task and setting occurred at a low but measurable rate.

Two indices were used to measure the breadth of fact coverage, namely the total number of different fact citations out of a possible forty-three and the total number of key fact citations out of a possible fifteen during the entire deliberation process. These statistics are critical measures of the thoroughness of deliberation. The average jury in any of the decision rule conditions covered about 85 percent of the relevant coded categories. Thoroughness dropped with the decision rule requirement, and both these differences reached the $p < .01$ level of statistical significance.

References to Judge's Instructions

The primary measures of each jury's application of legal principles were based on the contents of deliberation divided into subcategories according to references to legal issues cited in the trial judge's instructions (Table 5.2). About 25 percent of the remarks in deliberation made reference to the instructions. The same pattern of decision rule effects that was apparent with respect to trial testimony appears here. All measures of volume of entries reflect deliberation times and are directly related to the decision rule requirement. When proportions are considered, almost every decision rule effect vanishes. The sole exception to this generalization is the difference in proportions of deliberation time devoted to the evaluation of witness credibility. This difference, which is .03, .04, and .06 for the three decision rules, is marginally significant ($F[2,63] = 4.34$, $p < .017$). It also accords with an impression, based on examination of the deliberation videotapes, that eight-out-of-twelve juries frequently exhibited a discounting strategy in the evaluation of testimonial evidence, whereby witnesses were classified as either absolutely reliable or absolutely unreliable ("Do we believe the policeman *or* the defendant?"). An integration strategy, whereby portions of testimony were compared and combined, seemed more common in twelve-

Table 5.2. Discussion of legal issues.

Legal issue	Decision rule			$F(2,63)$ p value
	12/12	10/12	8/12	MSe
Standard of proof	13.8	12.5	7.8	1.01 .37
(Proportion of total discussion)	(.01)	(.01)	(.01)	179
Reasonable inference	4.3	4.0	1.3	2.69 .07
	(.00)	(.00)	(.01)	23
Witness credibility	44.7	46.8	40.3	.06 .944
	(.03)	(.04)	(.06)	1,159
Inadmissible evidence	4.1	3.9	2.3	1.54 .22
	(.00)	(.00)	(.00)	16
Verdict preference	64.3	48.0	34.2	2.90 .06
(not included in total issues)	(.05)	(.05)	(.05)	1,711
Verdict elements	146.0	123.6	81.5	3.51 .04
	(.11)	(.12)	(.12)	6,465
Verdict definitions	161.8	151.5	94.0	4.55 .015
(not included in total issues)	(.12)	(.15)	(.13)	4,656
Verdict-evidence relationships	99.3	84.2	55.7	2.44 .12
	(.08)	(.08)	(.08)	3,928
Total legal issues	312.1	274.9	188.9	2.95 .06
	(.24)	(.26)	(.27)	23,944
Different legal issues	21.0	21.3	17.9	2.99 .05
(Proportion of 39 possible issues)	(.52)	(.54)	(.43)	23,945
Total fact-issue pairings	171.3	150.3	112.8	1.52 .22
	(.13)	(.14)	(.16)	8,567
Different fact-issue pairings	71.1	63.1	47.2	2.69 .07
				889
Total speaking entries	1306.4	1041.3	702.3	

out-of-twelve juries ("The policeman's testimony needs to be qualified by consideration of his opportunity to observe, and the defendant's remarks may be biased").

The discussion of the standard of proof, beyond reasonable doubt, occurred at a very low rate in all juries. Although there is no standard amount of discussion that should concern the standard of proof, expert observers and the experimental coders were disturbed at the extremely low amounts of deliberation devoted to the issue. Again, the deliberation videotapes yielded a plausible explanation for the apparent procedural error. In general, jurors did not understand that the reasonable doubt standard was relevant to their verdicts, given that the defendant was unquestionably the agent of the decedent's death. Research using different trial materials supports this point. When a probabilistic issue, such as the possible identification of the perpetrator of a crime as the defendant, is the focus of the trial, then discussion of the standard of proof is prominent in deliberation. However, when the standard of proof is applied to intuitively less probabilistic elements of the crimes charged, such as the defendant's state of mind, then the jury fails to heed the trial judge's instruction that each element of a crime must be established beyond a reasonable doubt to return a guilty verdict.

Considerations of the judge's instructions on inadmissible evidence, such as references to the decedent's personal character or statements made by the defendant prior to the Miranda warning at arrest, were brief. Typically, one juror raised the topic of the stricken testimony explicitly in the form of a question ("Should we talk about the victim's reputation for violence?"). A brief discussion ensued, which concluded that such considerations were illegitimate. Thus, a clear finding emerges that the judge's instructions were extremely effective in stopping discussion that would ordinarily, without the instruction, have occurred during deliberation.

This result may have arisen from the experimental nature of the research task. One plausible reason that jurors were well-behaved when the discussion of inadmissible testimony was at issue may be their knowledge that in the mock jury they were being observed by outsiders. Furthermore, the mere fact that the jury does not discuss the stricken testimony does not establish that the testimony does not affect individual juror decisions. Experiments have been conducted to detect the subtle and possibly unconscious impact of inadmissible testimony on juror decisions (Hans & Doob, 1976; Sue, Smith, & Caldwell, 1973). They have consistently obtained evidence that stricken information does influence judgment. These demonstrations are a warning that the jury study's method, focusing on overt responses, such as deliberation content, is not a sensitive test of the influence of inadmissible testimony. Even the results showing that memory for stricken testimony is abnormally poor do not demonstrate that such testimony has no effect on judgment. Poor memory may reflect forgetting processes that are independent of initial comprehension and judgment effects.

One conception of the jury's task emphasizes its function to relate general legal categories and procedures to the evidence in a specific case. This means that the frequency with which instruction (issue) codes are paired with evidence (fact) codes is a critical measure of jury performance. For example, frequent evidence-instruction pairings include applications of the judge's remarks concerning credibility evaluation to determine the weight accorded to testimony or comparisons between crime event features and verdict category elements during the later stages of the verdict rendering process. Two measures of fact-issue pairings are total pairings and different pairings. Both measures show the typical volume effect of decision rule with the frequencies of both indices increasing with decision rule strictness. In this case the trend across decision rules reverses for the total fact-issue pairings measure when proportion of speaking entries are considered. Proportionally more discussion of fact-issue pairings occurs in the nonunanimous decision rule conditions ($F[2.63] = 3.33$, $p < .042$). This marginally significant difference is attributable to the larger proportion of discussion spent on credibility issues in these juries. Most credibility evaluation is comprised of pairings of references to testimony and to the credibility issue.

Functional Types of Communication

The major function of discussion during deliberation is to generate a pool of shared information relevant to the case under consideration. However, linguists and social psychologists have identified a variety of more specific pragmatic functions served by information exchange. All entries measuring speaking and nonspeaking events during deliberation were classified by functional type (Table 5.3). Statements asserting or conveying information are the most frequent functional type by far, making up about three-quarters of the deliberation content under all decision rules.

Two categories of statement, errors and corrections of errors, are of special importance in the deliberation process. An analysis was made of the specific content of remarks that were classified as errors. For the stimulus case, more errors occur in citation of the judge's instructions than in references to testimony. Fact errors occur at about one-half of the rate with which judge's instruction errors occur in twelve-out-of-twelve and ten-out-of-twelve juries (.36 and .38 of total errors were errors of fact respectively). In eight-out-of-twelve juries fact and instruction error rates are about equal (.47 of total errors were fact errors). The findings on postdeliberation memory and on deliberation content converge on the conclusion that difficulties with comprehension, memory, and application of the trial judge's instructions are major obstacles to proper jury performance.

Another critical factor is the rate at which a juror corrects an error once it has occurred. The frequencies of corrections under the three decision rules are .50, .30, and .50. The ten-out-of-twelve decision rule jury error correction rate (.30) is significantly lower than the comparable rates (.50 and .50) in the other experimental juries ($F[2,63] = 5.31$, $p < .01$). The analysis of jury verdicts (Chapter 4) found that first-degree murder verdicts occur with a slightly higher frequency under the ten-out-of-twelve rule.

Table 5.3. Discussion classified by functional types of contributions.

Function	Decision rule			$F(2,63)$	p value
	12/12	10/12·	8/12	MSe	
	Verbal discussion				
Statement	987.0	784.3	531.3	5.28	.008
	(.76)	(.75)	(.76)	186,104	
Error	14.7	13.2	7.2	4.61	.01
	(.01)	(.01)	(.01)	79	
Correction	6.2	3.7	3.1	5.29	.008
	(.00)	(.00)	(.00)	13	
Question	113.1	93.0	63.0	3.37	.04
	(.09)	(.09)	(.09)	3,681	
Direction	110.8	86.0	59.7	5.38	.007
	(.08)	(.08)	(.09)	2,472	
Irrelevant	12.8	8.3	3.6	3.97	.02
	(.01)	(.01)	(.00)	142	
Verdict statement	62.0	52.9	34.7	6.88	.002
	(.04)	(.05)	(.05)	598	
Total	1306.4	1041.3	702.3		
	Nonspeaking events				
Formal voting (hand or written ballots)	5.9	6.7	3.8		
Dynamite charge	0.4	0.1	0.0		
Request for information from the judge	2.1	2.1	1.1		
Outburst	42.3	28.7	23.0		

The five first-degree murder juries did have slightly lower error correction probabilities (.26 versus .30 for second degree and .39 for manslaughter verdicts), but the difference was not statistically significant. For some unknown reason, experimental juries reaching all verdicts under the ten-out-of-twelve decision rule generated corrections at a relatively low rate.

Questions occur at a fairly constant rate, in about 10 percent of the speaking entries, across all decision rules. The same is true of organizational directives, individual suggestions, or imperatives to take specific actions such as voting or setting a topic for discussion. Expressions advocating specific verdict positions also occur at a constant rate across decision rule conditions. Deliberation task-irrelevant remarks occur at a negligibly low rate (about 1 percent of total speaking entries). Again, jurors may be especially well-behaved in this regard when they are aware that they are being studied by social scientists.

Formal voting rates show a different pattern across the three decision rule conditions. Votes occurred, on the average, about once every 23.4 minutes for unanimous rule juries. Votes occurred at a higher rate, averaging every 15.4 minutes and every 19.7 minutes, in the nonunanimous juries. This difference may reflect a strategic variation between unanimous and nonunanimous juries. The need for unanimous agreement may induce an integrative, evidence-driven deliberation style, while the lower verdict requirement in nonunanimous juries produces a discounting, verdict-driven deliberation style (see Chapter 8).

Deadlocked juries were routinely presented a videotaped instruction requesting further consideration of the case and another vote. Wording of this dynamite charge followed current precedents in Massachusetts trial courts (*Commonwealth v. Rodriguez*, 1973; *Commonwealth v. Tuey*, 1851; *Yale Law Review*, 1968). Eight juries under the unanimous decision rule received the charge, and five of these rendered verdicts, always in accord with the largest faction's preference (four second-degree murder and one manslaughter). Three juries in the ten-out-of-twelve condition received the charge, and all rendered verdicts, one for first degree murder, one for second degree murder, and one for manslaughter. Only one jury in the eight-out-of-twelve condition received the charge, and it remained deadlocked.

One of the most dramatic endings to a deliberation occurred in a unanimous jury that ultimately deadlocked with a majority of eleven opposed by a lone holdout. In this instance the *Commonwealth v. Rodriguez* (1973) instruction was presented after three hours of deliberation, when the jury declared itself deadlocked, ten jurors versus two. The instruction exerted a positive influence not by encouraging jurors to reconsider their own views but by stimulating discussion by the holdouts. After an attempt to express and defend his position, one of the two holdouts joined the majority. The final holdout made a short-lived attempt to express his viewpoint and then refused to engage in further interaction with the other jurors, thus terminating deliberation. Jurors, in short, do not respond to the dynamite charge by arbitrarily changing their stands on the verdict decision. Rather the charge appears to work by encouraging jurors who have been relatively uncommunicative to engage in discussion. Their own effort to express themselves is the critical factor that facilitates opinion change.

Requests for clarification of the trial judge's instructions occurred in sixteen of the twenty-three unanimous juries, in fourteen of the ten-out-of-twelve juries, and in eight of the eight-out-of-twelve juries. The lower frequencies of instruction requests under the majority rules doubtless reflect the shorter, less thorough character of deliberation in these juries. This is especially worrisome because of the high error rates noted for both postdeliberation juror memory and discussion during deliberation. Furthermore, repetition of the judge's instructions appeared to affect individual verdict preference shifts. The probability of shifting verdict preferences was considerably higher immediately following the presentation of instructions than at other times during deliberation. This suggests that changes in beliefs about the verdict category definitions, such as the contents of the instructions that were repeated, are an important, if not the most important, basis for shifts in verdict preferences.

Group outbursts, when five or more jurors spoke simultaneously, occurred on the average about once every three minutes of deliberation in all decision rule conditions. The rate of outburst events was not related systematically to other signs of disorganized deliberation, such as error rates or jury verdict choice.

Equity and Rate of Participation

Some general characteristics of discussion that are not captured in direct measures of frequencies or proportions of participation in deliberation involve equity of participation across jurors and the pace of discussion (Table 5.4). Variance in speaking volume for a single deliberation is a measure of equity in the division of deliberation time. The measure is based on individual jurors' contributions to deliberation. Each of the twelve jurors was assigned a single number representing the proportion of total speaking entries produced during the entire deliberation. These twelve numbers were percentages that would total 100. If participation was perfectly equal across jurors during deliberation, these percentages would all be equal to about 8.5 percent and the variance would approach zero. To the extent that a few jurors dominate deliberation and others participate at a lower rate, the differences between juror contributions will increase, and variance will also increase. Thus, the speaking variance measure is sensitive to inequity in deliberation participation.

The speaking variance measure shows a nonsignificant trend with higher

Table 5.4. Variance and rate of speaking in deliberation.

| | Decision rule | | | $F(2,63)$ p value | |
	12/12	10/12	8/12	MSe	
Variance in individual juror speaking entries	437	423	538	1.84 .16 38,935	
Speaking rate (events/minute)	9.64	9.62	9.36		

variance, indicating less equity in discussion, in the eight-out-of-twelve rule condition (Fig. 5.1). When the curves relating mean proportion of speaking entries to participation rank are plotted, on the average, the most talkative juror (rank = 1) under the twelve-out-of-twelve rule contributed 23 percent of the speaking entries to deliberation. A comparison of the decision rule conditions reveals that the higher speaking variance for eight-out-of-twelve juries is produced by the relative elevation of speaking, to 26 percent of the entries, by the highest ranked juror. In about two-thirds of the juries the first-ranked juror was the foreman. Thus, the inequity in speaking rates is probably higher in the eight-out-of-twelve juries because the foreman dominates the relatively shorter deliberation to a greater extent than in twelve-out-of-twelve and ten-out-of-twelve juries.

The inequity in amount of participation across jurors within a jury reflects a consistent finding in many types of discussion groups (Stephan & Mischler, 1952; Kadane & Lewis, 1969). No general theoretical analysis has accounted for the shape of the participation rank curve, but it is doubtless created by a combination of factors, including individual differences in talkativeness, a dominance hierarchy within the group, and social conventions governing polite debate. A disturbing fact is that most juries include several members who virtually never participate in the group. For example, most juries, or 41 of the 69, included at least three members whose individual participation did not include more than 3 percent of the speaking entries during deliberation. These jurors barely expressed themselves outside of the formal balloting procedures, and they had no notable direct influence on the jury verdict decision. Nonetheless, they did have an opportunity to be heard. Furthermore, as they were typically members of large factions, it is plausible that they found their points of view being expressed by other jurors.

Absolute participation frequencies rather than proportions may be of interest in some evaluations of jury performance. The relatively shorter deliberations under nonunanimous decision rules result in many more jurors whose participation is minimal. For example, a juror who contributes as few as ten entries in an entire deliberation, including voting and verdict statements, is truly a nonparticipant in discussion. Such jurors appear much less often in unanimous juries than in majority rule juries: 24 jurors in twelve-out-of-twelve juries, 33 in ten-out-of-twelve juries, and 56 in eight-out-of-twelve juries.

Speaking rates are also measured as entries per minute. The differences between decision rule conditions on this variable were not significant. On the assumption that higher speaking rates might be associated with greater disorganization within juries, correlation coefficients were calculated between speaking rate and error rate ($r=-.06$, n.s.) and between speaking rate

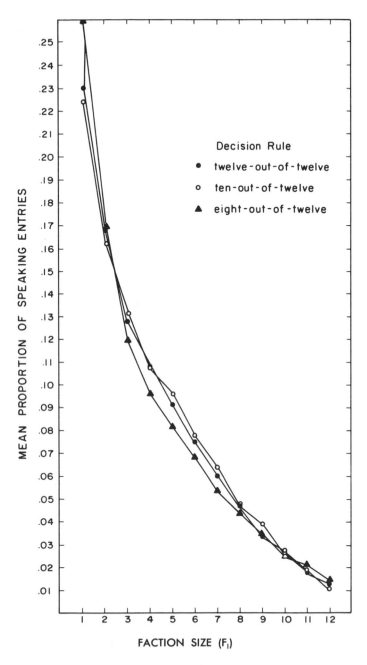

Fig. 5.1 Participation ranks for each decision rule.

and outburst rate ($r=+.11$). However, these correlations were not significantly different from zero, implying that the three measures of deliberation process coherence were not related.

The Time Factor

The full course of events during deliberation was analyzed by separating each jury's deliberation into quintiles of total time, each quintile being one-fifth of the total deliberation time for a particular jury. The sequence of events in deliberation measured as changes in the content of discussion during each quintile of the total deliberation time is quite similar across decision rule conditions. This conclusion was supported by the absence of significant decision rule by quintile interaction effects in the statistical analyses. However, the similarity in discussion sequences appears only when the data are partitioned into quintiles and would not be expected to hold if absolute time were the metric for analysis. For example, a comparison of discussion content during the first forty minutes of deliberation across decision rule conditions found clear differences in the amounts of discussion devoted to many of the content code categories, such as discussion of standard proof and verdict elements.

Sequential variations in the content of deliberation were parallel to the decision rule effects, as shown by statistical tests for quintile effects on the content measures derived from the observational coding data. Jurors' references to the testimony and evidence presented at trial tended to drop consistently across the five quintiles of deliberation. This trend was reflected in the means for key facts ($F(4,315) = 3.11$, $p < .02$) and the number of different facts cited per quintile ($F(4,315) = 3.35$, $p < .01$). The trend was paralleled by a tendency to discuss the credibility of witnesses at lower rates as deliberation progressed ($F(4,315) = 11.19$, $p < .0001$). Just the reverse trends emerged from analysis of jurors' references to material from the judge's instructions, particularly to verdict categories ($F(4,315) = 6.35$, $p < .0001$) and to the elements of the crimes ($F(4,315) = 8.04$, $p < .0001$). Similarly, references to the reasonable doubt standard of proof increased in frequency toward the end of deliberation ($F(4,315) = 9.03$, $p < .0001$). Generally performance under all three decision rule requirements exhibits a shift from factfinding to application of the law. First the jury reviews the evidence to create a "story" of the events described by testimony; then it moves on to specify the legal categories that are the focus of verdict decision; and finally it applies the decision procedures, such as the beyond reasonable doubt standard, to classify the case as a particular verdict instance.

Analysis of the content of deliberation in terms of functional types of remarks made by jurors yielded expectable findings. Statements conveying information and questions decreased in frequency across deliberation, while statements directing the jury to take an action and statements expressing verdict preferences increased. Formal voting was relatively frequent in the early and late quintiles of deliberation. Requests for further instructions from the judge occurred at a fairly constant rate across the last four quintiles of deliberation, but never in the first quintile. Judge's instructions to deadlocked juries were necessary only during the fourth and last quintiles.

Two general conclusions follow from this analysis of the sequence of deliberation content. First, it is unreasonable to conceptualize majority decision rule juries merely as unanimous decision rule deliberations that are cut off earlier than they would have been with the twelve-out-of-twelve requirement. The "cut-off" image would imply equivalent content at equal points in real deliberation time, whereas in fact there is sequential comparability in content across decision rules of equal proportions of real time. Second, the waxing and waning of discussion topics such as trial evidence, witness credibility, verdict definitions, and standard of proof, are consistent with the story-verdict-classification model for the jury decision process (see Chapter 2).

One critical comparison in assessing the effects of the decision rule on deliberation concerns the content of deliberation before and after verdict-rendering faction sizes are reached. For example, comparison of the quality of deliberation in twelve-out-of-twelve, ten-out-of-twelve, and eight-out-of-twelve juries preceding the point at which the largest faction reaches a size of eight members yields a relatively pure comparison of deliberation quality among the three types of juries before any verdicts are rendered (Table 5.5).

There is a clear decision rule effect on deliberation before and after the largest faction size reaches eight by almost every measure of activity. This occurs because the volume of before-eight deliberation events varies directly with decision rule strictness. The volume difference actually reflects the fact that large factions grow more slowly in juries with stricter decision rules. If the deliberation events are converted to proportions of speaking events, the decision rule conditions are indistinguishable on any of the major measures of quality of deliberation.

Post-eight deliberation for each decision rule supports a different conclusion. Little occurs after the faction size reaches eight in juries deliberating under the eight-out-of-twelve rule. Deliberation continues for a few minutes, typically less than five, after the necessary quorum of eight members is reached. This contrasts to the case for twelve-out-of-twelve juries where approximately 20 percent of deliberation occurs after the largest faction contains eight or more members. The ten-out-of-twelve decision rule case is

Table 5.5. Content of deliberation before and after reaching an eight-member faction.

Content	12/12		10/12		8/12	
	Pre-eight	Post-eight	Pre-eight	Post-eight	Pre-eight	Post-eight
Trial evidence	557.7	129.2	506.5	48.5	360.3	14.5
Non-key testimony	338.5	77.4	311.0	28.5	224.5	11.2
Key testimony	219.2	51.8	105.5	20.0	143.8	3.3
Legal issues	246.0	66.0	254.8	20.0	186.3	2.6
Standard of proof	9.2	4.7	11.6			
Fact-issue pairings	136.1	35.2	139.0	11.3	108.1	4.7
Errors	11.7	3.4	11.9	1.3	6.8	.4
Correction of errors	4.7	1.5	3.2	.5	2.8	.2
Requests for additional instructions	1.5	.6	1.9	.2	1.0	.1
Total speaking entries	1046	260	945	96	656	47

intermediate, with about 10 percent of the total deliberation time occurring after a largest faction size of eight is reached.

The critical question is whether important procedural or legal events are likely to occur after the largest faction reaches a size of eight. The twelve-out-of-twelve decision rule condition gives evidence that the last twenty to thirty minutes of post-eight deliberation are important. In seven juries the largest faction reached eight but failed to render the final verdict favored by that faction. Three of these juries finished deliberation in a deadlocked state with the largest faction favoring a manslaughter verdict. In four juries deliberation in the post-eight period reversed the largest faction's verdict to produce unexpected final verdicts, shifting from a majority of nine for second degree murder to a unanimous verdict of manslaughter, from nine for first degree murder to second degree murder, from eight for manslaughter to second degree murder, and from nine for second degree murder to a manslaughter verdict. Thus, in seven out of twenty-three juries, or over 30 percent, the conclusion of deliberation was not determined at the point that a majority faction of size eight had been attained. Moreover, in twelve-out-of-twelve juries several important procedural events occurred during the post-eight period. Twenty-seven percent of the requests for additional instructions from the trial judge, twenty-five percent of the oral corrections of errors made during discussion, and thirty-four percent of the discussion of the beyond reasonable doubt standard of proof occurred during the post-eight period. Furthermore, substantial amounts of the discussion of trial testimony (20 percent) and of the judge's instructions (21 percent) occurred during the post-eight period.

Similar calculations can be made for ten-out-of-twelve decision rule juries. However, because the post-eight period is much shorter in these juries, much less of consequence happens. The period following the point at which the largest faction reaches a size eight is thus an important part of deliberation in unanimous juries. This period includes some reversals of opinion and many important procedural events.

Such a broad-stroke picture of the content and form of discussion during deliberation is limited not only by the particular case materials in the study but also by the fact that the surface content of discussion does not provide a view of the underlying individual decision processes that are also part of the jury process. However, no other research has attempted to provide this total view of deliberation content for any case materials.

By any measure of volume of discussion, the stricter the verdict quorum requirement, the greater the volume of discussion produced during deliberation. This result follows from the differences in total deliberation time that are associated with the different decision rules. Slightly over half of the remarks made during deliberation cited testimonial material from the trial evidence. Discussion did not appear to focus on the key facts that experts had indicated were determinants of the central decision issues in the case. Rather, discussion focused on both key and non-key facts introduced as testimony at trial. In the average jury approximately 90 percent of both key and non-key facts were covered in typical deliberations under the unanimous decision rule, with a slight drop in breadth of coverage in the eight-out-of-twelve decision rule.

Typically about one-quarter of the remarks made during deliberation cited material from the judge's instructions on the law. Discussion of the judge's definitions of the verdicts and his instructions on the evaluation of witness credibility dominated references to the instructions. Discussion of credibility took up a larger proportion of discussion in nonunanimous than in unanimous decision rule juries. The disturbingly low rate of reference to the beyond reasonable doubt standard of proof during discussion was perhaps due to jurors' failure to understand when to apply this standard of proof. Paired references to evidence and to legal issues were probably of particular significance in the jury's task of finding facts and applying the law. A substantial proportion of the discussion made simultaneous reference to both facts and legal issues. In this case again there was a decision rule effect; the stricter the decision rule, the lower the proportion of joint fact-issue references.

When the content of deliberation was classified by functional type, most remarks were clearly motivated to communicate information concerning the case from one juror to the others, with about 75 percent of the remarks falling into this category. A low but non-negligible proportion of these remarks were errors, and most of these errors concerned references to the trial judge's instructions. The rate at which these errors are corrected by other members of the jury is a critical factor in the jury process. Correction rates were moderately high, with over 40 percent of the errors typically corrected by other jurors, except in the case of first degree murder verdict juries, where the correction rate was 26 percent, considerably lower than the rate for juries rendering other verdicts.

The volume of remarks contributed by individual jurors showed considerable variation across jurors. Most juries included a few members who did not participate in oral discussion at all. Their presence was registered only in their votes during formal balloting procedures. A larger inequity in speaking participation rates occurred in the eight-out-of-twelve jury than in the ten-out-of-twelve and twelve-out-of-twelve juries. This inequity stemmed from a tendency for foremen in these juries to dominate discussion to an even greater extent than they did in the ten-out-of-twelve and twelve-out-of-twelve decision rule conditions.

When the content of deliberation was analyzed by quintile to give a sense of the sequence of discussion, decision rule effects did not show up as simple differences in deliberation cutoff points. Although deliberation sequences were uniform across decision rules when compared quintile by quintile, deliberation contents differed across decision rules when compared at absolute times, such as the events occurring thirty minutes into deliberation under each decision rule. Sequential effects were consistent for all three decision rule conditions: references to evidence and testimony decreased as deliberation proceeded, references to verdict categories and definitions increased, references to issues of credibility decreased, organizational directives increased, questions and efforts to convey information decreased, and balloting increased.

An analysis of the types of events occurring in deliberation before and after the largest faction in a jury reached a size of eight members is pertinent to policy decisions concerning the proper jury decision rule. In unanimous decision rule juries a number of important events, including reversals of the most popular verdict choice, substantial portions of the discussion, and requests for further instructions, occurred during the period after the largest faction exceeded eight members. This and other findings in the analysis of deliberation content strongly imply that the unanimous decision rule should be preferred over majority decision rules.

6

Dynamics of
Jury Deliberation

The deliberation process extends across time, and among its most important characteristics are the dynamic changes that take place from moment-to-moment. The most important dynamic events in the deliberation process are the movement of individuals from verdict preference to verdict preference, the pattern of communication among jurors, and the growth of dominant factions.

The Development of Factions

The most visible dynamic event in deliberation is the formation and development of verdict-favoring factions. During the study special note was taken of jurors' statements of verdict preferences. Any clear expression by a juror of a preference in hand or written balloting or in oral discussion was marked. Factions were defined on the basis of common verdict preferences. Thus, for example, jurors were grouped together as a faction if each juror's most recently expressed verdict preference was second degree murder.

The initial distribution of verdict preferences was expressed on the predeliberation written ballot taken by the experimenters. The relationship between initial predeliberation preferences and final postdeliberation preferences under each decision rule can be summarized in the form of three verdict-to-verdict transition matrices (Table 6.1). The one anomaly in these

By Hastie

probabilities is the high frequency of first-degree murder verdicts on initial ballots under the ten-out-of-twelve decision rule. This small concentration of harsh verdict preferences was partly responsible for the observed increase in first-degree murder jury verdicts under this decision rule.

The probabilities of moving from one verdict state on the initial predeliberation ballot to another verdict state by the end of deliberation are conditional on the totals. These totals, to the right of each matrix, are the frequencies of mock jurors favoring each verdict (or undecided) at the beginning of deliberation. Thus, for example, under the twelve-out-of-twelve decision rule there was a .02 probability of starting deliberation with an initial vote for first degree murder and of remaining in favor of first degree murder throughout deliberation. Similarly, the movement from first degree murder as an initial vote to second degree murder at the end of deliberation occurred with the probability of .67, and the movement to a verdict of manslaughter occurred with the probability of .31 for jurors who initially preferred first degree murder.

The three verdict transition matrices have several features in common. First, deliberation accomplishes its goal in the sense that no jurors remain undecided at the end of deliberation, although a sizable fraction, almost 10 percent of the jurors, started deliberation with undecided views on the verdict. Second, under all decision rules the most popular initial verdict choice is manslaughter. However, by the conclusion of deliberation, the most popular verdict has changed to second degree murder. Because the study used only one stimulus case, it is difficult to determine whether this shift is motivated by a desire for harsher verdicts, for more correct, second degree murder verdicts, or for some other reason.

There are also differences in the transition probabilities under each decision rule. The sharpest difference concerns individuals who do not change from initial verdict to final verdict. These probabilities are comparable across decision rules for the verdicts of manslaughter and second degree murder. However, the initially less popular verdicts of not guilty and first degree murder reveal a dramatic difference. Jurors in the twelve-out-of-twelve decision rule condition are unlikely to remain in these initial verdict positions, while jurors voting initially for first degree murder and not guilty under the nonunanimous decision rules are much likelier to remain in those verdict positions at the end of deliberation. This is another example of the holdout effect that appears at several places in the data. Jurors in the nonunanimous deliberation rule may remain in their initial unpopular verdict categories without deadlocking the jury. A statistic directly reflecting this difference is the ratio of nonchanging jurors to total jurors under each decision rule. These ratios are .33, .44, and .50 in the twelve-out-of-twelve, ten-out-of-twelve, and eight-out-of-twelve decision

Table 6.1. Verdict-to-verdict transition probabilities for juries in each decision rule condition.[a]

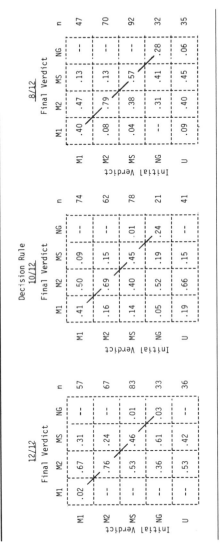

Decision Rule

12/12

	Final Verdict				
Initial Verdict	M1	M2	MS	NG	n
M1	.02	.67	.31	--	57
M2	--	.76	.24	--	67
MS	--	.53	.46	.01	83
NG	--	.36	.61	.03	33
U	--	.53	.42	--	36

10/12

	Final Verdict				
Initial Verdict	M1	M2	MS	NG	n
M1	.41	.50	.09	--	74
M2	.16	.69	.15	--	62
MS	.14	.40	.45	.01	78
NG	.05	.52	.19	.24	21
U	.19	.66	.15	--	41

8/12

	Final Verdict				
Initial Verdict	M1	M2	MS	NG	n
M1	.40	.47	.13	--	47
M2	.08	.79	.13	--	70
MS	.04	.38	.57	--	92
NG	--	.31	.41	.28	32
U	.09	.40	.45	.06	35

a. The major diagonals, indicated by broken lines in each matrix, represent the probabilities of not changing verdict preferences from the start to the finish of deliberation.

rules, respectively. Another related statistic is the ratio of individuals changing toward harsher verdict categories over individuals changing toward either harsher or more lenient categories. Calculation of this harshness shift over total shift ratio yields proportions of .51, .58, and .59 for the three decision rules.

The movement of jurors from verdict category to verdict category across the five quintiles of deliberation in the three decision rule conditions can also be translated into fifteen transition matrices, each of which indicates the likelihood of moving from one verdict category to another from the beginning to the end of a quintile of deliberation (Table 6.2). Jurors who are initially undecided and unable unequivocably to select a single verdict position at the beginning of deliberation are a special case. First, changes from the undecided category to any other verdict category occur with a much higher probability than other type of change. No jurors remained in the undecided category at the very end of deliberation. Furthermore, jurors leave the undecided category more quickly in the unanimous jury than in the nonunanimous juries. For example, only one individual juror remains in an undecided category at the beginning of the final quintile of deliberation for the unanimous decision rule, while larger numbers of jurors are undecided under the nonunanimous decision rules at this point in time (six and eleven jurors, respectively).

The most consistent difference between the unanimous and the ten-out-of-twelve and eight-out-of-twelve decision rules is that in unanimous rule juries there are major shifts from initial verdict to end-of-quintile verdict throughout deliberation. These shifts in the twelve-out-of-twelve decision rule condition are especially apparent for the categories of not guilty, first degree murder, and manslaughter. The proportion of jurors shifting to a more lenient verdict preference, once a shift has occurred, excluding undecides, is much higher for the unanimous juries than for the nonunanimous juries at every point in deliberation. The most dramatic changes in verdict preferences under the three decision rules occur in the final quintile of deliberation. At that point there is a sharp difference in the rate at which jurors move away from not guilty and into the other verdicts. In the twelve-out-of-twelve unanimous decision rule this shift is almost universal, with only one juror failing to defect from the not guilty category. However, for the nonunanimous juries the likelihood of remaining in favor of acquittal is above 50 percent.

The proportion of lenient to total shifts for individuals who shift verdicts changes in the last four quintiles of deliberation, when shifts toward leniency occur at a slightly higher rate for the twelve-out-of-twelve unanimous juries than for the nonunanimous juries. The tendency in nonunanimous juries at that point is to shift toward harshness, while in the unanimous jury

Table 6.2. Verdict-to-verdict transition probabilities for each quintile of deliberation.

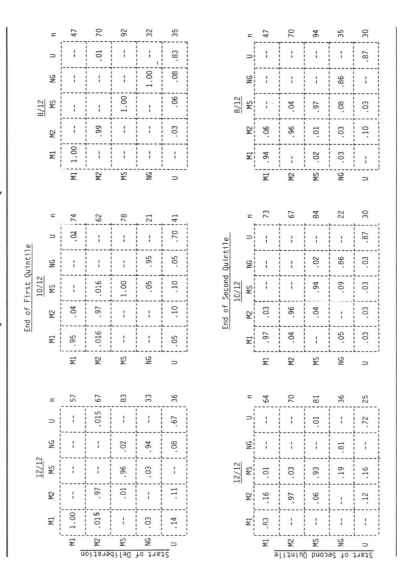

Start of Deliberation

12/12

	M1	M2	MS	NG	U	n
M1	1.00	--	--	--	--	57
M2	.015	.97	--	--	.015	67
MS	--	.01	.96	.02	--	83
NG	.03	--	.03	.94	--	33
U	.14	.11	--	.08	.67	36

End of First Quintile

10/12

	M1	M2	MS	NG	U	n
M1	.95	.04	--	--	.01	74
M2	.016	.97	.016	--	--	62
MS	--	--	1.00	--	--	78
NG	--	--	.05	.95	--	21
U	.05	.10	.10	.05	.70	41

8/12

	M1	M2	MS	NG	U	n
M1	1.00	--	--	--	--	47
M2	--	.99	--	--	.01	70
MS	--	--	1.00	--	--	92
NG	--	--	--	1.00	--	32
U	--	.03	.06	.08	.83	35

Start of Second Quintile

12/12

	M1	M2	MS	NG	U	n
M1	.83	.16	.01	--	--	64
M2	--	.97	.03	--	--	70
MS	--	.06	.93	--	.01	81
NG	--	--	.19	.81	--	36
U	--	.12	.16	--	.72	25

End of Second Quintile

10/12

	M1	M2	MS	NG	U	n
M1	.97	.03	--	--	--	73
M2	.04	.96	--	--	--	67
MS	--	.04	.94	.02	--	84
NG	.05	--	.09	.86	--	22
U	.03	.03	.03	.03	.87	30

8/12

	M1	M2	MS	NG	U	n
M1	.94	.06	--	--	--	47
M2	--	.96	.04	--	--	70
MS	.02	.01	.97	--	--	94
NG	.03	.03	.08	.86	--	35
U	--	.10	.03	--	.87	30

Table 6.2. (continued)

End of Third Quintile

Start of Third Quintile

12/12

	M1	M2	MS	NG	U	n
M1	.77	.19	.04	--	--	53
M2	--	.91	.09	--	--	86
MS	--	.18	.82	--	--	89
NG	--	.03	.38	.55	.03	29
U	--	.32	.16	.05	.47	19

10/12

	M1	M2	MS	NG	U	n
M1	.81	.16	.02	--	--	76
M2	.04	.93	.03	--	--	70
MS	.04	.21	.75	--	--	82
NG	.05	--	.36	.50	.09	22
U	--	.39	.19	--	.42	26

8/12

	M1	M2	MS	NG	U	n
M1	.89	.09	.02	--	--	47
M2	.05	.89	.04	.01	--	75
MS	.04	.04	.92	--	--	98
NG	.03	.03	.33	.53	.07	30
U	.04	.19	.11	.08	.58	26

End of Fourth Quintile

Start of Fourth Quintile

12/12

	M1	M2	MS	NG	U	n
M1	.49	.39	.12	--	--	41
M2	.03	.87	.09	--	.01	111
MS	.03	.18	.77	.02	--	97
NG	--	--	.41	.59	--	17
U	--	.40	.40	--	.20	10

10/12

	M1	M2	MS	NG	U	n
M1	.77	.19	.03	.01	--	69
M2	--	.99	--	.01	--	104
MS	--	.19	.81	--	--	79
NG	--	.09	.09	.82	--	11
U	.08	.31	.15	--	.46	13

8/12

	M1	M2	MS	NG	U	n
M1	.92	.08	--	--	--	52
M2	.025	.95	.025	--	--	81
MS	--	.04	.96	--	--	107
NG	--	--	.05	.95	--	19
U	--	.23	.06	--	.71	17

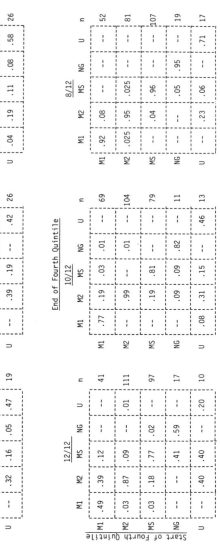

Table 6.2. (continued)

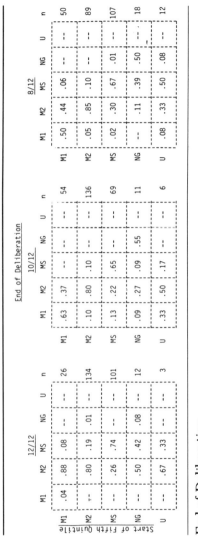

End of Deliberation

12/12

	M1	M2	MS	NG	U	n
M1	.04	.88	.08	--	--	26
M2	T-	.80	.19	.01	--	134
MS	--	.26	.74	--	--	101
NG	--	.50	.42	.08	--	12
U	--	.67	.33	--	--	3

10/12

	M1	M2	MS	NG	U	n
M1	.63	.37	--	--	--	54
M2	.10	.80	.10	--	--	136
MS	.13	.22	.65	--	--	69
NG	.09	.27	.09	.55	--	11
U	.33	.50	.17	--	--	6

8/12

	M1	M2	MS	NG	U	n
M1	.50	.44	.06	--	--	50
M2	.05	.85	.10	--	--	89
MS	.02	.30	.67	.01	--	107
NG	--	.11	.39	.50	--	18
U	.08	.33	.50	.08	--	12

Start of Fifth Quintile

End of Deliberation

the lenient-harsh shifts are about balanced. This is not true, however, for the first quintile of deliberation, when there appears to be a striking shift toward leniency in the nonunanimous juries but a shift toward harshness for the unanimous jurors.

Faction Size and Attractiveness

Faction size is the most important determinant of the outcome of deliberation (Hawkins, 1962; Davis, 1973). One measure of faction size effects is the probability of leaving a faction under each decision rule, excluding undecided jurors. These values were obtained by dividing the number of times an individual juror left a faction of each size, one through twelve, by the number of times such a faction existed (Table 6.3). These probabilities can also be displayed in curves for each decision rule, "smoothed" by replacing each value by the mean of itself and the two adjacent points (Tukey, 1977; Fig. 6.1), that reveal the important features of the data. First, jurors are much less likely to defect from large factions than from small ones. Second, the lower the jury decision rule requirement, the less likely that an individual will defect from a relatively small faction. This characteristic arises from the fact that there are substantial numbers of holdout jurors in nonunanimous juries. These jurors remain in nonmajority factions in eight-out-of-twelve and ten-out-of-twelve verdict-rendering juries at the end of deliberation.

Table 6.3. Probability of leaving a faction (number of times a juror defected/number of times a faction of size F_I existed).

Faction size (F_I)	Decision rule		
	12/12	10/12	8/12
1	.754	.592	.377
2	.465	.311	.358
3	.423	.299	.279
4	.190	.342	.250
5	.162	.214	.214
6	.166	.100	.156
7	.063	.104	.040
8	.137	.036	.034
9	.063	.031	.055
10	.042	.000	.025
11	.006	.000	.000
12	.004	.000	.000

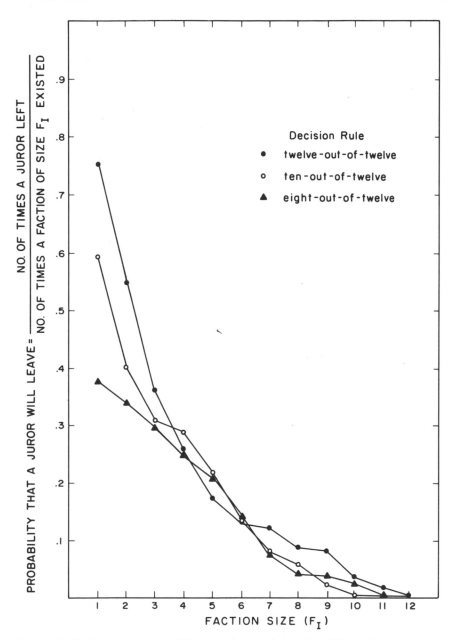

Fig. 6.1 Probability that a juror will leave a faction of size $F_I = 1, 2 \ldots 12$.

A more incisive empirical question concerns independence of the verdict and size effects on movement from faction to faction. The two potential causal factors are confounded, for larger factions tend to favor second degree murder of manslaughter verdicts, whereas smaller factions invariably favor not guilty. Small faction sizes of one to four members make it possible to compare the independent effects of verdict category and size on movement from faction to faction. Such a comparison reveals a clear effect of faction size, in that jurors are less likely to desert larger factions, but only a hint of an effect of verdict category, in that jurors are unlikely to desert the second degree murder verdict and are relatively likely to desert the not guilty verdict when faction size is held constant. The meager data must be stretched quite far to produce these findings, which are suggestions rather than confirmed conclusions.

The suggestion of a faction size effect is consistent with all theory-based and data-based expectations from a broad range of research on small group performance, and it emerges clearly in the present mock jury study. The verdict category effect is more tentative. The effect is doubtless dependent on the specific evidence structure for the stimulus case, and it is not exceptionally strong in the data. The suggestion that second degree murder has a special drawing power beyond faction size effects is plausible in view of the argument that this verdict has the most merit as a proper verdict for the case. The same argument implies that not guilty is the furthest from the truth and should therefore have the least juror-retaining power.

Faction Size and Speaking Rates

Just as movement from faction to faction is a function of faction size and verdict associated with the faction, so are speaking rates (Hawkins, 1962; Zeisel, 1963). An index of speaking probability was calculated by dividing the number of spoken remarks made by members of a faction by the number of remarks made throughout deliberation while that faction existed. Speaking probabilities in large factions tend to be based on data drawn from later phases of deliberation, where larger factions are likelier to exist, and from factions advocating second degree murder or manslaughter verdicts, which are the typical final verdicts. Nonetheless, the speaking probability calculations include a fair variety of composition and deliberation phase samples for each faction size and faction verdict summary. In addition, faction size and verdict preference have independent effects on speaking.

The probability of speaking, calculated for groups of jurors in each verdict-favoring faction under each decision rule, ranges from .08 for unde-

Table 6.4. Proportion of speaking events per speaker.

Faction size (F_I)	Decision rule		
	12/12	10/12	8/12
1	.130	.088	.081
2	.112	.102	.089
3	.096	.094	.096
4	.087	.094	.084
5	.074	.074	.091
6	.075	.077	.070
7	.097	.074	.077
8	.075	.077	.080
9	.070	.079	.074
10	.071	.077	.093
11	.075	.081	.083

cided jurors under the ten-out-of-twelve decision rule to .38 for second-degree murder jurors under the unanimous decision rule. These results are not conditioned on the number of jurors within factions and so are a rough measure of the extent to which the various factions, not individuals, dominated discussion. Second-degree murder factions, which were larger than other factions, were the most dominant, doubtless because of their size.

The proportion of speaking events per speaker was tabulated as a function of speaker's faction size under each decision rule, excluding undecideds (Table 6.4). These values were obtained by dividing the proportion of speaking events contributed by a juror in each of the faction sizes one to eleven by the number of speaking events that occurred while such faction sizes existed. These proportions are also displayed in curves for each decision rule, smoothed by replacing each value by the mean of itself and two adjacent points (Fig. 6.2).

The twelve-out-of-twelve unanimous decision rule shows a decreasing likelihood for an individual to speak as faction size increases, as has been frequently observed (Hawkins, 1962). That is, the larger the faction size, the less likely that any specific faction member will speak. The ten-out-of-twelve decision rule also exhibits this decreasing likelihood of speaking as a function of increases in faction size. However, one notable difference between the two rules is that jurors in small factions of one to two jurors are extremely likely to speak out relative to members of large factions in the twelve-out-of-twelve decision rule, while they are much less likely to speak in the nonunanimous ten-out-of-twelve rule. This tendency is further exaggerated in the eight-out-of-twelve decision rule, where members of small

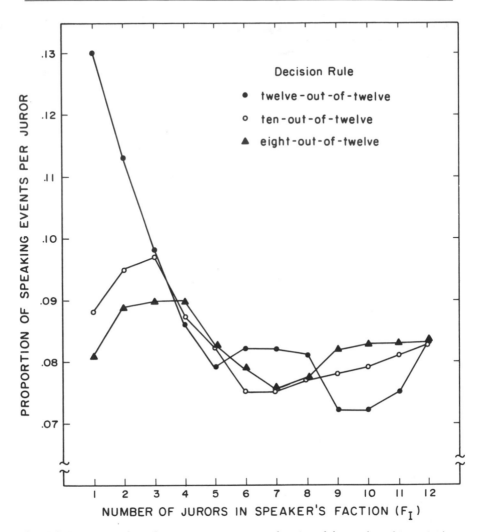

Fig. 6.2 Proportion of speaking events per juror as a function of the number of jurors in the speaker's faction (F_i).

factions are quite unlikely to speak, and where the largest factions, with nine to eleven members, even tend to increase their likelihood of speaking relative to intermediate-sized factions. In summary, the probabilities for factions of sizes three to eight are fairly close to one another in the three decision rules. For small faction sizes, the likelihood of speaking is elevated considerably in the unanimous decision rule but is only slightly elevated, relative to intermediate faction sizes, in the ten-out-of-twelve and eight-out-of-twelve decision rules. For large faction sizes the tendency is reversed, with higher likelihoods of speaking associated with larger factions for the eight-out-of-twelve decision rule juries in comparison to the unanimous rule condition.

Faction size is related to probability of speaking in unanimous juries (Table 6.4; Fig. 6.2). This relationship is similar to a function obtained in other mock jury research (Hawkins, 1960, 1962). Three explanations can be suggested for the monotonically decreasing function. One is that the personality characteristics which make jurors active talkers also make them more resistant to persuasion. Minority factions thus tend to be made up of high participators with this tendency increasing across deliberation. Another explanation is that social pressure depends on the number of jurors who oppose a juror. Jurors in minority factions are thus pressed to talk, even if they do not want to, by large factions of opposition jurors. A third possible explanation is that certain positions, such as verdict preferences, provide more material for discussion than others. When these positions are relatively unpopular, namely preferred by smaller factions, then higher rates of speaking will be associated with smaller factions.

There are four results that imply only one of these factors is the determinant of the relationship. First, although certain individual differences are correlated with speaking rates, these factors are not correlated with initial verdict preferences, final verdict preferences, measures of "stubborness," or size of faction. Thus, individual differences are an important determinant of speaking rate but do not mediate the relationship between faction size and speaking probability. Second, when individual difference factors, verdict preference, and point of time or quintile during deliberation are controlled, the relationship of faction size to speaking probability continues to appear. Thus, within the limits of the ability to identify and statistically remove the individual difference, verdict position, and deliberation sequence effects, the "pure" effect of faction size emerges when obvious alternate causal factors are controlled.

The third and probably the most compelling argument for the importance of group pressure is the effect of decision rule on the relationship of faction size to speaking probability. It is relatively easy to explain why changes in the patterns of group pressure on small versus large factions result from variations in decision rule. However, it is difficult to understand why the personalities of jurors moving into or out of different-sized factions or why rate of speaking for one verdict position or another would also depend on decision rule. Therefore, the clear dependence of faction size and speaking probability on decision rule, technically called the interaction effect of faction size and decision rule on speaking probability, supports the group pressure explanation of the relationship.

Fourth, as in the case of the faction-to-faction shift probabilities, the relationship of faction size and verdict category to individual speaking probability can be explored separately. Faction size effects are clear, with jurors in larger factions less likely to speak in factions favoring all verdict categories. Verdict category effects are less definite, but undecided jurors talk the least, followed closely by not guilty jurors, regardless of faction size. First-degree murder jurors are the most talkative, but they are barely distinguished in talkativeness from second-degree murder and manslaughter jurors. This pattern of results is sensible: undecideds are quiet, waiting to be persuaded; not guilty arguments are convoluted and abstract, therefore difficult to articulate; and first degree murder arguments follow from a simple, easily expressed story line. However, because of the small amount of data and the lack of inferential statistical support, the conclusion that verdict preference is related to speaking probability is suggestive rather than final.

These four arguments, particularly the interaction of faction size with decision rule, strongly implicate the group pressure explanation for variations in speaking probabilities. The group pressures affecting individual participation rates may take three forms. First, members of minority factions may assess the probability that their verdict position will either prevail in deliberation or at least prevent opposition positions from rendering a verdict. The perceived probability of affecting the outcome of deliberation, by reversing the majority preference or by deadlocking, may thus decrease as the decision rule requirement drops from unanimity to an eight-out-of-twelve majority. Second, members of majority factions may make the same assessment, and their perceptions of the likelihood of controlling the outcome of deliberation may then increase as decision rule requirements decrease, especially in cases with more than two verdict alternatives. Third, the closer the members of a faction perceive it to be to attaining its desired outcome, the more highly motivated its members may be to contribute to deliberation and to direct persuasive communications toward dissenters.

One more factor may be relevant. The "social climate" of deliberation in many of the majority rule juries appeared to be quite adversarial, even combative, in contrast to a deliberate, ponderous atmosphere in many of the unanimity rule juries. It may be that larger factions in majority rule juries adopt a more forceful, bullying, persuasive style because their members realize that it is not necessary to respond to all opposition arguments when their goal is to achieve a faction size of only eight or ten members. Thus, they are not concerned that their persuasive tactics will leave a few opposition jurors untouched or even frozen into defensive postures.

Growth of the Largest Faction

The verdict is the most important product of jury deliberation, and the path followed during deliberation to reach the final verdict is the most important aspect of the jury's behavior across time. The path to the final verdict can be traced by following the growth of the winning or verdict-rendering faction through deliberation. A statistically unbiased description of the growth of the largest faction can be calculated as the relationship between deliberation time and the probability that the winning or verdict-rendering faction has reached a size of eight members, excluding hung juries (Fig. 6.3). This relationship measures the rate at which the winning faction grows. Such relationships for all decision rule conditions show a common S-shape, with gradual positive acceleration at first followed by negative acceleration as the final probability of 1.0 is approached. However, there is an orderly difference in relationships across the three rules, with winning factions in eight-out-of-twelve and ten-out-of-twelve decision rule juries reaching size eight more rapidly than in unanimous juries. Analyses of variance performed on the data for the minute at which the winning faction first reaches size eight show that the decision rule effect is significant whether or not hung juries are included ($F(2,66) = 6.73$, $p < .002$) and ($F(2,62) = 5.46$, $p < .006$). Similar analyses using faction sizes of six and ten as criteria support the same conclusion. Large factions form relatively quickly in the nonunanimous rule juries.

To ensure that statistical artifacts were not responsible for the apparent decision rule differences, two related analyses were performed. First, the average time in minutes at which the winning faction size reached six, eight, or ten members was calculated. Juries that never reached the criterial largest faction size were excluded from these calculations. These analyses agreed substantially with the finding that the size of the largest faction increased more quickly under majority decision rules than under the unanimous rule. Second, the growth of the winning faction size across time, analyzed at ten-minute intervals, supported the conclusion that growth rates differed across decision rules.

The decision rule effect on the growth of the winning faction was independently replicated in a jury simulation experiment conducted West Virginia University (Foss, 1981). When the disagreement among jurors on the verdict of a murder case was measured, ten-out-of-twelve majority rule juries moved toward agreement more quickly than unanimity rule juries. The basic phenomenon was the same as the differential growth of the winning faction obtained in the present study.

The growth rate differences are an indication that the decision rule conditions are not qualitatively equal, differing only in duration. Something about the process of deliberation is reflected in the different faction growth rates that are produced by the manipulation of decision rule. Because the growth of the largest faction is central to any theory that would explain or predict the jury's verdict, almost every psychological factor relevant to jury behavior is implicated in hypotheses to explain the differential growth rates across decision rules. Ten alternate, but not exclusive, hypotheses may

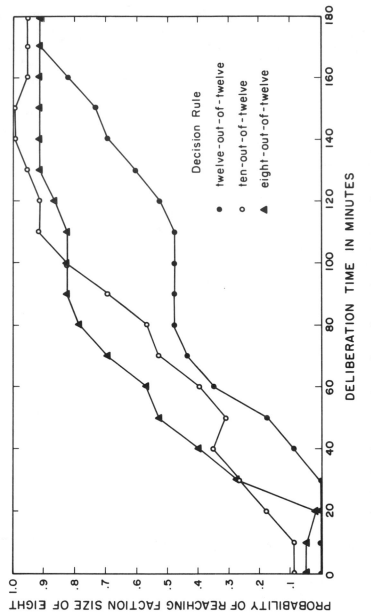

Fig. 6.3 Probability that the winning faction has at least eight members as a function of time for each decision rule.

account for the differences in the results from the mock jury study.

Two causal accounts focus on differences between decision rule conditions in the rate at which ballots are taken or at which individuals express their verdict preferences. The notion is that voting or verdict preference statements occur at a faster rate under the less strict decision rule conditions and thus faction sizes appear to grow at a faster rate under these decision rules. That is, since faction size is defined by the rate at which jurors express their opinions, a condition under which opinion expressions occur at a faster rate would also show factions growing at a slightly faster rate. There is a problem with this account, which has to do with the rate at which votes are taken or verdict statements are expressed. Verdict statements do not occur at a higher rate during deliberation in the nonunanimous decision rules as compared with the unanimous rule. Formal voting rates for both hand and written balloting do increase slightly for majority rule juries, which vote every 15 minutes for ten-out-of-twelve juries and every 20 minutes for eight-out-of-twelve juries, as compared to unanimous juries, which vote every 23 minutes. However, this sequence of twelve-out-of-twelve, eight-out-of-twelve, and ten-out-of-twelve does not reflect the growth rate differences. Furthermore, there is no correlation between voting rates and verdict change rates, or between verdict preference expression rates and change rates across quintiles or across juries within decision rule condition. Thus, there seems to be little empirical evidence that the apparent differences in growth of the largest faction are produced by higher rates of discussion or expression of individual verdict preferences under the less strict decision rules.

Another causal account involves the characteristic motivational state or mood induced in individual jurors by the decision rule. The notion is that decision rule affects the seriousness or gravity with which an individual juror addresses the decision making task. A lessened feeling of seriousness or gravity produces lowered motivation to review information thoroughly in the case before changing verdict preferences. This results in faster, less considered movement from initial verdict preferences to the most popular verdict within the jury. This concern was voiced in the Supreme Court opinions concerned with decision rule requirements, especially by Justice Douglas (*Apodaca et al. v. Oregon*, 1972; *Johnson v. Louisiana*, 1972). The postdeliberation rating data in the mock jury study lend support to this possibility, for jurors in the majority decision rule conditions rated deliberation as less serious and less thorough than jurors in the unanimous decision rule condition.

A fourth causal factor, which raises the issue of generalizing from the experimental setting to a real jury setting, concerns variation in experimental realism across the three decision rules. According to this view, jurors in the nonunanimous decision rule took the entire experimental experience less seriously than jurors in the unanimous decision rule condition because the nonunanimous rule did not apply to criminal cases in the jurisdictions where the study was conducted. However, the data are not consistent with this view. For example, the rate at which comments about experimental realism occurred during deliberation did not vary as a function of decision rule. Furthermore, the filmed materials and experimental procedures were rated as just as highly realistic in all three decision rules. This suggests that variations in acceptance of the experimental task across decision rules do not account for differences in the seriousness of deliberation.

A fifth possible explanation for the differences in growth of the largest faction across the three decision rules involves a shift toward harsher verdicts that is amplified in majority decision rule conditions. There was a consistent tendency to shift from less lenient to more harsh verdicts across the course of deliberation, and this shift was more pronounced in the majority rule juries. However, it would be imprudent to label this a shift to conviction or harshness. A more favorable and equally defensible label would be a shift to accuracy. For the stimulus case the most appropriate verdict is second degree murder, but the most common initial verdict preference was manslaughter. Thus, for this case, shifts toward a slightly harsher verdict are also shifts toward a more accurate or appropriate verdict. A further problem with the harshness shift account is that it is merely a descriptive label and does not provide a useful psychological explanation for the phenomena it describes.

One explanation for a conviction shift, which is hinted at in some opinions by Supreme Court justices, is that there is a diffusion of responsibility in the majority rule conditions (*Apodaca et al. v. Oregon*, 1972; *Johnson v. Louisiana*, 1972). Jurors feel less responsible for the final verdict of the jury when they are operating under a majority decision rule. The problem here is that a subjective sense of lowered responsibility is not clearly associated with majority decision rules. In fact, on the surface, a juror in a verdict-rendering majority under a nonunanimous decision rule is more likely to feel responsibility. Typically fewer jurors render the verdict, and often they render the verdict in the face of persistent opposition from an outvoted minority faction. These conditions would seem to be associated with a greater, not lesser sense of individual responsibility for the verdict on the part of the verdict-rendering jurors. However, if responsibility is defined as the ability of an outside observer to identify an individual juror's verdict preference at the end of deliberation, the unanimous decision produces the greatest sense of individual responsibility in that the observer can be certain of every juror's final vote. The majority rule decisions are associated with lowered responsibility in this sense, because an outsider might never be sure who was in the majority and who was in the minority. This interpretation would be consistent with the conclusion that heightened individual responsibility is associated with slower growth of the largest faction. The problem is that in a typical major felony case the jury is polled individually in court after the verdict is rendered. Jurors in the mock jury study were aware of this practice. Furthermore, no individual opinions were anonymous, under any decision rule condition, and jurors were fully aware that researchers were observing their deliberations. Thus, even this subtle version of the diffusion of responsibility account does not apply to actual trial procedures.

A sixth possibility, which emphasizes cognitive factors rather than motivational incentives, is that individual jurors translate the jury decision rule into a personal standard of proof. Under this hypothesis, the juror's perception of the beyond reasonable doubt standard would be affected by the group decision rule. The more lenient the group decision rule, the lower the personal standard of proof. This possibility was not considered in the study, but ninety other mock jurors who were not part of the original sample and who did not deliberate in mock juries were shown the stimulus trial, including the three decision rule instructions. They were then asked to give quantitative ratings of 0 to 100, to indicate an acceptable level of confidence in their judgment to render a verdict "beyond a reasonable doubt" for the case. The median rating of confidence was 92, and it did not vary with decision rule. This finding casts the cognitive, standard-of-proof explanation in doubt.

A seventh possibility is that certain final states are particularly aversive at the end of jury deliberation. In particular, under majority deliberation conditions, it is possible to finish deliberation as a minority faction member in a verdict-rendering jury. Any minority faction members at the end of deliberation under a unanimous decision rule would necessarily be jurors in a deadlocked jury. Thus, under unanimous decision rule conditions there are only three possible final states for individual jurors: majority faction members in verdict-rendering juries, majority faction members in hung juries, and minority faction members in hung juries. Under nonunanimous decision rules, a fourth state is possible: dissenting faction members in juries where a verdict has been rendered by the dominant majority faction. It seems likely that this fourth state is particularly aversive to jurors. If a juror finishes deliberation in this state, it usually means that he or she has worked hard but fruitlessly to advocate a position and perhaps received a dose of social abuse without affecting the product of deliberation. Thus, jurors may change verdicts to avoid the minority faction-majority rule jury state.

An eighth incentive to change verdicts, closely related to the motive to avoid minority faction membership, may be to put the jury "over the top," to be the juror who makes the decisive, verdict-rendering shift. The avoidance motive could be characterized as a desire to avoid being on the "losing team," while the over-the-top motive could be viewed as an incentive to "win" deliberation by scoring the final point. It is not possible in the present study to distinguish between these two incentives, namely to avoid losing versus to approach winning. One implication of both hypotheses is that jurors who change to avoid being in the minority faction in a verdict-rendering jury or who change to put the jury over-the-top are conforming behaviorally but not cognitively. That is, such jurors change verdicts, but without resolving basic intellectual issues, to join jurors in a more attractive faction. The derived measures of agreement among jurors on key case issues yielded lower values for late changing jurors in majority juries as compared to unanimous juries. The implication is that late-changing jurors in majority rule juries are motivated to join the largest faction by considerations other than changes of opinion about fundamental issues in the case.

A ninth explanation for differences in the growth of the largest faction derives from normative social influences in juries. In nonunanimous juries faction definition is more explicit or more frequently expressed, so a larger faction's normative prominence is defined more frequently and more clearly to all jurors. The problem here is that voting patterns and verdict statements during deliberation are not correlated with the rate at which the largest faction grows (see discussion of first explanation above).

A final explanation for growth rate differences of factions focuses on the effect of information pooling in deliberation. The decision rule is hypothesized to affect the motivation of majority faction members to talk during deliberation. This effect is such that under the unanimous decision rule majority faction members dominate discussion to a lesser extent (generate fewer valid and novel arguments) relative to minority faction members in contrast with nonunanimous decision rule conditions. These differences in volume and quality of deliberation create different informational pressures to change on members of minority factions under the different decision rules. The greatest pressure to change, measured by the volume of opposition arguments, occurs under the least strict decision rules. There is considerable evidence for this hypothesis. Not only were differences in probability of speaking a function of a juror's faction size, but this effect interacted with decision rule. Members of small factions in unanimous decision rules were relatively likely to speak compared to members of small factions in majority decision rules. Just the reverse was true for the members of large factions: unanimous decision rule jurors in larger factions were relatively less vocal than members of comparable factions in unanimous juries. Thus, if sheer volume of speaking is the measure of information communicated, informational pressure to motivate change out of minority factions is greater in nonunanimous decision rules than in unanimous rules.

In short, four of the ten explanations for differences in the rate of growth of the largest faction were supported by results of the mock jury study. The notion that jurors take their task less seriously or with less gravity in nonunanimous decision rule conditions as contrasted with unanimous decision rule conditions found support in the postdeliberation ratings of jury seriousness. The argument that jurors are highly motivated to avoid ending deliberation as members of minority factions in verdict-rendering nonunanimous juries found support in the postdeliberation ratings of between-juror agreement on opinion issues relevant to the case. Jurors appear to be motivated to shift to the largest faction to put the jury over-the-top of the quorum requirement or to shift out of small factions to avoid finishing as dissenters. Finally, the role of informational influence in jurors' faction-to-faction shifts was supported. The largest faction grew most quickly under majority decision rule conditions where it also generated the highest proportion of discussion content.

In summary, among the dynamic characteristics of behavior during deliberation are individual juror movement from verdict-favoring faction to verdict-favoring faction, speaking rates by jurors aligned in factions, and the growth of the largest faction across deliberation. Jurors' movements from verdict to verdict provide a comparison of the decision rule effects on performance. All initially undecided jurors eventually moved to join verdict-favoring factions. There was a shift from a modal initial juror verdict of manslaughter to a modal final juror verdict of second degree murder. The most obvious difference between majority rule juries and unanimous juries was signaled by the relatively large numbers of jurors who remained in favor of first degree murder or not guilty verdicts at the end of deliberation under majority decision rules, most of whom were holdout jurors. Jurors in majority rule juries also tended to shift toward harsher verdicts at a slightly higher rate than jurors in unanimous decision rule juries. Faction size was a major determinant of individual jurors' movements from verdict to verdict, although faction size effects were moderated by the holdout effect in majority rule juries. Finally, faction size had a definite effect on jurors' decisions to move from verdict category to verdict category, and there was a relatively strong attraction to the second-degree murder verdict category.

Faction size was a determinant of the probability that an individual juror would speak. The effect of faction size was such that the larger a faction, the lower the probability that any individual member would speak. This faction size effect was moderated by decision rule. The tendency for members of very small factions to speak with a relatively high probability reached its extreme in the unanimous decision rule jury and diminished in the majority rule juries. Group pressure factors as well as other motivational and social considerations were probably responsible for the diminished participation rates of small faction members under majority rule jury conditions. The verdict favored by a faction was also related to speaking rates, independent of the influence of faction size. In this case, first-degree murder verdicts seemed to be associated with the highest speaking rates, while manslaughter and not guilty verdict categories were associated with relatively low speaking rates.

Finally, differential rates of growth of the largest faction within the jury were observed in juries assigned different decision rules. The largest faction attracted new members at a lower rate under the unanimous rule as compared to majority rules. Four accounts, based on both motivational and cognitive principles, were retained as viable explanations for the phenomenon, while six accounts were rendered implausible by the results of the present experiment. Factors such as the seriousness of the deliberation climate, jurors' desire to avoid holdout status on verdict-rendering majority rule juries, and persuasive influence produced by information exchanged during discussion were judged to contribute to the occurrence of the effect.

7

Individual Differences among Jurors

Individual differences in background, including demographic characteristics, attitudes, and personality factors, are related to behavior as a juror. Demographic factors, such as age, social class, and gender, and role, such as jury foreman, have effects on verdict preferences, performance during deliberation, and postdeliberation ratings, including ratings of each juror by others.

Juror Stereotypes

Within the legal profession it is commonly assumed that differences between jurors in background, personality, and attitudes will influence a juror's decision making. This assumption acquires particular significance in states where attorneys are given an opportunity to examine prospective jurors, the jury *voir dire*, before the jurors are impaneled. The attorneys may challenge any jurors who exhibit demonstrable bias in a particular case (challenges for cause), and they may also exercise a limited number of challenges at their own discretion (peremptory challenges).

Various selection strategies have evolved that are designed to alert trial attorneys to characteristics which supposedly reveal a juror's biases. Advice on the types of questions to ask includes references to virtually any demographic characteristic, such as occupation, wealth, ethnicity, religion, marital status, or age; attitudes toward the law, courts, police, and related

By Penrod and Hastie

subjects; and probes to identify jurors with various personality traits (Bailey & Rothblatt, 1974; Belli, 1954; Ginger, 1975; Keeton, 1973; McCready, 1954). In fact, trial lawyers have been given so much often contradictory advice on what kinds of jurors to select, that the average practitioner would have no difficulty finding at least a few prospective jurors who possess the proscribed characteristics or answer questions in the wrong way.

On the subject of occupation, for example, attorneys are told to avoid jurors having a special knowledge of areas about which expert witnesses will testify, for these jurors will think they know more than the other jurors and more than the experts (Heyl, 1952). The unemployed, pensioners, and people on relief are thought to be generous, but teachers, clergy, and lawyers should generally be rejected (White, 1952). The defense should accept jurors with the same occupation as the defendant (Biskind, 1954). Farmers are desirable for criminal prosecution and civil defense, for they believe in strict liability, whereas waiters and bartenders are forgiving (Belli, 1954). Avoid jurors with expertise in fields involved in the trial (Davis & Wiley, 1967). Bankers are bad for criminal defendants in robbery and theft cases but are good in white-collar crime cases (Campbell, 1972). Unless the defendant is a veteran with a good military service record, retired police, military men, and wives are undesirable, for they adhere to strict codes (Bailey & Rothblatt, 1974).

On the question of gender, attorneys are instructed to avoid women in all defense cases (Darrow, 1936). Women are sympathetic and extraordinarily conscientious (Goldstein, 1935). With a woman as client, take all men (Heyl, 1952). Take women if the defendant is a handsome young man (Appleman, 1952). Women are unpredictable and influenced by their husbands' experience (Bodin, 1966). Women forgive male criminal defendants, but men are better jurors when counsel wants to avoid intuitive and sympathetic thinking (Belli, 1954). Females are good for all defendants except attractive female defendants (Katz, 1968–1969; Karcher, 1969).

On the question of ethnicity, attorneys in a criminal defense are advised never to drop an Irish person, for the Irish identify with defendants (Darrow, 1936). The emotionalism of ethnic groups is ranked, on a scale from high to low: Irish, Jewish, Italian, French, Spanish, and Slavic. Nordic, English, Scandinavian, and German jurors are preferable if it is necessary to combat emotional appeals (Goldstein, 1935).

On the question of demeanor and appearance, attorneys who are suing in an assault case should select weak jurors who would be frightened by a fight (Cornelius, 1932). Take smiling jurors, especially if they smile at the attorney (Darrow, 1936; Bodin, 1966). Avoid dominating types, for they will not change their minds and may sway others (Biskind, 1954). Take a favorable looking leader and argue the case to that juror (Keeton, 1973; Adkins,

1968–1969). Avoid jurors who feel imposed upon and who resent being called for jury duty. Be wary of smiling jurors who are trying to disarm attorneys; they want to get on the jury and "murder" them (Harrington & Dempsey, 1969). Avoid jurors who have been mistreated by life, lest they spread their misery for the sake of company (Donovan, 1887).

On the question of wealth and social status, attorneys are warned that wealthy people will convict, unless the client is accused of a white-collar crime (Darrow, 1936). On the matter of religion, attorneys who are defending are advised that Presbyterians are too cold; Baptists are even less desirable; and Lutherans, especially Scandinavians, will convict. Methodists may be acceptable. Keep Jews, Unitarians, Universalists, Congregationalists, and agnostics (Darrow, 1936). However, some experts warn that information on religion is not usually helpful (Appleman, 1952).

On the question of marital status, married people are said to be good for civil plaintiffs and criminal defendants, for they are more experienced in life and more forgiving (Belli, 1966). And on age, younger persons are said to favor the defendant (Appleman, 1952). The elderly are generally lenient but in criminal matters are sometimes severe (Adkins, 1968–1969).

Despite the conflicts in this advice, its reliance on ethnic, sexual, and other stereotypes, and its basis in idiosyncratic experiences rather than in more reliable forms of data, it has had enduring currency among practicing trial attorneys. In fact, these rules of thumb have produced stirring testimonials to the attorney's perspicacity, such as, "Trial attorneys have developed a perceptiveness that enables them to detect the minutest traces of bias or inability to reach an appropriate decision" (Begam, 1977, p. 78).

Systematic Jury Selection

Social scientific methods have been used to assist trial attorneys in jury selection. These methods typically use individual differences as a basis for determining which jurors should be challenged and which should be retained. Survey research techniques were first used in jury selection in the 1971 Harrisburg Conspiracy Trial, in which seven co-defendants were charged with conspiring to raid draft boards and with other antigovernment activities (Schulman et al., 1973; Etzioni, 1974; Tivnan, 1975; Saks, 1976; Herbsleb, Sales, & Berman, 1978). Social scientists who supported the defendants and were themselves antiwar activists volunteered to assist the defense. As a first step, these social scientists conducted 840 telephone interviews of a cross-section of residents of the eleven counties from which jurors were to be drawn. Next, follow-up interviews were conducted with 252 members of the original 840-person sample, to explore such topics as their knowledge of the case; media exposure; demographic characteristics; attitudes toward government, religion, trial issues, and antiwar activities; organizational memberships; and leisure activities.

The research found that religion was significantly linked to attitudes relevant to the specific case, and that low levels of education and media use identified conservatives in the community. Using such information, the social scientists formulated profiles of both desirable and undesirable jurors for use by the attorneys in making peremptory challenges. A total panel of 465 jurors was thereby reduced to 46. The 419 rejected jurors were excused for various reasons, such as their knowledge of the case, biases, or unwillingness to serve. The survey information almost certainly played a significant role in guiding the selection of jurors. The defendants were acquitted.

Similar methods were used by a group of psychologists to aid Angela Davis' defense attorneys in the selection of a jury for her 1972 murder, kidnapping, and conspiracy trial (Sage, 1973). A graphologist was also employed to examine prospective jurors' handwriting. Similarly, a group of psychologists aided the attorneys for Daniel Ellsberg and Anthony Russo in their conspiracy trial (Ungar, 1972). Defendants of other political persuasions have also made use of social science methods, as in the Mitchell-Stans-Vesco conspiracy trial (DiMona, 1974; Zeisel & Diamond, 1976).

Systematic jury selection methods have been criticized by both legal and social science authorities. Referring to defense tactics in the Joan Little murder trial, defense attorney Edward Bennet Williams characterized social scientific jury selection as "bunk," whereas criminologist Marvin Wolfgang called it a "more formal and systematic process that reflects what attorneys have always done through intuition" (Tivnan, 1975, p. 31). These methods have also been assailed as "social science jury stacking" (Etzioni, 1974). Questions involve the extent to which one side's juror profiles ought to be made available, through legal "discovery," to the opposing side (Herbsleb et al., 1978). There is little evidence that the method makes any difference in trial outcomes (Saks, 1976; Sperlich, 1977). Adherents argue that the methods help to ensure that juries will be impartial (Bonora & Krauss, 1979).

Although the methods used by social scientists have undergone modifications over the years, the general procedure is unchanged (Schulman et al., 1973; Kairys et al., 1975; Saks, 1976; Berk, Hennessey & Swan, 1977; Berman & Sales, 1977; McConahay, Mullin & Frederick, 1977; Bonora & Krauss, 1979). A random sample survey, such as the one in the Harrisburg Seven case, provides the basic data for the development of juror profiles. The survey method has three aspects that are of critical importance to its effectiveness, namely sample representativeness, questionnaire design, and data analysis.

First, care must be taken to ensure that the individuals sampled in the survey are representative of the population from which the jury venire is to be drawn (Berman & Sales, 1977). There may also be reasons for oversampling certain types of potential jurors. For example, if the defendant is black, it may be desirable to oversample from the black population.

The second critical consideration is that questionnaire items provide valid measures of jurors' case-relevant attitudes, beliefs, and attributes. The questions selected for the survey should generally cover three areas: attitudes about the particular case and issues in the case; knowledge of the case and the defendants; and background characteristics, such as demography, general attitudes, personality traits, media use, and leisure activities (Adorno, Frenkel-Brunswik, Levinson, & Sanford, 1950). A problematic aspect of question design is the choice of a measure of the respondent's verdict-rendering tendency. Ideally, the survey should make it possible to predict accurately how a juror with a particular profile will vote on the case at hand. Yet, no one interviewed in the survey will have actually heard the case evidence or been confronted with the task of deciding the defendant's guilt or innocence. Questions must therefore be included in the interview to represent the interviewee's probable verdict on the case. It is extremely difficult to specify precisely which responses will serve as an adequate predictor of how an individual will vote on a given case. Constraints of this kind have typically led to the use of factor analysis as a statistical method of data reduction. This analysis is designed to yield a variable that can serve as a surrogate for verdict preference or prejudgment.

The third requirement is that proper statistical procedures be used to analyze the data. Once a measure of the respondent's tendency to favor or oppose one side in the case is chosen, two methods of data analysis are employed, either separately or in combination. The first, called the Automatic Interaction Detector (AID), systematically searches data for interactions between variables by a step-wise procedure that initially hunts for the single predictor variable which, when split dichotomously, yields the maximum explained variance on the verdict dependent variable in the two resulting groups (Sonquist, Baker, & Morgan, 1973). After the first split is made, a search begins for another variable that, when split, maximizes the explained verdict variance in the resulting groups. This process is repeated until the sample has been subdivided into a large number of groups all of which meet a minimum size requirement.

AID is used primarily as an exploratory tool, presumably because of its propensity to capitalize on error variance or "noise" in data (Sonquist, 1970). The relationships it detects may not accurately reflect relationships that actually exist in the general population represented by the interview sample. In a sense, this analysis may be overly sensitive to relationships in the sample interviewed and yield conclusions that are not general to the real population of potential jurors. The use of these results in jury selection is difficult because AID provides only relative comparisons rather than overall judgments of particular juror types (Berk et al., 1977). A method must still be devised for deciding which types to challenge and which types to accept.

The second method of data analysis tyically used to predict the dependent variable is multiple regression (Kerlinger & Pedhazur, 1973; Cohen & Cohen, 1975). Essentially, regression analysis is used to construct a predictive equation in the form of an additive combination of independent variables. For example, if data are collected on prospective jurors' verdict preferences for a particular case and on their characteristics such as age (in years), income (in dollars), education (in years), and political liberalism (on a 7-point scale), a regression analysis might show that jurors' verdict preferences (akin to the probability a juror would vote to convict) are an additive function of these variables such as:

Preference for conviction = .008 (age) + .001 (income in thousands) − .015 (years of education) − .03 (liberalism score)

According to this equation, a forty-year-old person earning $20,000 per year with sixteen years of education and a liberalism score of 3 would have a preference score of .19. An older person would have a higher score, while a better educated person would have a lower score. A regression equation that perfectly predicted all jurors' scores would account for 100 percent of the variance in juror preferences, but actual jury regression models have typically accounted for about a quarter of the variance (Berk et al., 1977). Significantly, reports on the strength of the relationship between juror votes and the dependent variables used in regression analysis are only anecdotal. Furthermore, regression analysis is susceptible to the same problem as the AID method of "overfitting" a sample, making it difficult to generalize to true population relationships.

There is little evidence that these systematic techniques of jury selection do or can work (Saks, 1976). The empirical foundations of the survey profile methods are questionable, as is the generalizability of results obtained from individuals who have not heard the evidence. Most experimental studies of jury decision making have failed to detect systematic predictors of juror behavior, but they do suggest the strong influence of evidence on decision making. Similarly, research on the relationship between attitudes and behavior has failed to produce consistent or striking relationships.

In fact, estimates of the method's efficacy are not precise. An accuracy rate of 70 percent has been claimed (Kairys et al., 1975; Silver, 1978). However, if half of all jurors are expected to vote for conviction, simple guessing or coin-flipping would yield a 50 percent accuracy rate. And if 80 percent of the jurors prefer conviction, either in a single case or across cases, an 80 percent accuracy rate can be achieved by always predicting conviction.

Efforts to select jurors on the basis of their demographic, personality, or attitudinal characteristics also have not enjoyed much success (Berman & Sales, 1977). The few relationships observed do not provide significant advantages in jury selection. In one study 780 jurors viewed the same videotaped burglary trial and then deliberated, as juries, to a verdict (Saks, 1977). Demographic and attitudinal information from the jurors was used to predict their votes. The single best predictor, a question on whether crime was mainly the product of "bad people" or of "bad social conditions," accounted for only 9 percent of the variance, and the four best predictors together accounted for less than 13 percent.

The relationships between juror behavior and juror attitudes, personality, and demographic characteristics are not well understood. More than 160 jury studies provide little systematic evidence that personality variables, such as authoritarianism, locus of control, and legal attitudes, provide the predictive power needed to detect and challenge biased jurors, even assuming that requisite information on prospective jurors is available in voir dire (Berg & Vidmar, 1975; Buckhout, 1973; Boehm, 1968; Jurow, 1971; Buckhout et al., 1979; Sosis, 1974; Kauffman & Ryckman, 1979). Furthermore, deliberation may operate to nullify biases that exist before deliberation (Kaplan & Miller, 1978). On the whole, this implies low efficacy for jury selection strategies based on personality characteristics.

But attitudes about crime in general, particular crimes, or particular cases are a fruitful source of information on juror bias. Public opinion polls find that jurors who are strongly opposed to the death penalty tend to be less conviction prone than jurors who are not strongly opposed (Bronson, 1970, 1980; Harris, 1971; Ellsworth & Fitzgerald, 1983). Data from posttrial interviews with actual jurors and simulated juror decision-making studies are also consistent with the conclusion that those strongly opposed to the death penalty are likelier to vote for acquittal (Zeisel, 1969; Goldberg, 1970; Jurow, 1971; Ellsworth, Thompson, & Cowan, 1983). Researchers found that jurors' attitudes regarding rape are also related to their decisions in rape cases (Feild, 1978). Attitudes on punishment were found to be the best attitudinal predictor of recommended sentence in both a precipitory rape case and a nonprecipatory rape case.

In one study 367 experienced jurors were presented 30-minute, audiotaped summaries of four different trials—murder, armed robbery, rape, and a civil case—which included opening and closing arguments, witness testimony, and instructions by a judge (Penrod, 1979). Analysis of the jurors' attitudinal and demographic characteristics showed that no variable had a strong relationship to actual verdict preferences, the highest correlation being +.18. In addition, multiple regression techniques showed an average of 11 percent explained variance for the verdict preferences in the four cases, with the highest $R^2 = .16$ for the rape case. This implies that anyone who is aware of the relationships between the attitudes, demographic factors, and verdict preferences in the rape case can, in principle, do better than chance in predicting juror preferences. If half the jurors in a jury venire vote to convict at the end of the trial, those relationships would accurately predict the verdict preferences of 70 percent of the jury venire, as opposed to the 50 percent accuracy rate obtained by coin flipping. Of course, this assumes that all the appropriate attitudinal and demographic data are available to the jury selection team. It is quite unlikely, however, that the usual systematic methods of jury selection will yield a criterion as reliable as the verdict preferences obtained in the Penrod study.

AID analyses were also performed in Penrod's study. The results were similar to the regression results; in none of the four cases was it possible to predict verdict preference at high levels of accuracy. Although the AID analyses could sometimes account for as much as 25% of the variance in verdicts, subsequent tests demonstrated that much of the variance "accounted for" was actually error variance. In effect, no research has provided evidence that social scientific methods can be a powerful aid to attorneys in the task of detecting juror bias. However, attitudes, particularly case-relevant attitudes, such as toward the death penalty or rape, appear to be the most powerful individual difference predictors of verdict preference that have been studied to date.

One purpose of the present mock jury study was to evaluate jury selection techniques. The 828 jurors provided information on their personal backgrounds in a postdeliberation questionnaire, including age, gender, occupation, residence, education, political party, ideology, marital status, income, race, number of previous cases heard as a juror, and number of previous criminal cases heard as a juror. This information was entered into a step-wise multiple regression, with variables such as occupation and residence included to reflect socioeconomic status, and using predeliberation verdict preference as the dependent variable, assuming equal interval values ranging from one for first degree murder to four for self-defense. Only four variables produced significant F's (overall $F [5, 742] = 5.22$). Employed versus nonemployed, including retired, entered first with the highest correlation $r = .119$. Juror gender ($r = -.073$) brought the multiple R to .145, number of previous criminal cases as jurors ($r = -.059$) raised R to .155

and number of previous cases (criminal or civil) as jurors ($r = .054$) raised R to .179. No other variable added as much as 1 percent to R. At the fourth step the R^2 was only .032.

A subsample of 269 jurors completed a more extensive questionnaire that covered additional background characteristics, including years of employment, spouse's occupation, spouse's years of employment, years of residence at current address, number of children, newspaper most often read, frequency of newspaper reading, ethnic origin, and degree of ethnic identity. Self-perception questions were also asked concerning the extent to which jurors thought their verdict choices would be affected by the fact that a defendant had young children, the prospect of an unusually harsh sentence if the victim "got what was deserved," or the prospect of a death penalty. They were also asked whether someone should be punished simply because they caused another person's death. Finally, jurors rated their general attitudes toward the judges and the police.

Analysis showed that five factors contributed significantly to predictions of verdict preference, namely residence in a wealthy suburb ($r = -.20$), attitude toward punishing someone who causes another's death ($r = -.16$, $R = .30$), marital status ($r = -.13$, $R = .32$), and newspaper read ($r = -.08$, $R = .33$). These factors accounted for 11 percent of the variance in verdict preference. Thus, even when a reliable measure of verdict preferences is available, as in the mock trial initial verdicts, predicting a particular respondent's preference is difficult. For example, using a discriminate function analysis only 45.6 percent of the jurors were correctly classified by verdict preference. When the jurors were divided into only two groups, those voting to convict for murder and those not voting for a murder conviction, 61 percent of the jurors were correctly classified. This is better than chance performance but is not an impressively powerful lever for use in courtroom selection procedures.

Furthermore, in actual applications of the survey method in jury selection, there is no access to the jurors' verdict preferences, and it is not clear what measure could be substituted for these preferences. None of the attitudinal or demographic measures that might serve as a criterion in the analysis had more than a 20 percent correlation with the jurors' verdict preferences. The best that can be done in such a situation is to attempt to account for variance in a stand-in variable that is plausibly linked to verdict preference.

Although there is no hard evidence that current systematic jury selection methods are useful in typical felony cases, there are five applications of the method which may be more promising. First, the survey method has been employed most frequently in relatively unusual types of cases, often cases with political implications. In some of these cases biased sentiments may have influenced the jurors' decisions, in contrast to typical criminal cases in which systematic juror biases would be difficult to detect.

Second, even in criminal cases there can be substantial variability in the verdict judgments made by jurors. Although trial evidence accounts for most of the variability in verdicts across cases, the variability in opinions within cases must be attributable largely to individual juror differences of some sort. The juror's world knowledge concerning the domain of events that are relevant to a case is the most important individual ingredient in the juror's decision. For example, in the stimulus trial in the present research the juror's knowledge of social customs that might govern barroom quarrels, the effects of alcohol on physical coordination, and the acuity of visual perception under various viewing conditions were directly pertinent in the verdict decision-making process. The juror's general attitudes toward events and individuals involved in a case or toward relevant legal institutions, procedures, or standards are also inputs to the decision process. For example, the juror's attitudes concerning police officers, rape laws, or the death penalty would be expected to influence verdicts when the decisions require consideration of related issues, such as the credibility of a police officer's testimony, consent of the victim of rape, or a capital crime. However, personality factors, such as authoritarianism, introversion versus extroversion, and the need for achievement, or demographic factors, would not be expected to influence verdicts unless these factors are related to cross-relevant knowledge or attitudes. For example, juror income or residence might be related to verdict performance in a case, such as the stimulus trial, where knowledge of lower-class social habits, such as behavior in barroom environments, would make one construction of the evidence more or less plausible than another construction. Thus, a juror from a lower-class environment might believe (world knowledge) that men frequently carry knives or other weapons without specific plans to use them, whereas a juror from an upper-class environment might see possession of a knife as a rare event and infer malice or premeditation from possession.

Third, survey methods are not the only techniques employed by social scientists who aid in jury selection. Various nonverbal clues in the courtroom during voir dire may provide useful information about potential juror biases (Suggs & Sales, 1978). Another jury selection technique labeled the "Community Network Model" employs members of the local community or private investigators as informants to acquire background information about jurors whose names appear on the jury list from which trial jurors are to be selected (Bonora & Krauss, 1979).

Fourth, even if survey methods fail to assist social scientists and trial attorneys at the voir dire stage of the trial, these methods are useful to attorneys who seek to change the location of the trial, or venue, on the grounds that it is not possible to obtain a fair trial in the place where the trial was initially scheduled. A survey can also be used to challenge the composition of the jury pool by demonstrating that certain segments of the population are systematically underrepresented (Bonora & Krauss, 1979).

Fifth, social science strategies have been designed to optimize the effective use of peremptory challenges. These strategies, based on normative models from game theory and probability theory use the information available to an attorney about juror biases to maximize the advantage to one side of the case (Brams & Davis, 1978; Kadane & Kairys, 1979; Roth, Kadane, & DeGroot, 1977; Penrod et al., 1979). Thus, even when predictive information is weak, as in most voir dire situations, a significant competitive advantage may be obtained using scientific methods.

The relationships between juror characteristics and performance during deliberation and jurors' perceptions of the trial and their own deliberation offer insights into the deliberation process and the influence of individual differences on that process. In collecting background data from the jurors who participated in the present study, five standard demographic characteristics were used, namely education, occupation, income, political ideology, gender, and age; two role variables, namely prior juror experience and foreman status; and a small number of variables that are based on juror performance during deliberations, including persuasiveness and open-mindedness as rated by other jurors, initial verdict preferences, and holdout status at the conclusion of deliberations.

Some of these characteristics are dependent on one another. For example, education has a moderately strong relationship to persuasiveness and other characteristics that reflect socioeconomic status, such as occupation, income, and age (Table 7.1).

The six juror characteristics of education, occupation, political ideology, gender, age, and prior jury experience were used to predict eighteen aspects of jury behavior, ranging from verdict preference to status as a holdout against a majority of other jurors (Table 7.2). The percentage of variance in jurors' behavior that is accounted for by juror characteristics ranges from less than 1 percent for holdout status to over 18 percent for persuasiveness during deliberation. It is thus not possible to make a confident prediction of whether a juror will end up as a holdout during deliberation on the basis of juror characteristics. But juror characteristics can be used to predict whether a juror will be persuasive. For example, if such characteristics were used to predict whether a particular juror would be above or below average in persuasiveness, the predictions would be correct over 59 percent of the time.

The standardized regression coefficients that make up the regression equation for each of the dependent variables are the weights that are at-

Table 7.1. Correlations among juror characteristics. [a]

Characteristics	Education	Occupation	Income	Political ideology	Gender	Age	Criminal trial experience	Foreman status	Persuasiveness	Open-mindedness	Holdout status
Occupation	-.32										
Income	.34	-.21									
Ideology	-.14	.01	.05								
Gender	-.08	.23	-.08	-.07							
Age	-.24	.27	.04	.26	.08						
Criminal trial experience	.02	.01	.02	.06	-.09	.11					
Foreman	-.13	.12	-.10	.00	.10	.02	-.11				
Persuasiveness	.34	-.22	.24	-.05	-.26	-.16	.10	-.14			
Open-mindedness	.19	-.07	.12	-.02	-.08	-.09	.11	-.20	.42		
Holdout status	.00	-.05	-.07	.01	.01	-.04	-.02	.00	-.05	-.17	
Verdict preference	-.02	.10	-.07	.00	.06	.01	-.08	.02	-.16	-.02	.03

a. Critical values: $r = .091$, $p < .01$; $r = .099$, $p < .005$; $r = .116$, $p < .001$.
Values of individual difference variables:

Education: 1 = grade school, 2 = high school, 3 = some college, 4 = college, 5 = postcollege
Occupation: 1 = professional and managerial, 4 = skilled labor, 5 = unskilled labor, 6 = unemployed (incl. housewife and student)
Income: 1 = $1000 per annum or less . . . 100 = $100,000 or more per annum
Political ideology: 1 = very liberal, 9 = very conservative
Gender: 1 = male, 2 = female
Age: 20 to 69 years
Criminal trial experience: 0 = none . . . 6 = service on six criminal cases
Foreman status: 0 = not foreman, 1 = foreman
Persuasiveness: 1.0 = lowest persuasiveness . . . 4.8 = highest persuasiveness
Open-mindedness: 1.4 = lowest open-mindedness . . . 4.9 = highest open-mindedness
Holdout status: 0 = not holdout, 1 = holdout
Verdict preference: 1 = first degree murder, 2 = second degree murder, 3 = manslaughter, 4 = not guilty

Table 7.2. Standardized regression coefficients for multiple regression models.

Criterion: Predictors	Verdict preference	Entries	Facts	Issues	Key facts	Verdicts	Fact-issue relationships	Questions	Organization	Mean	s.d.
Education	.10	.21	−.07	.29	.03	−.22	.22	.04	.21	2.74	1.15
Occupation	.01	−.10	.02	−.08	−.09	.07	−.09	.00	−.05	3.90	3.52
Political ideology	.01	−.02	−.02	−.04	.02	.03	−.05	−.03	−.04	5.18	2.02
Gender	.03	−.13	−.10	−.17	−.12	.16	−.17	.06	−.07	1.43	.50
Age	−.02	.06	−.07	−.03	−.03	−.09	−.06	.06	.10	45.05	12.93
Criminal trial experience	−.06	−.00	.03	.04	.01	.02	.02	−.06	.10	1.17	1.07
R^2	.015	.092[a]	.019	.165[a]	.034[b]	.095[a]	.133[a]	.012	.074[a]		

Criterion: Predictors	Irrelevancies	Different facts	Different issues	Different key facts	Different fact-issue relationships	Foreman	Persuasiveness	Open-mindedness	Holdout	Mean	s.d.
Education	−.02	.25	.31	.23	.28	−.10	.28	.17	−.02	2.74	1.15
Occupation	.04	−.10	−.10	−.09	−.12	.07	−.06	.02	.07	3.90	3.52
Political ideology	−.03	−.04	−.06	−.03	−.04	.01	−.02	−.00	.03	5.18	2.02
Gender	.08	−.14	−.16	−.15	−.16	.07	−.22	−.08	.04	1.43	.50
Age	.05	.08	.05	.05	.02	−.03	−.07	−.06	−.05	45.05	12.93
Criminal trial experience	−.05	−.00	.02	−.01	.01	−.10	.08	.12	−.01	1.17	1.07
R^2	.018	.111[a]	.165[a]	.103[a]	.156[a]	.039[a]	.183[a]	.057[a]	.008		

a. $p < .0001$.
b. $p < .001$.

tached to each of the predictor variables. Each of the variables has been standardized to have a mean of 0 and a standard deviation of 1. Although standardization has the disadvantage of changing the scales for predictor variables, such as age being no longer in units of years, it has the advantage of putting the weighting coefficients on roughly the same scale and allows a crude comparison of the relative sizes of coefficients. The comparisons have to be made cautiously whenever predictor variables are correlated with one another. For those juror performance variables in which the overall regression equation attains statistical significance, the basic pattern of regression coefficients is similar. Juror education is the dominant predictor of juror performance.

Jurors were classified according to individual differences and their performance was compared in five respects. First, their contributions to deliberation were compared. One of the principal aspects of behavior during jury deliberation is the substantive contributions made by jurors during deliberation. These include relatively gross measures of contribution, such as total speaking time and the number of statements recorded per juror. At a more fine-grained level the contributions of jurors are compared in terms of the proportion of statements in critical areas of discussion, such as references to the facts of the case, the legal issues raised in the case, the central or disputed facts in the case, labeled key facts, and the relationships between facts and legal issues. Jurors were also compared in terms of the numbers of different facts, issues, key facts, and fact issue relationships credited to each speaker. The overall frequencies of such references provide insight into the relative levels of participation in deliberation. The proportion of such references among the different categories also indicates the relative importance to jurors of particular categories of statements. And the number of different types of entries within the categories index the jurors' contributions in terms of their thoroughness or exhaustiveness in raising and discussing relevant aspects of the case.

Second, jurors were asked to assess such aspects of the trial as the performance of the attorneys, the judge's fairness, the usefulness and clarity of the judge's instructions on the law, and the extent to which the jurors felt they understood the instructions. Third, jurors were asked to rate their jury's deliberation for thoroughness, seriousness, and the amount of pressure they felt from other jurors to change their verdict preferences. Fourth, jurors were asked to rate the difficulty of their decision-making task, their confidence that their jury had reached a just verdict, and the extent of their agreement with the verdict.

The final area in which jurors were compared was memory. They were evaluated in terms of their recall of the judge's instructions, particularly their memory for the legal definitions of the four verdict alternatives: first degree murder, second degree murder, manslaughter, and not guilty by reason of self-defense. Jurors were also compared on their overall recall of case evidence.

Education

Education is correlated with such individual differences as occupation $(-.32)$, income $(.34)$, age $(-.24)$, and ideological orientation $(-.14)$. Education effects cannot be entirely separated from occupational, income, and other effects in the present analysis because these factors are all correlated with one another. As a result, the effects for various individual differences cannot be added together to arrive at an index of the overall effect for an individual juror with particular characteristics. For example, the effects expected for a high-income professional male with a liberal ideology are not the sum of the effects for high income, professional occupation, male sex, and liberal ideology.

Five educational levels of jurors were identified: jurors with less than a high school diploma $(n = 120)$, jurors with a high school diploma $(n = 281)$, jurors with some post-high school or college education $(n = 195)$, jurors with a college degree $(n = 167)$, and jurors with some education beyond a college degree $(n = 57)$.

Other studies on the relationship of education to juror performance and attitudes have found that less educated as compared to highly educated jurors participated less in discussions, devoted a smaller percentage of their deliberation statements to procedural and legal matters, were more likely merely to agree with other jurors, received lower ratings from other jurors for their contributions to deliberation, and were less effective at changing other jurors' opinions (James, 1959). As for the relationship of education to verdicts, college educated jurors were found to be less likely to acquit on grounds of insanity than less educated jurors (Simon, 1967). Similarly, better educated jurors more frequently voted for conviction (Reed, 1965). However, simulation studies using adults qualified for jury duty found that educational level was related to verdict preferences in only one of four cases, a rape case, where less educated jurors were more likely to convict (Sealy & Cornish, 1973a). Another study using adult "jurors" also reported that education was unrelated to sentencing (Gray & Ashmore, 1976).

In the present mock jury study, more educated jurors tended to participate more frequently in deliberation than less educated jurors. On the average, jurors from the five education levels, ranging from grade school to postcollege, contributed 74, 76, 83, 119, and 120 remarks respectively to deliberation $(p < .0001)$. As education level rose, the proportion of statements concerning legal issues and the problems of relating the case facts to those legal issues increased, while the relative number of simple expressions of verdict preference declined. Educational attainment was also clearly related to the number of different facts generated by jurors, to the number of different issues mentioned, to the number of different key fact categories, and to the number of fact-legal issue relationships noted.

There are two reasons why these results do not necessarily imply that highly educated jurors are likely to produce superior decisions. First, it is not clear that a jury composed of relatively better educated jurors will generate the same set of facts, legal issues, and fact-issue relationships for discussion during deliberation as will a jury with a wider range of educational backgrounds. Second, it is unnecessary to have more than a few jurors who generate a variety of facts and issues in order to ensure that a broad variety of factors are considered during deliberation. This was shown in the mock jury study by a crude analysis of jury exhaustiveness in which the average level of education in entire juries was kept uniform. Juries were divided into four groups ($n = 18, 17, 17, 17$) based on mean educational level. The difference across groups was only marginally significant in terms of the number of different facts generated ($F [3.65] = 2.90$, $p = .041$) and moderately significant in terms of the number of different key facts generated ($F [3.65] = 3.36$, $p = .024$), but these effects were not directly related to education level. There was no relationship for the number of different issues generated ($F [3.65] = 1.57$, $p = .200$) nor for the number of different fact-legal issue relationships ($F [3.65] = 2.17$, $p = .100$).

Juror ratings of the trial judge's fairness did not vary as a function of educational attainment, nor did their ratings of their comprehension of the judge's legal instructions and the helpfulness of the instructions. However, as educational levels rose, jurors rated both the defense attorney and the prosecutor as less skillful ($p < .05$ and $.0001$ respectively) and the judge's instructions as less clear ($p < .01$). The higher levels of juror recall associated with greater educational attainment may have highlighted the difficulties inherent in trying to reach a verdict while conforming to the instructions, thus producing lower ratings of instruction clarity. The implications of the education-attorney rating relationship are unclear. Possibly the better educated jurors have higher standards for performance or have personal experience with better attorneys than do less educated jurors.

On perceptions of deliberation, jurors were asked to evaluate their jury's thoroughness, the pressure to change votes that they felt from other jurors, and the seriousness with which they thought their jury approached the decision making task. Jurors' assessments of thoroughness and pressure did not vary as a function of educational level, although ratings of seriousness declined slightly as educational attainment increased ($p < .01$).

In their perceptions of decision making, jurors did not differ in their ratings of the difficulty of reaching a verdict, their confidence that the jury reached a just verdict, or the extent to which they agreed with the final verdict.

On recall tests, jurors' recollections of the judge's instructions and the facts of the case revealed a direct relationship between education and recall. Higher levels of education were associated with superior recall of the four verdict definitions and for eight different trial facts. For example, jurors who had not completed high school recalled less than 25 percent of the content of instructions on verdict definitions, while college graduates recalled more than 60 percent of the same material. Similarly, recall for facts from testimony was at 48 percent for the lowest levels of educational attainment and over 70 percent for the highest levels (all significance levels $p < .0001$).

Occupation

Several jury studies have treated occupation as an individual difference. In experimental juries in metropolitan areas of the Midwest, higher status jurors were slightly over-represented as foremen, and occupational status was positively associated with participation in deliberation and with ratings by other jurors of helpfulness (Strodtbeck, James, & Hawkins, 1957). In a mail survey, occupational status was positively associated with higher rates of conviction (Reed, 1965). Teachers and housewives were somewhat more likely than other jurors to convict in a negligence case involving an injury to a child (Green, 1967). A study of the voting behavior of over six thousand civil jurors provided a litany of occupational differences, such as, "butchers . . . vote for the plaintiff 88 percent of the time versus 28 percent for retired executives" (Hermann, 1969–1970, p. 151). A greater disparity was found in the occupational status of the jurors and defendant in convicting juries than in acquitting juries (Adler, 1973). But a weak relationship was reported between occupational status and verdict preference on only one of three cases examined in a British study of mock juries (Sealy & Cornish, 1973a).

Jurors who participated in the present mock jury study were classified into one of six occupational categories: professional ($n = 169$), managerial ($n = 114$), clerical ($n = 180$), blue collar ($n = 194$), housewife ($n = 92$), and retired and nonworking ($n = 79$). The last two categories were combined in order to avoid small sample sizes and because the two groups are roughly equal in standard "prestige" ratings. The correlation between these six occupational categories, with lower numbers associated with higher status occupations, and the Duncan Socioeconomic Index is $-.91$ (Duncan, 1961;

Yankelovich, 1979). There is also a moderately high correlation between juror education and occupational categories ($r = .32$). Higher levels of education are associated with professional and managerial groups as compared to blue collar and housewife groups. Again, many of these occupation effects cannot be separated from the education effects.

On their contributions to deliberation, there was a clear pattern of differences in participation rates across the six occupation categories, with members of higher status occupations participating more than members of lower status occupations. The average number of contributions ranged from 109 to 113 for professionals and managers to 62 for nonworking and retired ($p < .0001$). These differences may be a function of not only the types of experiences that jurors are exposed to in their work settings but also the differential educational experiences of jurors. However, there are a few differences across occupational groups in types of contributions to deliberation. For example, occupation groups discussed evidentiary facts at a uniform level, but occupation was linked to different rates of discussion of legal issues, verdicts, and organization (all significance levels, ($p < .0001$). Members of higher status occupations spent relatively more time discussing legal issues and making organizational suggestions but less time stating verdict preferences than did lower status jurors.

The importance of occupation in deliberation is further underscored by the significant variability in the number of different facts generated by individual jurors in various occupational groups, the number of different legal issues, and the number of different fact-issue relationships. Again, higher status occupations were associated with greater breadth or variety of contributions ($p < .0001$).

On jurors' perceptions of the trial, deliberation, and decision making, essentially no differences owing to occupational status were obtained. The occupation-recall results closely paralleled the results obtained for education. Jurors in higher status occupations remembered more than lower status jurors; the differences were highly significant ($p < .0001$) and of magnitudes comparable to those obtained for education.

Income

The relationships between juror family income and juror behavior were assessed by forming four income groups: annual family income under $12,000 ($n = 162$), family income between $12,000 and $17,000 ($n = 139$), family income between $17,000 and $25,000 ($n = 215$), and family income over $25,000 ($n = 126$). A total of 186 jurors (22 percent) did not indicate their family incomes. Income was correlated with education ($r = .34$) and occupational status ($r = .21$), and the patterns of significant differences for total speaking and other forms of participation were virtually identical to those obtained for education and occupation. However, there were no significant relations between income and ratings of the trial, deliberations, or the jury decision process. Memory test results were in the expected direction, with superior memory associated with higher income, but differences were smaller in magnitude and typically reached lower levels of statistical significance ($p < .01$ rather than .0001).

Political Ideology

Few studies have examined the relationship between self-assessed political ideology and verdict preference. The political values of some college subjects may have affected their decision making, but no empirical evidence for this relationship has been reported in the few relevant studies (Nemeth & Sosis, 1973). Political beliefs did not predict verdict preferences in four cases examined in a study conducted in Massachusetts jury pools (Penrod, 1979). The methods of jury selection developed and advocated by social scientists sometimes rely on estimates of the relationship between political values and jury decision making (Schulman et al., 1973). In highly political trials such relationships may exist and might be detected with appropriate case-specific questions, but no such relationships are documented. Yet some attitudes, such as those toward the death penalty, and some personality traits, such as authoritarianism, which are related to political orientation may affect juror decisions.

Jurors in the mock jury study reported their ideological orientation on a nine-point scale, which was collapsed to form four groups: left ($n = 237$), liberal ($n = 256$), conservative ($n = 201$), and right ($n = 106$). On contributions to deliberation, juror ideology was unrelated to total speaking contributions to deliberation. And while the four ideological groups differed in the number and percentage of references to fact-issue relationships ($p < .001$), the relationship was not direct and is difficult to interpret.

On perceptions of the trial, more liberal jurors tended to characterize the judge's instructions and general conduct as favorable to the prosecutor, while conservative jurors perceived the judge as favoring the defense ($p < .01$). The left-leaning jurors rated both the prosecution and defense attorneys as lower in ability than did the more conservative jurors ($p < .01$ and $p < .001$). The ideological groups did not differ in their assessments of the helpfulness of the judge's instructions, but the more conservative jurors rated the instructions as clearer ($p < .01$).

On perceptions of deliberation and decision making, the left jurors gave the lowest ratings for jury thoroughness and seriousness ($p < .001$ and $p < .0001$). However, verdict confidence, decision difficulty, and agreement with the jury's final verdict were unrelated to ideological orientation.

The pattern of differences in recall of legal definitions and case facts were consistent and significant but puzzling ($p < .0001$ for all measures except recall of second-degree murder elements). Left-oriented and conservative jurors exhibited similar and high levels of recall compared to lower levels for liberal and right-oriented jurors.

Gender

The individual difference that has received the most attention by empirical researchers is juror gender. Most research on gender effects has used jury simulations, generally with student jurors, and typically the goal has been to find differences in conviction rates and recommended sentences.

Neither student nor citizen judgments for typical criminal case materials have revealed differences between male and female verdict preferences (Simon, 1967; Gray & Ashmore, 1976; Bray & Noble, 1978). No gender differences showed up in student judgments of a murder trial based on the stimulus trial in the mock jury study (Eisen & McArthur, 1979). Actual jurors who rendered verdicts on four different sets of trial materials also exhibited no gender differences (Penrod, 1979).

Some differences as a function of juror gender have been observed in sentencing recommendations and other judgments related to the verdict-rendering process (Rose & Prell, 1955; Griffit & Jackson, 1973). In an automobile theft case there were no gender effects on verdicts, but male students did think the defendant was more likely to be guilty, regarded the crime as more serious, and, presumably offsetting the higher likelihood of guilt, required a higher standard of reasonable doubt for conviction (Kerr, 1978). In another study, although males began deliberations preferring harsher sentences than females, jurors converged to favor similar penalties during deliberation, yielding no main effects of gender on verdicts (Bray et al., 1978). No relationship appeared between the gender of student jurors and their sentencing judgments, although women prescribed slightly more lenient sentences for women (Richey & Fichter, 1969). Jurors were less likely to convict same-gender defendants (Stephan, 1974). And males were more influenced by defendant attractiveness than females (Efran, 1974).

The picture differs for rape cases, where female jurors appear to be somewhat more conviction-prone than male jurors (Miller & Hewitt, 1978). For example, male students were more inclined to think that a rape victim made a causal contribution to the rape, attributed more fault to the victim, and characterized her more negatively than did female students (Calhoun, Selby, & Warring, 1976; Rumsey & Rumsey, 1977). Male student jurors gave more lenient sentences in rape and robbery cases when victims did not resist, while females gave harsher sentences under the same conditions (Scroggs, 1976).

In a rape case female students favored conviction more often than males before and after deliberation, but there were no differences in male and female probability thresholds for conviction using different definitions of reasonable doubt (Kerr et al., 1976). Another study using essentially the same case also obtained gender differences in verdict preferences and ratings of the defendant's guilt, with males more lenient (Davis et al., 1977). But with this case female student jurors were more likely than males to change votes from guilt to innocence, so that verdict differences largely disappeared by the end of deliberation (Nagao & Davis, 1980).

Other research has failed to find gender differences among adult mock jurors in verdict preferences on two theft cases and one rape case (Sealy & Cornish, 1973a). However, in a second rape case based on circumstantial evidence, women were more likely to vote for conviction. In another rape case there were interaction effects between gender and intelligence on verdict judgments (Hoiberg & Stires, 1973). But, in yet another study of college student mock-jurors, no gender differences emerged in rape case decisions (Jones & Aronson, 1973).

In research using civil case materials, no gender differences were found in verdict preferences (Green, 1967). However, in another study males awarded plaintiffs more damages than did females (Stephan & Tully, 1977).

As for the effects on deliberation, differences between adult male and female interaction patterns have been observed in mock jury deliberations (Strodtbeck & Mann, 1956). Males participated more actively than females and were rated as more helpful, even when occupational status was equated (Strodtbeck, James, & Hawkins, 1957).

Male and female students did not differ in preferred verdicts for a muder case (Nemeth, Endicott, & Wachtler, 1976). In a large sample of 474 students, males were slightly more likely to sit at the head of the table at the start of deliberations, and males tended to communicate more suggestions, opinions, and information and to receive more suggestions and opinions, though the differences were quite small.

The safest generalization that can be made from all research on gender differences is that female students are more likely than male students to regard the defendant in a rape case as guilty and that males participate at higher rates in deliberation than females.

In the present mock jury study the participation rates of male and female jurors varied significantly. First, males produced 40 percent more speaking entries than females, averaging 98 and 69 remarks during deliberation respectively ($p < .001$). In addition to these overall differences, the men and women in the juries allocated the substantive content of their statements in different ways. Males made more references to case facts ($p < .01$), legal issues ($p < .0001$), the disputed key facts ($p < .0001$), and organizational matters ($p < .01$). Females made more verdict statements ($p < .0001$) and had a higher share of irrelevant statements ($p < .01$).

The male jurors were more talkative than the females, generating more total facts and more key facts, and they generated larger numbers of different facts, different key facts, different issues, and different fact-issue pairings ($p < .0001$) during their speaking time. The numbers of unique facts, issues, and key facts generated by jurors and their ability to link relevant facts and legal issues are useful indices of jurors' contributions to deliberation. However, because of the other systematic differences between male and female jurors in the sample, such as education, occupational status, and experience in decision making contexts, these differences cannot necessarily be ascribed to gender per se.

There were not sizable differences between male and female jurors on measures of their perceptions of the trial and deliberation. And men and women were equally adept at recalling the definitions of first and second degree murder and manslaughter as well as the facts from testimony, but men had slightly superior recall for the self-defense definitions ($p < .001$).

Age

To assess the relationship between juror's ages and their behavior as jurors, four roughly equal-sized age groups were formed: jurors under the age of 34 ($n = 200$), jurors aged 34–46 ($n = 184$), jurors aged 47–56 ($n = 224$), and jurors aged 57 and older ($n = 206$). Because age was related to educational level ($r = -.24$), the large number of differences among jurors that were a function of educational attainment suggested differences would be found among the age groups as well. In addition, other research has found age differences (Strodtbeck & Mann, 1956; Plutchik & Schwartz, 1965; Scroggs, 1976; Green, 1967; James, 1967; Sealy & Cornish, 1973a; Gray & Ashmore, 1976).

On contributions to deliberation, the oldest and youngest jurors in the mock jury study tended to participate slightly less than jurors in intermediate age groups (34–56), although this difference was only marginally significant ($p < .05$). Age groups differed in the number of references to legal issues and fact-legal issue relationships ($p < .0001$) but not in other respects. The same pattern held for references to different facts ($p < .01$), legal issues

($p < .001$), key facts ($p < .001$), and fact-issue pairings ($p < .0001$), with the highest contribution levels by members of the 34–56 age groups.

Jurors in different age groups did not differ in their perception of the trial judge or the defense attorney, but their ratings of the district attorney increased as a function of juror age ($p < .01$). Ratings of instruction helpfulness ($p < .01$), instruction clarity ($p < .0001$), and comprehension ($p < .0001$) also increased as a function of juror age. Actual comprehension of the instructions bore an inverse relationship to age. Older jurors exhibited relatively low recall of specific components of the instructions but gave high ratings for instruction clarity and comprehensibility.

Older jurors rated the deliberations as more serious ($p < .0001$) than did younger jurors. Jurors in different age groups did not differ in their assessments of deliberation thoroughness, of the persuasive pressure from other jurors, of the correctness of their own decision, or of the extent to which they agreed with their jury's verdict.

There was a clear relationship between age and recall of the judge's instructions and recall of case facts ($p < .0001$). Once again, the oldest group of jurors displayed markedly poorer performance than younger jurors.

Prior Jury Service

The influence that prior juror service has on subsequent decision making in juries is a subject of legal folklore. Perhaps the most common notion concerning prior service is that it will tend to make jurors more conviction prone. The argument is that as jury service continues, a juror is repeatedly exposed to similar crimes, similar legal arguments, similar issues, and similar alibis; jurors grow weary of hearing the same arguments over and over again and grow irritated with those who apparently commit crimes.

There is little systematic research on the effects of prior jury service, although district attorneys in many areas where jurors serve for extended periods of time maintain tallies of jurors who have served on cases and of how they have voted, with an eye to using this information to aid in jury selection (Ginger, 1975). Most accounts of prior service effects are anecdotal and inconclusive (Broeder, 1965). Research on prior service reveals a complex pattern of results. Jurors with prior experience were significantly more likely to convict in some cases but not in others (Reed, 1965; Sealy & Cornish, 1973a). Subtle relationships between the nature of earlier cases decided and subsequent decisions have been uncovered (Center for Jury Studies, 1981b; Kerr, 1980). For example, jurors who initially judged severe crimes were later less likely to convict those charged with minor offenses (Nagao & Davis, 1979).

Jurors in the present mock jury study were asked about their prior juror service and about the total number of civil and criminal cases on which they had served as jurors. Four groups were formed based on the number of prior experiences on criminal trials: zero experience ($n = 214$), one ($n = 366$), two ($n = 152$), and three or more ($n = 73$). The number of experiences as a juror on criminal cases was not strongly related to any of the other measured individual differences. Even the age of a juror, which might be linked to opportunities to serve as a juror, barely correlated with prior experience on criminal cases ($r = .08$). The reason for this low correlation may be that for most jurors their entire previous juror experience occurred during the same month of service that they were participating in the study. Thus, the measure of prior jury service was largely a measure of recent jury service.

On contributions to deliberation, neither prior jury service nor prior criminal juror service was related to speaking entries. This was unexpected, since experienced jurors should have a clearer notion of how jury decision making proceeds and should be more comfortable with participation. Not only did overall rates of participation remain constant, but experience-related differences were negligible with respect to the generation of various types of remarks during deliberation. The only significant difference was on the proportion of organizational statements, with more experienced jurors making slightly more such remarks than less experienced jurors ($p < .01$). Prior experience was unrelated to the number of unique facts, issues, key facts, and fact-issue relationships generated by jurors.

Prior experience was also unrelated to ratings of the judge, the attorneys, the instructions, the pressure from other jurors, the thoroughness or seriousness of deliberation, the difficulty of decision making, and agreement with the jury verdict. Moreover, although prior juror experience should sensitize jurors to aspects of the trial that are most relevant to their decision making task, such as case facts and the judge's instructions on the law, causing the jurors to attend more to those trial aspects and therefore to recall more of the relevant information at the conclusion of the trial, experience was unrelated to recall for the legal definitions of the jury's four possible verdict alternatives and was unrelated to their overall recall of case facts.

The Jury Foreman

Research has found that jury foremen tend to be of higher status and male. They also provided approximately one-quarter of the total jury discussion, far more than the average juror (Strodtbeck, James, & Hawkins, 1965; Simon, 1967).

Foremen in the present mock jury study spoke nearly three times as much as the average nonforeman juror (200 entries versus 74, $p < .0001$). The foreman's speech also differed from the other jurors'. Foremen devoted a greater proportion of their statements to legal issues ($p < .0001$) and made organizational statements at five times the rate of other jurors ($p < .0001$), but they made a lower percentage of verdict statements ($p < .0001$). In the remaining areas foremen did not differ from other jurors; their contributions were similar to those of other jurors, albeit more frequent. The fact that foremen, as compared to other jurors, made fewer verdict preference statements suggests that they attempted to execute their leadership role with some neutrality respecting their juries' verdicts.

With their higher rates of speaking, foremen also generated significantly larger numbers of different facts, legal issues, key facts, and fact-issue relationships ($p < .0001$). Even allowing for the fact that foremen frequently repeated in summary form the points raised by other jurors—as evidenced by the fact that they generated three times as many statements but only twice as many novel facts, legal issues, or key facts—the magnitude of the differences suggests that the foremen contributed disproportionately to the exhaustiveness of jury deliberations.

Foremen did not differ from other jurors in their perception of the trial or of the deliberation process. The two groups also did not differ in their recall of the legal definition of manslaughter. Although foremen did recall more about the definitions of second degree murder and self-defense and about the facts of the case ($p < .001$), the magnitude of these differences was rather small.

The Persuasive Juror

A variety of individual characteristics are associated with measures of juror persuasiveness, based upon ratings provided by fellow jurors in the present mock jury study. Foremost among these individual differences is education ($r = .36$). Other individual differences that are related to education are also related to persuasiveness, such as income ($r = .24$), social status ($r = .23$), and occupational status ($r = .22$). Additionally, juror gender is related to persuasiveness ($r = .28$), with males viewed as more persuasive.

In the mock jury study persuasiveness was analyzed in a manner similar to other individual differences. Jurors were divided into four equal groups according to their persuasiveness as rated by other jurors, using a scale from 0.0 for the least persuasive to 5.0 for the most persuasive. The mean levels of persuasiveness for each of the four groups were 2.02, 2.74, 3.33, and 4.01.

Persuasiveness was strongly related to the amount of speaking credited to jurors. On the average, the four persuasiveness categories, starting with the least persuasive, made 42, 66, 94, and 151 statements respectively. Although sheer volume of contributions was strongly related to jurors' assessments of fellow jurors' persuasiveness, the relationship was not necessarily directly causal, because rated persuasiveness is linked to other factors, as indicated by the intercorrelations with factors such as education. Jurors in the four persuasiveness groups also did not vary in the proportion of facts and questions contributed to discussion, although there were major differences between groups in other contributions, such as the number of legal issues, key facts, fact-issue relationships, organization, and verdicts ($p < .0001$).

Thus, jurors with higher persuasiveness not only spoke more frequently during deliberation but also used their speaking time in different ways than jurors with lower persuasiveness. These differences in content were also reflected in the relationship between persuasiveness and the substantially greater numbers of different facts, issues, fact-issue relationships, and key facts generated by jurors ($p < .0001$). High persuasiveness was related to volume of production as well as to breadth or novelty of production during deliberation. Jurors' ratings of other jurors' persuasiveness provided a reliable reflection of the substantive contributions jurors made to the deliberation process.

Persuasiveness was not related to jurors' perceptions of the judge, the instructions, and the attorneys. While persuasiveness was also not related to the thoroughness or seriousness of deliberation, the less persuasive jurors indicated that they felt more pressure to change their verdict preferences than did the more persuasive jurors ($p < .01$).

The less persuasive jurors found decision making more difficult ($p < .0001$), expressed lower confidence in their initial verdicts ($p < .01$), and ultimately agreed less with the jury's final verdict ($p < .001$). The picture that emerged from these results was one of confident, talkative jurors who persuaded less confident and less articulate jurors to change their verdict preferences by placing verbal pressure on those jurors.

With their higher production of unique facts, legal issues, key facts, and fact-issue relationships, more persuasive jurors, not surprisingly, exhibited better memory than less persuasive jurors both for the legal definitions of the verdict alternatives and for the case facts ($p < .0001$).

The Open-Minded Juror

To analyze the behavioral characteristics of open-mindedness in the mock jury study, jurors were divided into four groups: highest open-mindedness ($n = 111$, mean = 4.54), moderately high ($n = 304$, mean = 4.04), moderately low ($n = 262$, mean $= 3.56$), and low ($n = 151$, mean $= 2.80$). The behavior rated as open-minded by jurors was correlated with the behavior rated as persuasive ($r = .42$).

Open-mindedness was associated with volume of speech (94 speaking entries for the least open-minded jurors, 131 for the most open-minded; $p < .0001$). Open-mindedness also correlated with discussion of legal issues ($p < .001$), fact-issue relationships, organizational directives, different facts, legal issues, key facts, and fact-issue relationships, but not with verdict statements ($p < .0001$).

In the area of trial and deliberation perceptions, rated open-mindedness was associated with lower perceived pressure from other jurors ($p < .0001$) and greater agreement with the jury verdict ($p < .0001$). Open-minded jurors were also most confident and most in agreement with their jury's verdicts (all $p < .0001$).

The pattern of recall was parallel to that found for persuasiveness. Open-mindedness was associated with slightly higher recall of legal definitions and case facts, although most of these differences were not statistically significant.

Initial Verdict Preferences

After the trial but before jury deliberations began, jurors, individually and privately, indicated their verdict preferences. Responses fell into five categories: approximately 14 percent of the jurors ($n = 115$) indicated that they were not certain about their verdict, but the remainder selected one of the legally appropriate verdicts. Twenty-two percent of the jurors ($n = 182$) expressed a preference for first degree murder, 24 percent ($n = 119$) preferred second degree murder, 31 percent ($n = 257$) preferred manslaughter, and 9 percent ($n = 75$) opted for not guilty by reason of self-defense. Jurors obviously differed in their perceptions of the trial evidence.

Jurors' initial verdict preferences were largely unrelated to contributions to deliberation. Initial verdict preferences were also unrelated to perceptions of the trial judge and the defense attorney. However, jurors preferring harsher verdict alternatives gave the prosecuting attorney slightly higher competence ratings ($p < .01$). While jurors' understanding of the legal instructions did not vary as a function of their initial verdict preferences, there was some variability in their ratings of the clarity of the instructions, with undecided jurors finding the instructions lowest in clarity ($p < .01$).

Initial verdict preferences were not significantly related to jurors' ratings of deliberation thoroughness, seriousness, and pressure to change verdicts. Jurors who initially preferred second degree murder as a verdict felt somewhat less pressure to change than other jurors. But since second degree murder was the modal jury verdict, jurors who preferred it from the start may have been subjected to the least pressure to change their preference. This interpretation is consistent with the finding that 100 percent of the initially undecided jurors adopted a verdict preference during deliberation, 72 percent of those jurors initially preferring first degree murder changed, 50 percent of those preferring manslaughter changed, 81 percent of those preferring acquittal changed, but only 21 percent of the jurors initially preferring second degree murder had adopted another verdict alternative by the conclusion of deliberation.

Jurors who began deliberation preferring the least popular verdict, not guilty, and those who began deliberation undecided on a verdict had more difficulty making a decision ($p < .0001$). Since jurors who initially preferred not guilty also reported more pressure to change verdict preference (mean $= 3.6$) than did the initially undecided jurors (mean $= 2.4$), the basis for reporting difficulty in their decision making may have differed for the two groups. For the undecideds, the process of actually determining an appropriate verdict may have been difficult, while for the not guilty jurors the difficulties may have arisen from the process of defending and then, in over 80 percent of the cases, changing their verdict preference.

The extremity of verdict preference was related both to jurors' assessments of the justness of their jury's verdict and to jurors' agreement with their jury's verdict. Again, jurors with more extreme preferences, and hence under the greatest pressure to change, were least satisfied with the results of deliberation ($p < .0001$).

There were no systematic differences in jurors' recall of the legal instructions, although it might be expected that jurors would be slightly better at recalling the legal definition of the verdict offense which they initially preferred and defended in the early stages of deliberation. Only in the definition of second degree murder did jurors initially preferring that verdict display marginally better recall of the definition ($p < .026$). The recall of instructions as a function of final verdict preference differed marginally only for the recall of the manslaughter definition. There was a small difference in recall of case facts, with initially undecided jurors scoring lower than other jurors ($p < .01$).

The Holdout Juror

Approximately one out of every seven jurors in the mock jury study were holdouts. These 120 holdouts consisted of jurors who did not vote with the majority of jurors in their jury at the conclusion of deliberation. This included some jurors from hung juries in the unanimous and eight-out-of-twelve decision rule conditions ($n = 16$), but for the most part holdouts were jurors left in the minority when a sufficiently large quorum of jurors in the ten-out-of-twelve and eight-out-of-twelve decision rule conditions reached a verdict.

No personal demographic characteristics differentiated holdouts from other jurors. Furthermore, the behavior and contributions of holdouts during deliberation did not differ substantially from other jurors. However, holdouts' perceptions of deliberation, of other jurors, and of some aspects of the trial differed from other jurors'.

Holdouts spoke as much as other jurors, and there were no significant differences between holdouts and nonholdouts in content of discussion. Holdouts and other jurors also viewed the judge and the legal instructions similarly, except that holdouts gave the prosecuting attorney slightly lower ratings ($p < .001$). But holdouts had a significantly lower perception of the seriousness and thoroughness of jury deliberations ($p < .0001$). Somewhat surprisingly, the holdouts reported no more pressure from other jurors to change than did the majority jurors, perhaps because jurors who did receive pressure from the majority and did change their verdict preference may have experienced great pressure from other jurors. Since these jurors were members of the majority, their ratings contributed to the fairly high mean pressure rating for the majority.

The holdouts expressed extreme disagreement with their jury's verdicts, and they were far less certain that their juries had reached just verdicts ($p < .0001$). However, holdout and majority jurors did not differ in their ratings of the difficulty of making a decision in the case. And although holdouts differed from other jurors in the verdicts they supported, both in speech and in voting, the two groups did not differ in their recall of the legal definitions of any of the available verdicts or material presented as testimony.

In summary, the relationship is weak between the background characteristics of jurors, such as demography, personality, and general attitudes, and their verdict preferences in typical felony cases. However, the jurors' world knowledge concerning events and individuals involved in the facts of the case does affect their verdict decisions. Deliberation performance and recall of instructions are most strongly related to the juror characteristics that reflect socioeconomic status, such as education, occupation, and income. Deliberation performance is also related to juror persuasiveness. This is an indication that both the rate of participation and the quality of participation form the basis of jurors' judgments of fellow jurors' persuasiveness. Participation and, to a lesser extent, recall is also related to juror gender and discriminates between jurors who serve as foremen and those who do not.

Jurors' perceptions of the trial and deliberation are largely unrelated to the socioeconomic factors. Perceptions of the defense attorney, the district attorney, the trial judge, and deliberation are weakly related to jurors' political ideologies, and perceptions of the judge's instructions are related to juror age. However, few significant relationships exist between juror characteristics and perceptions.

Some variables yield surprisingly few significant relationships. Previous jury experience is virtually unrelated to performance and perception. Initial verdict preferences are related to perceived difficulty of making a decision and agreement with other jurors but little else. Holdouts differ from other jurors chiefly in their perceptions of the quality of deliberation and agreement on the proper verdict.

8

The Deliberation Process

Deliberation processes can be illuminated by means other than quantitative analysis. Qualitative summaries of behavior, as well as impressions and intuitions that have accumulated over years of working with experimental juries, also provide valuable insights into jury performance. A sample of the contents of a typical jury deliberation reveals characteristics of the social persuasion process and juror motivations that are missing from quantitative analyses of the events tabulated in observational coding systems.

A Typical Jury Deliberation

The quality of deliberation can be made more concrete through a detailed description of one typical unanimous deliberation. The jury selected for this purpose was representative of the other unanimous juries with regard to its length (144 minutes), number of formal ballots (nine), errors (ten, four of which were corrected), and verdict (second degree murder). The mock jury panel was also representative of the local population and indistinguishable from panels deciding actual felony cases elsewhere in the same courthouse.

The foreman (Juror 1) was a sixty-one-year-old, white, male, insurance executive, married to an accountant and living in an upper income suburb. His initial verdict preference was manslaughter. He was a resourceful, directive foreman who dominated the discussion, contributing 25 percent of the comments during deliberation. His postdeliberation recollection of the

By Hastie

151

trial judge's instructions and of the evidence was highest on the jury. At the end of deliberation he was rated by other jurors as being the most open-minded and as second only to Juror 10 in persuasiveness.

Juror 2 was a twenty-five-year-old, white, female, business secretary, who was unmarried and living in a middle income suburb. Her initial verdict was not guilty. She was the major effective holdout for not guilty and manslaughter verdicts. Although she received high ratings for open-mindedness, she was rated as the least persuasive of the jurors.

Juror 3 was a twenty-seven-year-old, white, female, electronics assembler, who was unmarried and living in a middle income suburb. Her initial verdict was undecided.

Juror 4 was a fifty-seven-year-old, white, male, shoe factory foreman, married to a housewife and living in a middle income suburb. His initial verdict was manslaughter. Though talkative and confused, he did not make major errors in discussion.

Juror 5 was a thirty-four-year-old, white, male, insurance accountant, married to a housewife and living in a lower income suburb. His initial verdict was second degree murder. A talkative juror, he made major errors on both the evidence ("The doctor said Johnson was drunk") and the law ("Manslaughter has to be an accident").

Juror 6 was a fifty-seven-year-old, white, housewife, married to an electrical engineer and living in a middle income suburb. Her initial verdict was second degree murder. Talkative, she made significant errors on the relationship between manslaughter and second degree murder ("Unreasonable force is second degree murder"). Her abrasive, argumentative personal style earned her a rating as the least open-minded of the jurors.

Juror 7 was a twenty-two-year-old, white, male, college student, who was unmarried and living in the city. His initial verdict was undecided. A wavering, ineffective proponent of not guilty and manslaughter verdicts, he never fully accepted the jury's final verdict.

Juror 8 was a fifty-nine-year-old, white, housewife, married to a retired factory worker and living in middle income suburb. Her initial verdict was second degree murder. She never spoke during deliberation. However, her responses on the postdeliberation questionnaire showed that her memory for material from the trial was above average, and her evaluations of the other jurors and the deliberation task were unexceptional.

Juror 9 was a fifty-one-year-old, white, housewife, who was divorced and living in an upper income suburb. Her initial verdict was manslaughter.

Juror 10 was a thirty-eight-year-old, white, male, automotive mechanic, married to a department store clerk and living in a lower income suburb. His initial verdict was second degree murder. A plain-spoken but effective advocate of the second degree murder verdict, he was the second most talkative juror, after the foreman, and was regarded by the other jurors as the most persuasive.

Juror 11 was a twenty-one-year-old, oriental, stockboy, who was unmarried and living in an upper income suburb. His initial verdict was second degree murder.

Juror 12 was a forty-year-old, white, male, cook, married to a high school teacher and living in a middle income suburb. His initial verdict was second degree murder. This juror almost never spoke.

Juror 5 (reading). "Members of the Jury, harken to indictment No. 29211. Jurors for the Commonwealth present that Frank C. Johnson on the 9th day of May in the year of our Lord one thousand nine hundred and seventy-six, did assault and beat Alan Caldwell with intent to murder him by stabbing him, and by such assault and beating did kill and murder Alan Caldwell, against the peace of the Commonwealth aforesaid, and contrary to the form of the statute in such case made and provided. To this indictment the defendant has heretofore pleaded that he was not guilty, and for trial has put himself on his country, which country you are. You are now sworn to try the issue. If the defendant is guilty you will say so. If he is not guilty, you will say so and no more."

Foreman. Now, as the judge said, there are four possible findings in this case: murder in the first degree, second degree, manslaughter, and self-defense not guilty. But let's start with the facts and see if we can agree on some of them. We know that the defendant, Mr. Johnson, and the victim knew each other.

Juror 10. And there was bad feeling between them.

Foreman. Yes, it seems to be also true that they had been in this grill where the killing took place and they had had words early in the day. Have I got that right? There doesn't seem to be any disagreement that the defendant had a knife, was carrying that weapon, when the fight occurred later that day, that night, in the same grill. And am I right to say that there was consensus among the witnesses we heard that the victim also had a weapon on his person, a razor? Now, we can also say that the victim approached Mr. Johnson on the night in question; that the victim went up to Johnson in that grill and asked him to step outside. And then he went ahead and walked out of the grill and the defendant followed him. Are we agreed on that? And then there is no room for disagreement as to what happened next, as to who held the knife and who got stabbed and so forth. He obviously got killed, and the defendant admitted that he did it, that it was his knife, and that he held it. The point that's in disagreement is how he used it and why he used it. Is that right?

Now with that established, what we want to start discussing is, number one, why was he in that grill again? Did the defendant provoke that incident outside the bar? Can we believe him that the victim did pull a razor? And what were his motives if he did do these things, what did he have in his mind, was there malice? Maybe we ought to start talking around the room about these things, because that seems to be the key to the whole case here: why did he do these things? Does anyone want to volunteer?

Juror 4. I don't think that the razor was ever pulled.

Juror 9. It is inconceivable that after a mortal wound, that the razor could be put away.

Juror 10. Yes, and the doctor did testify to the fact that the razor was in his back pocket.

Foreman. Well, would you agree, well, two things here, that the victim did strike the first blow, that the defendant was hit on the jaw? And, two, that the razor was never in his hand, in the victim's hand? Right, we're agreed. Well, now we have the question of motive, of causes, of why did the defendant pick that knife up at home and carry it with him?

Juror 6. I think that it was provoked, that he was being prepared. I think that he did intentionally bring it with him.

Juror 9. Yes, or otherwise he would have had it with him earlier in the day.

Juror 11. I think that we should also discuss the fact that he was drunk, they took a blood sample.

Juror 4. But this was the victim.

Juror 11. Oh, this was the victim?

Foreman. So we have had testimony that he resisted the idea of going back to that bar, that he was talked into going back by his friend, because he didn't want to meet this guy again, the victim.

Juror 10. That's what the defense would have us believe anyway.
(*Discussion of the events referred to in testimony continued for another half-hour, and then the jury took a written poll of its members' opinions. The balloting showed six votes for a verdict of second degree murder, three votes for manslaughter, and three votes for not guilty. Discussion resumed with a consideration of the judge's instructions on verdict definitions.*)

Foreman. Manslaughter is where you kill someone without wanting to, or expecting to. In a way, it's an accident. For instance, an example would be when you kill someone by driving an automobile in a manner that's unsafe. So if he used this knife as a weapon, but not with the intent to kill. For instance, if this man, the victim, impaled himself upon the knife, then one could maybe get a manslaughter charge out of it. That is, he hadn't intended to use the knife in the manner in which it ultimately resulted in killing this man. But he had, you know, created the situation that made this thing happen.

Juror 11. But let's suppose that you had been in this bar in the afternoon and a man, the victim here, had pulled a straight razor on you. Why would you go back? Even though he did check for the car that night, there was the possibility that he could, the man with the razor could come back. That's what sticks in my mind.

Juror 4. That's right, he was showing he's not a chicken. "No one's going to bluff me."

Juror 8. No.

Juror 4. You don't understand, you've never been in those bars. It's a different breed of people that stay in bars on six or seven days a week.

Juror 11. When someone threatens you with a fist or something, that's one thing. But a straight razor, that's something else.

Juror 10. Because this gentleman had a reputation, I mean.

Juror 6. We're not supposed to take that, to discuss that testimony about his reputation.

Juror 8. That's right.

Juror 4. But to live in that neighborhood there, you can't stay out of that bar.

Juror 10. I agree with you there, but not that night, he could have waited a day.

Juror 6. I feel that way too. As a woman, I would have avoided that bar. Maybe men don't feel that way.

Juror 5. We were instructed by the judge that you have to exhaust all means of escape before you can justifiably stab someone.

Juror 8. Yes, well these people obviously think in terms of violence.

Foreman. Have you all got any further feelings on the charge of second degree murder? I mean, have you entertained any thoughts that it is or isn't in this area? Or maybe it's too early to bring this out?

Juror 5. I'd just like to state what I feel about what the term "second degree murder" might mean. Probably, I think, it has the same connotations as first degree except it wasn't . . . hmmm.

Juror 4. Premeditated.

Juror 5. Premeditated. He meant to kill him. He meant to thrust the knife in so hard, not enough to escape, but actually enough to kill him.

Juror 3. I just don't think that maybe you just fall onto a knife. I mean, maybe it's out there, but—I know things happen fast—I mean, I think he meant to kill him.

Foreman. So we have several possibilities here. The first is he meant to kill him. But then he could have wanted to hurt him.

Juror 3. That's a very big knife. I mean, getting back to that knife, they made the defendant out to be a, you know, wonderful family man.

Foreman. That's irrelevant.

Juror 3. Do we agree on the fight? Do we know why he had that knife out?

Juror 11. I'd like to say, the only person who was there, that saw that, like the cop, he's the only person that is trained for observation. No one else there is really trained for that type of thing. You know, they have—their eyes are just supposed to be trained for that type of thing. So the cop should know where the car is, where the people are, so forth, like that. You know, he's on his beat and it's at night and these people would come out after being inside in the light.

Juror 5. And he seems to be the most objective of the witnesses, too. He didn't have any interest.

Juror 11. Right, everyone else is a friend or something.

Juror 3. Right, a personal friend.

Foreman. Well, do you want to make this, I think it's an assumption, that the officer was objective? All these people were habitually around this area. The policeman may have his friends and enemies as well. Just because you have a uniform on doesn't make you not have friends that you help, and enemies you hurt.

(*Discussion of the judge's instructions on the law, the credibility of witnesses, and the implications of testimony continued until the end of the day.*)

Foreman. It isn't something that I feel happy with. And I think that we should all acknowledge that there's no certainty in our vote. I've also done things that I regret afterwards. But there's no way to come to a "no doubt" decision.

Juror 7. It's late, I would like to get out of here for tonight.

Foreman. Well, would you like us to take one more vote? If we're still locked, we'll start up again tomorrow, all right?

Juror 3. We'll take a vote, and if we're still locked, we're going to be back tomorrow.

(*The written ballot showed ten votes for second degree murder and two votes for manslaughter. Jurors 2 and 7 were voting in the minority.*)

Foreman. All right, gentlemen and ladies, I have a suggestion. It doesn't have to be done, but it might help us to move ahead from where we are today. And that is, I was going to send a question to the judge. And I worded it this way: "Please give exact statute definitions of second degree murder and manslaughter. Also the difference between the two." Because I have a feeling that while each of us has been trying to explain what he thought each of these were, we may not be correct. So, if it's the will of the jury, I'll ask this question before we go beyond it.

(*The next day, the jury spent half an hour listening to the trial judge repeat his instructions concerning second degree murder and manslaughter before resuming deliberation.*)

Foreman. I hope that the judge's answer was helpful to you. I know it was for me. Now, yesterday we were deciding between manslaughter and second degree murder. Do we want to reconsider any of the charges that were discarded yesterday? No. All right, the meeting is open.

Juror 7. I think that the judge said it, that as far as manslaughter, he says, you go after a sudden conflict and a reasonable provocation, and that sounds exactly like what happened. They're both angry at each other, the guy had fear of bodily harm, Mr. Johnson had fear of bodily harm, there was definitely a sudden conflict. He walked outside and there was a fight, that's definitely pretty sudden. And I think he was provoked, with the thought in his head that the guy had a razor there on him someplace. So he pulled out his equalizer and got there first. That's why I would say it was manslaughter, just as the judge said.

Juror 10. Did he use excessive force?

Juror 7. That would eliminate self-defense. So, whether or not he used excessive force, that's already been eliminated.

Juror 5. My interpretation was that excessive force was second degree.

Juror 7. No, malice is the key word.

Juror 6. My interpretation is that this was not their first encounter, they had encountered earlier in the day, and he went home and he got the knife, so that was malice. If these were strangers and were maybe meeting for the first time—

Juror 3. Yes, then I could say manslaughter. But no, not with the earlier confrontation, that's what's really bothering me.

Juror 10. I think that what knocks out the manslaughter is that he may not have intended to kill him, but he did plan to take steps that would enable him to kill him. So, in other words, he prepared the situation. I don't mean he planned to kill him; it may have been in the heat of passion, in the fight, you know, but he went further.

Juror 2. I did a great deal of thinking last night. In fact, I missed my first subway stop. But it seems to me that the defendant did not exhaust all possible means, and that the victim still had the razor blade in his pocket, and after he threw the first punch, the defendant could have punched him back or he could have gotten help. But he didn't, he just pulled out the knife. And I do believe that he plunged the knife into the victim. And he did it with considerable force. And there's no question that if you're going to stick someone with a knife that there's a great possibility that that person's going to be killed. So, I think, yesterday when I left here, I didn't think that I could ever change my mind from manslaughter; I felt very strongly. But I've done a great deal of thinking, and I think I've had a change of heart, but I'd like to continue our discussion.

Foreman. I think that we should continue, because there are others who might like to change their minds. I would like to throw this out: you do have to look at the continuity of events. Number one, there was the bad feeling. Number two, you do have to admit that the defendant had every reason to expect that the other man had a razor in his back pocket. Three, he deliberately took a knife, and it's reasonable to suppose he took it in case he was to have an encounter with this man. Then in the bar, when the victim came up to him, he made a decision to have it out with him, whatever the consequences. He chose to have a showdown whatever that resulted in. Therefore I feel, at least this is how my thinking goes, that there was real malice between these two. Mr. Johnson took that knife, not under passion, but before passion occurred. If he felt he needed it, that's a passionless decision.

Juror 2. Well, I thought of this example—Oh, I'm sorry.

Foreman. No, no, go ahead; I think I've said about everything I've got.

Juror 2. I thought of this example last night. Well, say the victim threw the first punch, and the defendant punched him back. Then the victim went up against the wall, cracked his head, and then died. That would be manslaughter because, you see, when the defendant punched him, he didn't intend, so it was sort of an accident, and that would be manslaughter. But the defendant had his knife in his hand, and the victim didn't even have a chance to pull out his blade.

Juror 3. Right, should we take a vote?

Foreman. Well, it's up to you. I don't want to cut anything off. Do you all feel like you want to take a vote?

Juror 10. How does everybody feel?

Juror 3. Well, we could take a vote and see what happens.

Foreman. All right, we're voting on second degree murder. (*Written ballot taken.*) Well, we have a verdict, and he is guilty on the count of second degree murder. Are we in full agreement? (*General assent.*) Well, thank you. That's it, second degree murder.

The following summary provides more details from this example jury deliberation. Following an introductory speech by the foreman, the jury discussed in turn the defendants' motives in returning to the bar and using the knife, the direction of knife thrust, witness credibility, reasonable care and use of force, the defendant's reasons for carrying the knife, and the personal characters of defendant and victim. The general format of discussion was first to agree on as many facts as possible and then, once these had been resolved, to relate the facts to potential verdict categories. Due in large part to the foreman's strong sense of organization and forceful leadership, most of the major facts were agreed upon relatively quickly. Therefore, as deliberation progressed, the issues discussed became both more abstract and more verdict-related.

Discussion was generally polite and well ordered, though not particularly deep. An effort was made to disregard inadmissible and hearsay evidence, and anecdotes were kept to a minimum. Although some jurors spoke more often and more aggressively than others, in particular Juror 10, participation rates were not badly skewed. Pressure on dissenters tended to be subtle, aside from a few remarks by Juror 10, and jurors were fairly supportive of each other. However, their persuasive styles were no doubt tempered to some extent by the fact that the lone dissenter for much of the deliberation was a soft-spoken young woman, Juror 2. Another dissenter, a man of about the same age, received slightly more pressure from the dominant faction, and on two occasions he quickly switched to the majority verdict without stating his reasons. He also seemed generally less certain of his opinions, and he was sitting at the foot of the table, where he was much more visible than Juror 2.

At the outset, there was consensus on several points at issue, namely that Johnson and Caldwell had bad feelings for each other, that they had "had words" earlier in the day, that Caldwell approached Johnson in the bar that evening and struck the first blow, that Caldwell was in possession of a razor during the fight, and that Johnson stabbed Caldwell. Shortly afterward the jurors also agreed that Caldwell did not have his razor out at the time of the stabbing, that Johnson did not have the knife in his pocket when Caldwell threatened him during the day, that Johnson made an effort to avoid the situation by looking for Caldwell's car before entering Gleason's Bar, and that Caldwell approached Johnson with the specific intention of settling their differences, probably in a violent way. However, it remained to be determined whether or not Johnson provoked Caldwell once they stepped outside. As outlined by the foreman, the jury's task was to determine how and why Johnson used his knife. Did Johnson intentionally provoke the scene outside the bar; that is, was there premeditation? Who struck the first blow; that is, was Johnson in fear of his life? Was there malice on the part of the defendant?

Based largely on the conclusion that Caldwell initiated the encounter, premeditation was ruled out early in deliberation. Once the foreman became aware that the majority was not in favor of first degree murder, he suggested that a hand vote be taken on first degree murder alone, so that the verdict possibilities could be "winnowed down." The result was zero to twelve against murder in the first degree.

Next the other three verdict categories were defined, and discussion dwelt on the means of escape, the use of a weapon in self-defense, the credibility of Johnson's friend Clemens concerning the razor, the argument over the girl in the afternoon, Johnson's intent to defend or attack, Johnson's reason for carrying the knife, and the credibility of beat policeman Harris. The focus of this discussion was on who could be believed and, when credible testimony was identified, what picture of events was most consistent with the valid testimony. After about thirty minutes of discussion the foreman suggested that a vote be taken on murder in the second degree. He had withdrawn an earlier suggestion to this effect when the rest of the jury felt that they needed more time. The results of this vote were six to six.

Since those jurors voting in favor of second degree murder seemed unlikely even to consider self-defense, the foreman suggested that the jury see whether or not they could eliminate not guilty as a possible verdict. The result was a one to eleven vote against self-defense. Since the vote was not unanimous, the foreman stated that self-defense could not be completely eliminated from discussion, but in practice it was. The one juror who accepted self-defense, Juror 2, soon switched to manslaughter.

Next followed a discussion of the difference between first and second degree murder. When the tide seemed to be shifting in favor of murder in the second degree, the foreman suggested taking another vote. This and all future votes were written, at the suggestion of Juror 11. The result was eight to four in favor of second degree murder.

When the foreman asked those jurors voting for manslaughter or self-defense to present their reasons, ostensibly to see if they could sway others to their belief, the issue of intent emerged as central to the disagreements. Juror 4 seemed to have confused premeditation and malice. When corrected on this point by Juror 1, he changed his story to emphasize Johnson's desire for self-protection. Juror 7 felt that Johnson took out his knife only to prove his manhood. His intent was therefore to wound, not to kill. Juror 10 disagreed and pressed Juror 7 to explain how one went about planning a nonlethal stab. A third vote on second degree murder resulted in a ten to two split, with Jurors 2 and 7 voting not guilty.

While the foreman counted the votes, Juror 7 engaged in a bit of irrelevant conversation about the neighborhood where Gleason's Bar is located. He became progressively more uncomfortable and defensive as deliberation continued. At this point Juror 2 was silent. Juror 7 attempted ineffectively to explain both the depth of the stab wound and Johnson's failure to use any of the options available to him for avoiding further conflict. After a pause of several minutes he abruptly changed his vote, without stating any reasons. Immediately afterward, the foreman suggested taking another vote to make the change official. This left Juror 2 as the sole dissenter.

Juror 2 stated that she could never change her vote if this were a real case. In response to Juror 10's questions on reasonable doubt, she denied having any doubt at all. Her position was that Caldwell came at Johnson and that the latter acted in self-defense, without intending to kill. She agreed, however, that the knife was thrust. At this point the rest of the jury, but most emphatically Juror 3, attempted to delineate the difference between premeditated murder and murder involving malice alone. The foreman argued that, given Caldwell's character, Johnson would have thought it safer to kill him than to wound him. Before adjourning for the day, the jury took another vote on second degree murder. Again the tally was eleven to one. The foreman suggested that they all ("Not just Juror 2") give the problem some thought and mentioned the movie *Twelve Angry Men*.

The second session of deliberation opened with the request to the trial judge by the foreman: "Please give exact statute definitions of murder in the second degree and self-defense, also distinguishing the differences between the two." After hearing the judge's definitions, Juror 7 concluded that a manslaughter verdict was correct. He based this on the "sudden conflict" and "reasonable provocation" clauses in the manslaughter definition. When Juror 10 asked him whether Johnson used excessive force, Juror 7 replied, "That's the difference between self-defense and manslaughter." Juror 5 was similarly confused. Juror 2, in contrast, decided to change her vote to second degree murder on the grounds that the defendant did not exhaust all possibilities to avoid combat, the victim still had the razor in his pocket and therefore Johnson may have used excessive force, and the knife was thrust with considerable force. The foreman suggested that the jurors continue deliberating to determine if someone had changed a verdict choice. The next few minutes were spent "proving" that Johnson made a passionless decision to carry the knife with him, knowing that he might use it if provoked. Juror 2 now commented that she had resolved that pulling the kinife was evidence of malice, therefore she was truly convinced of the second-degree murder verdict rather than merely bowing to peer pressure. Following this comment, a final vote was taken. The result was twelve to zero in favor of second degree murder. Juror 7 had undergone a silent reconversion. Juror 2 said that she was glad she had held out, even though the final verdict was not affected, because she needed time to think about her decision. Other jurors remarked that she had "done the right thing."

The characteristics of a unanimous jury were typified by the example jury. References to testimony and evidence occupied about 50 percent of the content of deliberation, while about 25 percent of the discussion cited material from the judge's instructions. In the course of discussion, approximately 84 percent of all case relevant content from the testimony and 80 percent of the central or key evidentiary issues were mentioned at least once. About 59 percent of the judge's instruction material was cited. There was almost no discussion of the standard of beyond reasonable doubt. Ten errors were made, seven of which were incorrect verdict definitions and three incorrect references to testimony. All three testimony reference errors were corrected, but only one of the verdict definition errors was corrected.

Discussion of the testimony and witness credibility decreased throughout deliberation, replaced by discussion of the judge's instructions, particularly the verdict categories. Almost half of the deliberation period followed the point at which the largest faction reached a size of eight members, more than half of the jury's discussion of the judge's instructions occurred after this point.

Discussion was dominated by the foreman, who contributed almost 25 percent of all comments for the entire jury. The foreman was also the highest ranked member of the jury in terms of income, occupation, and years of education, and he was next to the oldest juror. However, aside from the foreman, whose role on the jury may have been chiefly responsible for his high participation rate, no clear relationships showed up for other jurors between social status, education, or age and speaking rate. Women, however, participated at a somewhat lower rate than men.

The sample jury also had a number of exceptional characteristics. Much of the responsibility for the character of the deliberation went to the foreman, who was well-organized and subtly directive. He conceived of his role as a guide and interpreter for the rest of the jury, and frequently he abstracted and rephrased arguments, which he then presented to the jury for approval. Later in deliberation he also took an active role in persuading other jurors of his own views.

The pattern of voting was unusually systematic in that the jury, on the foreman's suggestion, voted on single verdict distinctions, such as first degree murder versus all other verdicts, self-defense versus all other verdicts, and second degree murder versus all other verdicts. Typically in balloting each juror votes for one of the four verdict alternatives. Although agenda setting is not uncommon, this foreman was exceptional in the relentlessness of his efforts to eliminate verdicts through these tactics. His background experiences may have produced these organizational skills, for his occupation as an insurance executive must have included extensive practice in leading consensus-seeking business decision groups. The generalization of these skills from boardroom to juryroom would seem to be a natural accomplishment.

The most dramatic differences between unanimous and majority rule juries occur because deliberation typically ends when the requisite quorum is reached under majority rule. Thus, under an eight-out-of-twelve rule, deliberation in the sample jury would have ended after 80 minutes of discussion; under a ten-out-of-twelve rule, after 105 minutes of deliberation. In both cases the jury verdict would have been second degree murder, but with several holdout jurors in the majority rule juries.

Under a majority rule there would have been somewhat more extreme domination of discussion by larger factions, accompanied by more discussion of credibility issues than of other legal issues. Furthermore, the largest factions would have gained members at a slightly faster rate in real time in majority rule juries as compared to unanimous juries.

Styles of Jury Deliberation

The mock jury deliberations exhibited two contrasting styles of deliberation. Many of the juries opened deliberation with a public ballot, and then jurors, aligned in opposing factions by verdict preferences, acted as advocates for their positions. A common directive remark in these discussions was an imperative to members of one faction to summarize the evidence "for" their verdict. This deliberation style, which we label "verdict-driven," has four distinctive features. Deliberation begins with a public ballot. Individual jurors advocate only one verdict position at a time. Evidence is cited in support of a specific verdict position. And the content of deliberation contains many statements of verdict preferences and frequent pollings.

The other style, which we call "evidence-driven," has four different characteristics. Public balloting occurs only late in deliberation, and in extreme cases, only one ballot is taken to validate that a quorum has been reached. Individual jurors are not closely associated with verdict preferences but may cite testimony or instructions with reference to several verdicts. The evidence is reviewed without reference to the verdict categories, in an effort to agree upon the single most credible story that summarizes the events at the time of the alleged crime. And the early parts of deliberation are focused on the story construction and the review of evidence; not until toward the conclusion of deliberation does discussion emphasize the task of verdict classification. Thus, verdict statements and polling occur at a high rate later in deliberation.

The evidence-driven jury follows the decision stages outlined in the Story

Table 8.1. Content of deliberation in different styles of jury.

Deliberation content	Verdict-driven juries ($n = 19$)	Mixed juries ($n = 26$)	Evidence-driven juries ($n = 24$)
Total testimony	609 (56%)	648 (52%)	902 (51%)
Different fact codes	35	36	37
Total legal issues	211 (26%)	223 (24%)	334 (26%)
Different legal issues	19	19	21
Total fact-issue pairings	113 (14%)	124 (14%)	192 (15%)
Different fact-issue pairings	48	56	75
Persuasiveness[a]			
Self	3.15	3.33	3.47
Other	2.81	3.00	3.05
Open-mindedness[a]			
Self	4.10	4.26	4.21
Other	3.63	3.79	3.74
Seriousness[b]	7.90	7.88	8.09
Pressure to change opinion[b]	2.81	2.87	2.91

a. On a scale of 0 to 5.
b. On a scale of 0 to 9.

Model for individual juror reasoning, namely story construction, verdict category establishment, and classification of the story into the best-fitting category. In contrast, the verdict-driven jury appears to start with classifications arrived at by individual jurors, then moves backward toward the evidence. One result of this procedure is that complete stories are rarely presented in discussion in such juries. Thus, the evaluation of evidence for its credibility and implications appears to be more disjointed and fragmentary in verdict-driven than in evidence-driven juries. A similar distinction between jury types, labeled "deliberating in factions" and "deliberating in unity," has been proposed by researchers studying mock juries deliberating on a civil case (Hawkins, 1960).

To determine the characteristics of verdict-driven and evidence-driven juries, the juries in the present mock jury study were divided into three groups according to the time at which the first formal ballot was taken, whether hand or written. The three types were verdict-driven, with a ballot taken during the first 10 minutes (19 juries); mixed, with a first ballot between 10 and 40 minutes (26 juries); and evidence-driven, with the first ballot only after more than 40 minutes of deliberation (24 juries). Analyses of the differences between these three groups of juries revealed five important distinctions between jury deliberation styles (Table 8.1).

First, verdict-driven juries are more common under majority decision rules. There were four such juries for the unanimous rule condition, nine for the ten-out-of-twelve, and six for the eight-out-of-twelve rules. Second, verdict-driven juries reach their verdicts more quickly than evidence-driven juries. The mean deliberation time for verdict-driven juries was 83 minutes, for mixed 98 minutes, and for evidence-driven 131 minutes. However, there is no relationship between style and final verdict.

Third, the differences in total deliberation time among juries were accompanied by clear differences in the content of deliberation as measured by volume. However, the differences in proportions of speaking events were only slight. The most dramatic difference between the content of deliberation occurred in fact-issue pairings, which were higher in volume for evidence-driven than for verdict-driven juries, implying that the adversarial or verdict-driven style is not accompanied by a thorough development of testimony-instruction connections.

Fourth, persuasiveness and openmindedness were rated lower in verdict-driven than in evidence-driven juries. This suggests that jurors leave a verdict-driven deliberation with a lower evaluation of both their own and other jurors' contributions to deliberation than jurors from evidence-driven deliberation.

Finally, evidence-driven deliberation may be more robust than verdict-driven deliberation, as shown by jurors' higher ratings of the seriousness of the deliberation and of the perceived pressure from other jurors. In summary, verdict-driven juries, in contrast to evidence-driven juries, are relatively hurried, cursory on testimony-law connections, less respectful of their own and others' persuasiveness and openmindedness, and less vigorous in discussion. Verdict-driven juries are also somewhat more likely to appear under majority rule conditions than under unanimous decision rules.

Hung Juries

Juries that deadlock and are unable to render a verdict are a rare but important event in legal trials. Hung juries appeared in 5 percent or less of the cases reported in a survey of criminal trial judges (Kalven & Zeisel, 1966). In the present mock jury study, 4 out of 69 juries were deadlocked and unable to reach consensus even after being instructed by the judge to attempt to resolve differences and move to a verdict.

Hung juries have a conceptual and symbolic significance that is far greater than their frequency of occurrence would indicate. This is because they signal a failure of the jury institution to produce its desired result of a clear and unequivocal decision. However, the label of "failure" is misleading, for the hung jury is "a valued assurance of integrity" and has been interpreted as a sign that antidefendant bias was not present (Kalven & Zeisel, 1966, p. 453; *Ballew v. Georgia,* 1978).

The few hung juries in the mock jury study were similar to verdict-rendering juries in most respects. Initial predeliberation ballots from juries that later deadlocked showed that in every case they subscribed to a broad range of verdict preferences. The full spectrum of verdict opinions from not guilty to first degree murder was represented in these initial ballots for every hung jury. However, the distributions of initial opinions were neither distinctly flatter nor more varied than in non-hanging juries. Thus, initial verdict preference distributions were not distinctive for hung juries.

Three patterns of disagreement on the final ballot were apparent in the four hung juries. In one instance, there was a large faction at the end of deliberation voting for a manslaughter verdict and three relatively small factions, comprised of one or two jurors each, voting for first degree murder, second degree murder, and not guilty. In two instances, all jurors had been drawn to one of two large factions at the end of deliberation, favoring either second degree murder or manslaughter. In the fourth case a lone holdout opposed eleven other jurors.

Two dynamics appeared to be associated with the different distributions of final verdicts. The jury in which a lone holdout opposed a majority of eleven was distinctive in that the holdout was strongly isolated from all deliberation processes. For example, he did not speak at all until after 120 minutes of deliberation had elapsed. At the conclusion of deliberation, after receiving the judge's instructions to deadlocked juries, the holdout did attempt to speak but quickly withdrew from further interaction with the other jurors. If the holdout had been forced to speak out to articulate his position and to defend it publicly against argumentation from other jurors, he would perhaps have changed his mind and joined the majority faction. As it was, after about ten minutes of silence on his part, the other jurors gave up and terminated deliberation. Another characteristic of this jury, which may or may not have been a causal determinant of the final state, was its disorganized, confused discussion process. The jury exhibited an unusual degree of difficulty in reaching group consensus on issues such as what should be the focus of discussion, whether the jury should ask for further instructions, and other organizational issues.

The dynamic pattern of deliberation behavior associated with the other three hung juries seemed to be a product of the verdict-driven deliberation style. In these three juries, combative factions formed early, and individuals were unwilling to leave factions even when reasonable argumentation appeared to have undermined all of the bases for the initial verdict preference. These deliberations were also characterized by the prominence of extremely unreasonable but highly vocal individual jurors. These jurors appeared to "freeze" opposition jurors into their positions. It seemed as though the entire faction that included one of these vocal, unreasonable individuals was treated as unreasonable by the opposing factions. Furthermore, the high volume of argumentation by these few unreasonable jurors slowed progress in deliberation by occupying discussion time that might have been used by more reasonable, persuasive jurors favoring the same verdict.

The type of hung jury containing a stubborn, uncommunicative, isolate might be eliminated by more effective instruction from the trial judge encouraging interaction between jurors. Although current jury instructions are full of admonitions to communicate and to keep an open mind, they might be even more forceful in suggesting that the jury take time to consider each individual member's point of view in thorough detail. Such a consideration, in which the resistant isolate juror is encouraged to speak his or her mind at length, might produce a reconsideration of the position by the holdout. It is not so clear how to remedy the self-serving, irrational quality that appears to produce the other type of hung juries. An instruction that emphasizes the evidence-driven deliberation style might discourage the early formation of definite factions with their associated combative or defensive discussion style.

Reversal Juries

Another phenomenon of jury decisions is the reversal of an initially large faction by a smaller faction. If reversal is defined as occurring when a verdict-favoring faction is in the majority (seven or more members) but the final jury verdict does not match the initial majority's preference, the study had thirteen reversal juries. Seven of these reversal juries had unanimous decision rules (three of these juries ended hung); four such juries had ten-out-of-twelve rules; and two had eight-out-of-twelve rules (one of these juries ended hung). If the criterion of reversal is relaxed to include any jury that fails to render a verdict favored by a majority of the required quorum size, namely a faction of five under the eight-out-of-twelve decision rule or a faction of six under the ten-out-of-twelve rule, more than one-third of the mock juries were reversal juries.

Two types of events occurred in the thirteen juries that might have precipitated the reversal in verdict preference. First, the reversal typically occurred when a large number of jurors changed their interpretations of portions of the judge's instructions concerning the crime categories. In one reversal jury, for example, the discussion focused on the judge's definition of "malice." The judge had indicated that the use of a deadly weapon without justification is sufficient for the inference of malice. However, many jurors assumed that the defendant's possession of a knife was sufficient to infer malice on his part. Two potential errors follow from this reasoning: that possession alone, without use, is sufficient to infer malice, and that justification for use does not need to be considered. In this jury a repetition of the trial judge's instructions concerning malice produced several immediate shifts in jurors' verdict preferences, and these shifts started the reversal process.

The second event in some juries that may have precipitated the reversal was a kind of bellwether effect, in which one juror shifted and several other jurors were drawn after him or her. These bellwether shifts were clearest and probably most compelling when the juror preceded the shift with a cogent, valid restatement of his or her position.

First Degree Murder Verdicts

A first degree murder verdict is harsh enough and extreme enough to be labeled unreasonable in the stimulus case used in the present research. The six juries that rendered such a verdict were clearly misguided. In every one of these juries, serious errors concerning the judge's instructions on verdict categories were made in discussion and persisted throughout deliberation. Typical erroneous remarks made by jurors during deliberation in these juries, which were not corrected by other jurors, were: "According to the law, it's premeditated the minute he started to stab the guy." "The definition of the law says that when he reached for the knife, it was automatically premeditated." "Not returning was a means of avoiding combat, and he returned, so he didn't use all means of avoiding combat. If he was cornered and he couldn't get out, I think it is murder two, but because he could have gotten out of it, it's murder one." "Murder two is without premeditation, and he has to have been provoked. If it's murder two, then, there has to be provocation, and a punch isn't provocation." "If you believe at the time he stabbed him he intended to inflict serious bodily harm, whether to kill him or not, then it's murder one." And, "First degree murder doesn't have to be premeditated murder." Although over all, juries rendering a first degree murder verdict did not make more total errors of all types, a systematic pattern of errors concerned with verdict definitions appeared in the deliberations of first-degree murder juries. Systematic errors were made in definitions of manslaughter, second degree murder, and self-defense as well in these deliberations.

Aside from this systematic pattern of errors, there was little to distinguish these deliberations from deliberations of juries reaching alternate verdicts. First-degree murder juries were not less likely to request further instructions on the law. Four out of the six received a repetition of the judge's instructions on the definitions of first and second degree murder. These juries also did not arrive at aberrant versions of the evidence from the trial. In general, their stories of what happened based on the testimony were comparable to the conclusions reached by juries rendering other verdicts. Again, the distinctive feature was their interpretation of the trial judge's instructions on the law. One way to avoid these errors in the deliberation process might be to increase the efforts to put the instructions on law into the jury's hands, as by providing a written transcript of the judge's instructions or an audiotape of the oral instructions.

Initial Verdict Preferences

The three-stage Story Model that accounts for the juror's initial decision on a verdict is also relevant to events during deliberation, after most jurors have formed initial verdict preferences. We hypothesize that the deliberation process is largely a recapitulation at the group discussion level of processes that occur in the mind of each individual juror before deliberation. Evidence is combined with personal world knowledge to produce a story of "what happened." The judge's instructions are interpreted to yield verdict categories and classification rules. The story is assigned to a verdict category according to classification rules yields a verdict category classification.

The analogy between individual decision processes and group decision processes is reflected in the distinction between evidence-driven and verdict-driven juries. The story construction stage of the decision is the critical point at which individual jurors' predeliberation verdicts diverge. Variation across jurors in story structure is related to individual verdict choice, while variation at the verdict establishment and story classification stages is not. However, in deliberation, the verdict establishment and story classification stages appear to be the locus of causality for jurors' changes of opinion. For example, once jurors' constructions of the evidence, their stories of what happened, were formed and stabilized, these stories were relatively resistant to persuasive argumentation from other jurors. Jurors were much more likely to admit misunderstanding the judge's substantive instructions on the law or procedural instructions on the standard of proof, reasonable inference, and presumption of innocence. Thus, virtually every dramatic shift in juror verdict preferences, such as the reversal of a majority faction by a smaller faction, occurred because of changes in opinion about the law or jury procedures.

A serious deficiency in individual and group decision making in jury trials concerns the representation and application of the verdict categories given to jurors during the judge's instructions. The major problems involved in comprehending, remembering, and applying the categories doubtless derive from the complexity of the instructions and from the short space of time in which they are presented. Other problems arise from preconceptions and confusions concerning the unfamiliar and even arcane terminology of the law. For example, jurors often persisted in their belief that manslaughter was the only appropriate verdict when the death was accidental, as from a fall, or when the weapon used was not obviously deadly, such as a car or fists. Other inappropriate generalizations from other television or film trials were made, such as that manslaughter only applies to deaths arising in traffic accidents. Not even reinstruction on the law from the judge was sufficient to eradicate all of these errors.

Given the difficulty of comprehending and applying the instructions, many of the successful persuasive efforts to change verdicts during jury deliberation appeared to occur when the persuader focused on legal rather than evidentiary issues. Jurors seemed much more willing to admit that they were confused or even incorrect concerning legal issues than to admit that they misunderstood the evidence, misjudged the credibility of a witness, or put together their stories in an implausible fashion. Arguments concerning the reasonable doubt standard of proof were also persuasive. However, consideration of the standard of proof was surprisingly rare during deliberation, and typically the standard was applied erratically to some of the crime elements but not consistently to all elements. Nonetheless, on a few occasions jurors clearly shifted their opinions concerning the proper verdict by acknowledging that the standard of beyond a reasonable doubt made a harsh verdict inappropriate.

The clarity or detail in a juror's mental conception of an event or episode described in testimony was a major determinant of the perceived validity and significance of the event. A graphic illustration of this occurred in another study of mock juries deliberating on a robbery case (Hastie, 1982). The central issue in that case was the accuracy of an eyewitness identification. Many details of the crime event appeared to be probatively irrelevant and were therefore mentioned only briefly by the trial attorneys or were missing from the trial testimony. Nonetheless, jurors spent considerable energy trying to complete the picture of the crime with marginally relevant details, such as the model of the getaway car or the amount of money stolen. Failure to supply such details in testimony resulted in the devaluation of relevant evidence.

In the present study, there was almost no discussion of the attorneys' behavior or their tactics. The attorneys were well-matched, extremely competent, and instructed to try the case on its merits, so that there were few histrionics or other efforts to induce jurors to make misleading inferences, and few exaggerations in the opening and closing statements. But merely because jurors did not discuss the attorneys' performances does not mean that the attorneys' behavior did not affect their initial decisions.

Incentives Affecting Verdict Preferences

Various motives underlie jurors' behavior when choosing or changing verdict preferences during deliberation. Traditional psychological analyses of the bases of social influence in consensus-seeking groups provide a starting point for a typology of these motives (Deutsch & Gerard, 1955; Myers, 1982; McGuire, 1969). The first hypothesized basis for social influence, normative influence, exists because of the individual's need for self-esteem and a positive self-image. If the individual complies with a persuasive message, it is because he or she is motivated to conform to normative standards that prescribe how one ought to behave. The second basis for social influence, informational influence, occurs to the extent that rational information integration processes prescribe changes in belief. If compliance occurs, it is because novel, valid information changes an individual's beliefs about the true state of the world. A third basis, hedonic influence, occurs when an individual seeks reward or avoids punishment from others. If compliance occurs, it is because the individual is motivated by simple concerns for comfort or security.

Observations of the jury deliberation process suggest several ways in which this tripartite typology can be refined and extended. Patterns of discussion preceding and following jurors' opinion shifts and jurors' postdeliberation comments suggest several types of motives or incentives that lie outside of the traditional framework. Some of these distinctions may be specific to the jury task, such as behavior motivated to prevent the application of an unjust law, but most appear to be general to behavior in virtually any small consensus-seeking group.

The paramount goal of the juror, as expressed in instructions from the Court and in the juror's handbook, is to find the truth. More specifically, jurors attempt to avoid two types of errors: conviction of the innocent and acquittal of the guilty. These two types of errors may be weighted differently. For example, the British jurist William Blackstone suggested that ten errors of the second type, acquittal of the guilty, could be allowed for every one error of the first type, conviction of the innocent (Blackstone, 1962). Quantitative estimates of these factors cannot be generated on the basis of the present mock jury study, but common sense and remarks from the mock jurors support the notion that convicting the innocent is a more serious error than acquitting the guilty.

The second incentive that is frequently cited by jurors when discussing their performance is to do "a good job." Here the emphasis is not on the product of the decision, namely the accuracy of the verdict, but on the quality of the procedures that are used to achieve that product. Thus, many jurors argue that their job is to be thorough, to give all parties a fair hearing, and to follow the court's instructions to the letter. These goals do not prescribe specific verdict choices in particular cases, but they appear to be a common motivation for prolonging deliberation or a consideration that prevents jurors from shifting verdict preferences.

The third motivation is only occasionally cited by jurors in defense of their verdicts. It is the incentive to prevent a disagreeable law from being applied. That is, in certain cases jurors feel that a law should not be on the books, and during deliberation they urge other jurors to reject the Court's instructions and to refuse to apply the law either by acquitting the defendant or by refusing to render a verdict.

Fourth class of social motivations derives from an individual juror's desire to promote or hinder the wishes of other individuals or social groups. For example, many jurors appear to desire to follow the judge's will, to comply to the requests of an attractive attorney, or to respond to other more generally defined audiences, such as their circle of acquaintances or family outside of the courtroom or to the will of the general citizenry. In another form of this motivation, jurors seek to reward or punish other individuals within the jury as a group. Its most common manifestation occurs when a juror seeks the approval of other jurors and chooses a verdict on that basis. The reverse of this motivation occurs occasionally when the juror acts to punish other jurors by advocating an opposition verdict.

The last three mentioned incentives—to do a good job, prevent the application of an unjust law, and promote the wishes of an attractive reference person—can all be viewed as criterionological (Collingwood, 1940). The juror selects a verdict preference to match an internalized standard of proper conduct. Thus, these incentives fit the traditional normative influence category.

Less socially desirable motives also underlie juror behavior. In some cases jurors seem to be motivated to attack or protect members of certain social groups. For example, a juror might be biased against a defendant because of race or other social characteristics. A more general form of this motive appears when jurors, regardless of the evidence, attempt to protect or attack any defendant or the perceived class of criminals in general. This motivation is not unidirectional, for some jurors may be motivated to attack members of certain classes and other jurors may be motivated to protect members of these classes irrespective of the probative implications of the relevant evidence.

A sixth motivation is to escape deliberation. Deliberation is a rough and occasionally punishing experience, and jurors have commitments to other activities outside the jury room. These two factors, desire to escape punishment and incentive to seek rewards outside the context of the courthouse, doubtless explain some jurors' accession to other jurors' arguments.

Finally, two competitive motivations affect certain jurors' selection and adherence to verdict preferences. These are motives to win the deliberation or to dominate other jurors by exercising social power. Whether these motivations are consistently associated with individuals across situations inside and outside the jury room, or whether they derive from immediate situational factors, is not known.

This review of juror motivations during deliberation yields a more varied and more complete list of incentives than previous psychological or legal studies. The psychological analysis of social influence included three general bases for opinion change: normative, informational, and hedonic. However, this summary of motivations during deliberation distinguishes among seven classes of incentives: seek truth, follow instructions, prevent application of unjust law, conform to reference person or group norms, protect or injure a defendant, escape deliberation, and win deliberation. Legal studies of performance, based on trial judges' retrospective views of jury behavior, are in essential agreement with this analysis but yield shorter lists of motivations (Kalven & Zeisel, 1966). One major study focused on judge-jury disagreements and concluded that evidence factors, disparity of counsel, jury sentiments about the individual defendant, and jury sentiments about the law were primary bases for jury decisions.

In summary, behavior in unanimous rule juries contrasts with typical behavior in majority rule juries in six respects: deliberation time (majority rule juries take less time to render verdicts), small faction participation (members of small factions are less likely to speak under majority rules), faction growth rates (large factions attract members more rapidly under majority rules), holdouts (jurors are more apt to be holdouts at the end of deliberation under majority rules), time of voting (majority rule juries tend to vote sooner), and deliberation style (majority rule juries are slightly likelier to adopt a verdict-driven deliberation style in contrast to the evidence-driven style).

Juries systematically differ in general orientation to their decision task or in deliberation style. Verdict-driven juries vote early and organize discussion in an adversarial manner around verdict-favoring factions, as opposed to evidence-driven juries which defer voting and start with a relatively united discussion of evidence, turning to verdict categories later in deliberation.

Several of the phenomena identified in observations of deliberation are of considerable significance to legal policy makers; however, at present they lie outside the scope of theoretical explanation. Although only four juries were deadlocked and unable to render verdicts, three distinct patterns of disagreement among verdict-favoring factions existed at the end of deliberation: one medium-sized faction at odds with several small factions; two medium-sized factions; and one large faction versus a lone holdout. Both the reversal of initial large factions and the appearance of first-degree murder verdicts, deemed improperly harsh, appeared to hinge on jurors' comprehension of the judge's instructions on the law. Reversals were usually precipitated by changes in the jury's beliefs about the proper interpretation of the verdicts. First-degree murder verdicts were frequently accompanied by systematic, uncorrected errors on the law. Finally, an elaboration of traditional social psychological analyses of the bases of social influence was suggested to accommodate the variety of motivations or incentives that appear to underlie jurors' changes of opinion during deliberation.

9

A Model of
Jury Behavior

The most substantial theoretical contribution of the present research is a model of the jury decision process, named JUS, after the Latin word for justice. Psychological theories are being applied to practical purposes with increasing frequency and utility as the empirical foundations and conceptual sophistication of knowledge grow (Anderson, 1980; Broadbent, 1973; Estes, 1970; Hogarth, 1980). Occasionally psychological theory is applied to resolve legal questions, as when an expert on perception presents testimony at a trial about what, in principle, could have been observed under certain conditions; however, these applications are rare (Ellsworth & Getman, 1983; Loftus, 1979). More commonly, legal authorities, if they are willing to consider social science sources, accept only empirical results or tests with a minimum of theory and then draw their own implications.

Social science data and social science theories will inevitably play a larger and larger role in legal decision making. This will occur both because legal authorities will become more receptive and because scientific contributions will become more relevant and substantial. Three uses of theories of juror and jury behavior are generalization, projection, and conceptualization.

Psychological theories are important tools when deciding whether or not to generalize a conclusion from one setting to another. An evaluation of conclusion generalizability requires four steps. First, specify the conclusion and determine its internal validity in Setting One. Second, specify the characteristics of Setting Two and the relationships between Setting One

By Pennington and Hastie

175

("source") and Setting Two ("target"). Third, provisionally assume that the conclusion established in Setting One will generalize to Setting Two and attempt to reject this assertion. And fourth, qualify the assertion of generalizability with reference to both its apparent magnitude and repeatability in Setting One and the strength of plausible arguments that can be generated against generalization. Well-specified theories, in addition to informed intuitions, should play a role in deciding what characteristics of the two settings are relevant in defining the relationships between them and in generating and evaluating plausible objections to generalization.

The problem of projecting behavior under conditions that have not been closely studied and may only be imagined by policy makers is another aspect of the puzzle of induction that involves scientific theory. One solution to this problem is to design a general model of the relevant phenomena and then to study the behavior of the model under the conditions, whether existent or imaginary, about which conclusions must be reached.

The Supreme Court's consideration of variations in jury size and decision rule provides examples of this type of projection. The Court had to anticipate the behavior of juries under conditions that did not yet exist, such as seven-out-of-twelve majority rule juries or five-out-of-five unanimous rule juries, as well as to characterize the behavior of juries that did exist, which is also a difficult induction problem given the paucity of empirical research on the topic. Blackmun's opinion in *Ballew v. Georgia* (1978) provides an example of systematic consideration of projection from empirical results to legal practice.

In cases of expert testimony, usually in evidentiary hearings, scientists have introduced theoretical models of jury behavior and then used them to project to unstudied circumstances. Testimony in a hearing preceding the California Supreme Court's decision in *Hovey v. Superior Court of Alameda County* (1980) used a simple model of juror impanelment and decision processes to project from a survey study of death qualified jurors to populations of jurors in actual courtrooms. Similarly in a federal court hearing on *Grigsby v. Mabry* (1980) the JUS model was used to make projections concerning the effects of death qualification procedures on jury performance. An earlier version of the JUS model was used to project the effects of attorney jury selection strategies on jury composition and verdicts (Penrod et al., 1979).

One sign of progress in a scientific discipline is the replacement of common sense theories, also known as "fireside inductions," with scientific theories. In a few areas of behavioral sciences the sophistication of scientific theory now clearly surpasses common sense and intuitive analyses (Meehl, 1971). Several of these areas are relevant to jury decision making. Scientific theories cannot totally replace legal analysis, because empirical truth is only one component of the answer to legal policy questions. However, scientific theories and data can make important contributions to the legal analysis by organizing and sharpening legal questions and principles (Kalven, 1968). For example, modern theories of perception and memory provide useful, occasionally counterintuitive concepts for a legal analysis of eyewitness testimony (Woocher, 1977). And current judicial controversies over the competency of jurors to render acceptable decisions in complex cases could be sharpened and advanced by the application of theoretical principles from cognitive psychology (Sperlich, 1982).

The Computer Program

The JUS theory of jury decision making has been implemented in the form of a computer program model that simulates or mimics the major events which occurred in the deliberations in the mock jury study. This model is based on an earlier model, DICE, which was also represented in the form of a computer program (Penrod & Hastie, 1979, 1980). Although computer simulation models are becoming a dominant mode of theorizing in some areas of psychology, they are still quite novel in most social sciences (Newell & Simon, 1972; Anderson & Bower, 1973; Schank & Abelson, 1977; Kosslyn, 1980).

While the formal representation or implementation of JUS is a computer program written in the FORTRAN language, the theory behind JUS is a set of principles about how jurors, juries, and trials behave. Those principles are summarized verbally in this chapter, with an occasional mathematical equation. The computer as a machine, even as an abstract machine, is not considered analogous to the juror, the jury, or the trial court. The medium of a computer programing language is used as the representational device for theoretical formulations just as a set of algebraic equations or a series of English sentences might be used for the same purpose. The computer language offers a number of advantages over mathematical or natural language media.

First, computing languages are precise. The theorist is forced to specify in complete, explicit terms all aspects of any assumptions about processes and structures. Computing languages are also an explicit public medium for communication with other theoreticians. The ambiguities of natural language expressions are virtually eliminated in artificial computer languages.

Computer program models have unsurpassed deductive and computational power. Once the basic theoretical principles are implemented in a programing language, the theoretician is able to derive an almost limitless number of implications. In addition, when a phenomenon as complex as jury decision making is under study, an enormous amount of calculation is involved in summarizing all of the relevant characteristics of the model's performance and comparing them to empirical results. The computer is an ideal bookkeeper to produce, store, and compare both theoretical predictions and empirical results.

Moreover, several characteristics of the jury decision-making phenomenon require a theoretical medium with the properties of a computer simulation. First, the rich dynamic nature of the trial environment requires a theory that provides for elaborate representations of stimulus inputs and outputs. Second, the jury task occurs across a relatively long interval and typically involves an irregular sequence of qualitatively different substages. Third, the complexity of the components comprising the jury task and the variety of the principles underlying jury behavior require theory that is a system comprised of many principles or subtheories. For example, we distinguish between three types of psychological principles in JUS: assumptions about individual differences among jurors, assumptions about agendas and the jurors' representations of the decision alternatives, and assumptions about persuasive processes in deliberation. Other types of psychological and nonpsychological principles used in the model specify such matters as when voting will occur, or when a jury will deadlock. The model integrates many component subtheories and derives the implications of interactions among the components to predict the observable behavior of a jury and its members. In short, the computer program medium can represent complex and dynamic environments, model a sequence of qualitatively different substages, and deduce the implications of interactions among many distinct subprocesses in jointly causing observable behavior.

Finally, the computer program medium is flexible and general. This property is particularly important when the model is applied to behavior in several concrete settings, such as deriving theoretical predictions of the behavior of juries in California, Arkansas, and North Carolina. In each case, with information about the composition of the jury pool, jury selection procedures, jury size, and jury decision rule, it is possible to implement alternate versions of the basic model, tailored to local conditions, in order to predict jury performance in that setting, to evaluate the generality of the model, or to compare jurisdictions.

Two cautions are in order. First, the computer in this application is not treated as a metaphorical analogue to the jurors or juries. Rather, the computer is a tool for creating, communicating, and testing theories of juror and jury behavior. For example, if the computer program happens to represent information about jurors in a matrix of numbers or uses an algebraic equation to determine whether or not a theoretical juror will change verdict preferences, this does not imply that these matrices or equations, or even close analogues, exist inside the jurors and juries under study.

Second, we are not suggesting that either the jury or any other legal decision maker should be replaced by a computer program. Just as it would be nonsensical to talk of replacing a natural phenomenon, such as the weather, with a theoretical model of the phenomenon, so it would be foolish to speak of replacing the jury with the jury model. The standard by which to judge the jury model is its ability to predict patterns of jury behavior.

The analogy to a meteorological model that predicts weather conditions is also apt in that such a model would be relatively abstract compared to the phenomenon to which it applies. Just as a meteorological model does not actually "rain," the JUS model does not "hear cases" or "discuss" specific items of evidence. More generally, JUS does not include many of the mental subprocesses that occur when a juror forms a predeliberation verdict preference and generates arguments or reacts to communications from others during deliberation. Rather, the model is a general theory of the more macroscopic processes that are caused by or comprised of these subprocesses. Thus, the model does not "study" the evidence or the instructions for a trial. Rather, it simulates the distributions of verdict preferences that would result from such subprocesses.

The JUS model of jury decision making is evaluated against two major goals. First, the model should provide a realistic and psychologically plausible representation of the deliberation process. Second, the performance of the model, as measured by its outputs, should closely resemble the outputs produced by juries studied by jury researchers over a broad range of conditions. Providing a realistic and psychologically plausible model requires that all procedures and parameters have plausible interpretations. For example, JUS has two procedures called IMPANEL and BALLOT. The first procedure mimics the real life procedure of selecting the jurors, and the second mimics the voting procedure during jury deliberation. It would be unrealistic and implausible to have a procedure called REORGANIZE in which jurors who disagreed with the majority faction would be thrown off the jury and replaced with alternate jurors.

Similarly, the model's parameters should be interpretable within the context of particular juries and juror behavior. The values of the parameters differ according to circumstance. For example, one parameter is jury size, which is assigned a value each time the program is run. Another parameter corresponds to the average length of deliberation time for a particular case. As part of being realistic, hung juries should result when juries fail to reach the requisite majority for any single verdict, and the average deliberation time for hung juries should be substantially longer than the average deliberation time for verdict-reaching juries (Padawer-Singer & Barton, 1975).

Jurors and juries in a realistic model should display other general characteristics (Kalven & Zeisel, 1966; Saks, 1977). The verdict outcome is not random but is related to the distribution of the jurors' initial verdict preferences. The initial majority persuasion characterizes decision making in many cases. In a few cases, initial majorities do not prevail and are reversed or persuaded by the minority, or the jury fails to reach a verdict and "hangs." Individual jurors do not alternate repeatedly from one verdict preference to another but display relatively low frequencies of preference changing—not more than one or two, rarely three changes of preference during deliberation. Jurors are also unlikely to change the direction of movement once change has been made, such as voting manslaughter, then second degree murder, then acquittal. Finally, jurors differ in the extent to which they are susceptible to persuasion. For example, females change preference at higher rates than males, and jurors in hung juries change preference at lower rates than jurors in verdict-reaching juries (Davis et al., 1977; Padawer-Singer & Barton, 1975; McGuire, 1969).

If the deliberation process is accurately and realistically represented in the JUS model, its output will resemble the empirical data from the mock jury study. A model that produces only an aggregate distribution of verdicts would be unsatisfactory, for many plausible models could mimic such a distribution (Davis, 1973). The JUS model should fit empirical data on several characteristics of jury behavior across variations in jury size, decision rule, and verdict alternatives. Each run of the program is like an experiment whose outcome can be compared to actual behavior. When these outputs are compared to human behavior, discrepancies between the simulation performance and human performance provide information that is used both to identify gaps in our understanding of the phenomenon and to suggest modifications of the theory.

Components of the Model

The computer simulation model JUS is a conceptually simple collection of assumptions about the behavior of juries based on previous theoretical models, observations of ongoing deliberations in the mock jury study, and theories and intuitions about social behavior. The jurors' task is to study the evidence presented at trial in order to reach a consensus on the nature of the events described by the witnesses and exhibits. This consensus is expressed in the jury's verdict with reference to classification schemes outlined in legal statutes, which are categorical in criminal cases such as *Commonwealth v. Johnson,* namely first degree murder (M1), second degree murder (M2), manslaughter (MS), not guilty (NG), and hung (H). The process through which consensus is reached includes robust discussion in which all voices in the group are nominally accorded equal weight. Procedural rules also prescribe that the group's decision be registered by polling the group and that a final verdict classification be stated only when a requisite quorum is attained, such as a two-thirds majority or unanimous.

The operations performed in JUS can be depicted in flowchart form (Fig. 9.1). The first step in an application is to set the free parameter values.

A MODEL OF JURY BEHAVIOR

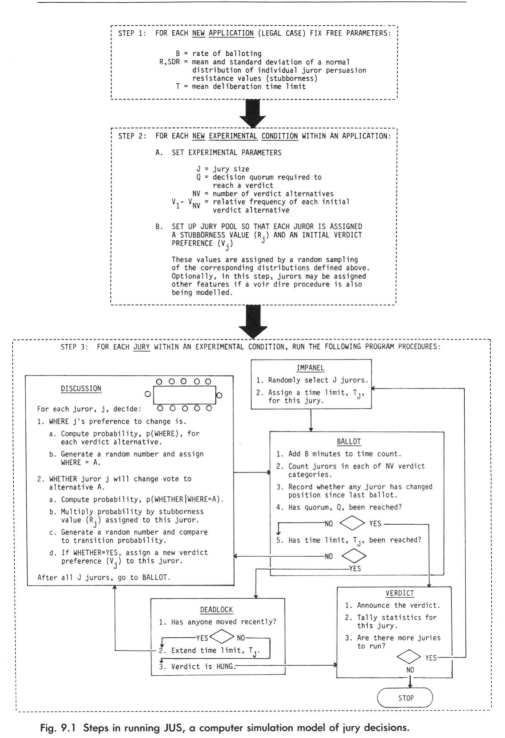

Fig. 9.1 Steps in running JUS, a computer simulation model of jury decisions.

While many aspects of the model remain constant across applications, a limited number of free parameters represent features of the model that are expected to depend on the particular application or environment being mimicked.

Allowing a few features of a model to vary across applications is a standard procedure in model fitting and testing. For example, in the formula, based on Galileo's experiments, used to calculate the velocity of a falling object,

$$\text{final velocity} = \text{initial velocity} + (32 \text{ ft/sec}^2 \times \text{time})$$

the gravitational constant, 32 ft/sec^2, is a free parameter, where the velocities are measured in ft/sec units and time is measured in seconds. If Galileo had conducted his experiments on another planet or at a different distance from the center of the earth, such as at the North Pole rather than Pisa, Italy, he would have used preliminary trials in the new environment to estimate a new value for the gravitational constant. The remaining trials would then have used the new constant to predict final velocities for different initial velocities and times. In the case of Galileo's formula for acceleration, its general principle is a scientific assertion. Similarly, in the case of the simulation model JUS, its general form is the theoretical assertion to be tested, assuming that free parameter values vary from application to application.

While the values of the free parameters may vary, the choice and interpretation of these parameters constitute theoretical assertions about jury and juror behavior. JUS is controlled by four free parameters: the rate of balloting (B), the mean and standard deviation of an individual juror's resistance to persuasion (R and SDR), and the mean of the time limit distribution (T). These four parameters must be estimated through preliminary simulation runs for each new application of the model. In other words, each of these parameters is like the gravitational constant in Galileo's formula, and each new legal case (new environment) is like a different planet.

The jury situation is somewhat more complicated than Galileo's since it has four free parameters instead of one. To find a set of four values that together produce the best fit to the empirical data requires a Monte Carlo estimation procedure. Three different values are assigned to each of the four parameters, the three values spanning a range of those that are likely to fit. In this application, these values were chosen to range around values that had been used in previous model applications. All combinations of the three possible values for the four parameters form a 3 X 3 X 3 X 3 factorial design, with eighty-one unique sets of values for the four parameters. Several hundred simulation runs were conducted for each of the eighty-one parameter-setting combinations evaluated. At the conclusion of these test runs, the performance of the model under each set of four parameter values was summarized.

Two sets of empirical data are needed from the new environment: the first set to fix the free parameters and the second to compare with the corresponding model output based on the chosen parameter values. In an ideal study, if there were enough data, the empirical data set used to fix the free parameters and the empirical data set used to test the model fit would be independent samples. In the mock jury study there is not enough data to do this. Therefore a limited portion of the data is used to determine the best-fitting parameter values. These data consist of final verdict distribution, deliberation time distribution, and the number of opinion changes for a single decision rule condition (12/12). The set of four free parameter values yielding the best fit to these data represent the fixed free parameter values for this application. If the general model formulation is valid, then the model output using this chosen set of parameters will pass three tests: the values for the parameters will be interpretable; the model simulation data will match empirical jury deliberation data on dimensions other than the ones used to select parameter values; and the model simulations using these parameter values will match data in the two decision rule conditions that were not used to choose the parameter values.

The first free parameter is rate of balloting (B). JUS needs to be instructed how frequently to poll the jurors for their verdict preferences. The frequency of vote taking depends in part on the case's difficulty, such as the number of witnesses and the complexity of the legal issues to be addressed by the jury. For this reason, the rate-of-balloting parameter indirectly reflects case difficulty. For application to the unanimous decision rule, the best-fitting value for the rate of balloting is 10, indicating that ballots are taken every ten minutes throughout deliberation. This frequency of balloting is about twice the empirically observed frequency for unanimous decision condition juries, which is once every 23 minutes. This discrepancy is due to a broader function currently assigned to voting in the model than is typical in empirical juries. The B value is equivalent to the mean deliberation time for empirical juries, divided by the average number of ballots needed to reach a verdict for simulated juries. Thus, this parameter directly ties the model operation to the empirical environment being simulated. However, the average number of ballots that the simulated jury deliberations require to reach a verdict is mutually dependent on the next model parameter, which controls how readily individual jurors will change their votes.

The second and third free parameters are the specified mean (R) and standard deviation (SDR) of the individual resistance distribution. Some jurors are more susceptible to group persuasion than are other jurors (Kerr et al., 1976). In JUS, all jurors are assigned individual persuasion resistance scores that reflect these individual differences. The scores are assigned by randomly selecting values from a normal distribution of values with a specified mean (R) and standard deviation (SDR). The best-fitting parameter values are 1.10 for mean persuasion resistance and .055 for the standard deviation. The resistance values can be interpreted as a likelihood ratio between the probability that a juror will not change verdict preferences on a given ballot owing to the individual's resistance and the probability that the juror will change. The low value of this ratio (1.10) indicates that on the average a juror is only slightly more likely ($p = .524$) to retain a verdict choice owing to internal resistance alone than to change verdict positions ($p = .476$). Jurors assigned extreme values from this distribution show up, on one extreme, as holdouts in hung and nonunanimous juries and, on the other extreme, as frequent opinion changers most susceptible to group pressure.

The fourth free parameter is the mean of the time limit distribution (T). Not all juries reach a verdict; often members of the jury decide that they can no longer make progress toward a verdict because individual jurors are entrenched in their preferred verdict positions. To simulate hung juries, JUS sets a limit on the time at which the jury begins to consider whether or not to continue deliberation. The time limit for any particular jury is assigned by randomly sampling a normal distribution of times with a specified mean (T) and standard deviation. The assigned value corresponds to the shortest elapsed time at which the jury may be declared hung. As estimated by the Monte Carlo procedure, the time limit mean is 240 minutes and the standard deviation is 24 minutes. The standard deviation for the time limit distribution is not considered a separate free parameter since it is fixed in the model as $.1 \times T$ independent of the application.

Four additional parameters in the model can be assigned values directly and do not depend on simulation trials to determine the best-fitting values. These are called experimental parameters, since different values for them refer to different experimental conditions simulated within an application. These parameters are reset for each decision rule condition in the current application.

The first experimental parameter is jury size (J). Although JUS can operate with any jury size, the simulations concentrate on six- and twelve-person juries. The jury size parameter is set to twelve for evaluation of model performance and to six to illustrate the predictive function of the model.

The second experimental parameter is the quorum required to render a verdict or the decision rule (Q). JUS can operate with any decision rule ranging from majority to unanimity. For example, in modeling the results from another study, the simulations used the two decision rules employed in it, unanimity and five-sixths majority (Padawar-Singer & Barton, 1975). In the application to the mock jury study, three decision rules are used: unanimity ($Q = 12$), five-sixths majority ($Q = 10$), and two-thirds majority ($Q = 8$). These simulations use the quorum values of eight, ten, and twelve to mimic the three decision rule conditions. Again, model simulation predictions are made for the corresponding decision quorums for six-person juries (4/6, 5/6, 6/6).

The third experimental parameter is the number of verdict alternatives (NV). JUS can simulate decisions between two or more decision alternatives. Previous applications of this model and of its predecessor DICE have been limited to the two-verdict case, acquit or convict (Penrod & Hastie, 1980). For application to the mock jury study this parameter is set to five, since a decision is required between four verdict alternatives: acquittal, manslaughter, second degree murder, and first degree murder, with a fifth category reserved for undecided jurors and hung juries. Four of these verdict alternatives, excluding undecided, are treated as discrete, ordered categories. Undecided is treated as nonordered with respect to the other four categories. In addition to the number of verdict alternatives, ordering relations, if any, may be specified.

The fourth experimental parameter is the initial verdict preference distribution (V1-V5). In this model, at the conclusion of a trial all jurors who have heard the evidence, or who might have heard it, are assumed to have formed an initial opinion of the case and to be inclined to vote for one of the verdict alternatives. In cases where a juror was not willing to indicate an initial verdict preference or has not formed one, the juror is considered to prefer the undecided alternative. The distribution depends on both the case itself, such as the strength of the evidence, and the characteristics of the jurors sampled, such as rural or urban. There are several models available suggesting that various influences converge to determine a juror's predeliberation verdict preference (Pennington & Hastie, 1981a). However, JUS requires only that a value be specified for each verdict alternative, including undecided, to represent the probability that a randomly selected juror will vote for that initial verdict category. The five probabilities are computed from the initial verdict votes of the 828 jurors who watched the murder trial in the study ($V1 = p[M1] = .21$, $V2 = p[M2] = .24$, $V3 = p[MS] = .31$, $V4 = p[NG] = .10$, $V5 = p[UN] = .14$). This initial verdict distribution represents the average over the three decision conditions in the study. In the empirical sample, however, different initial distributions were obtained for the three decision rule conditions. Therefore, the model simulation was run two times: first using different initial distributions that match the empirical distribution for each decision condition, and second using the same average initial distribution for each decision condition. The first set of runs shows how the model outputs match the empirical outputs, and the second set shows which decision rule effects are predicted by the model while holding initial verdict distribution constant.

The next step in an application of JUS is to assign specific values to jurors and to the jury for those parameters that are specified as distributions. JUS includes a POOL of simulated jurors with individual characteristics occurring in the same frequencies as in the Massachusetts Superior Court jury pools in the counties in which the research was conducted. Two individual juror parameters are significant in the model's decision processes: verdict preference parameters ($V1-V5$) and resistance to persuasion (R and SDR). The model is given the probability that a randomly selected juror will vote for a given verdict at the start of deliberation. JUS assigns initial verdict preferences to jurors in the POOL by sampling randomly from the multinomial distribution of initial individual verdict preferences $V1-V5$. The individual resistance to persuasion is assigned independently of the juror's vote preference by random sampling from a normal distribution of values with a mean and standard deviation as specified by model parameters (R, SDR).

Next JUS executes a subroutine procedure called IMPANEL, which provides for various impanelment and voir dire procedures. For example, attorney voir dire strategies are evaluated by instructing IMPANEL to seat or challenge certain types of jurors (Penrod et al., 1979). In the mock jury study the IMPANEL subroutine does nothing more than select twelve jurors (J) at random from the POOL, because the pretrial voir dire procedures did not exert any sharp selection pressures and the mock-juror characteristics matched those in the overall jury pool. This procedure also sets a specific time limit for the impaneled jury. This value is assigned by sampling from the normal distribution defined by the mean time limit (T).

The twelve impaneled jurors are then passed on to the BALLOT subroutine, and the cycle of subroutines that comprise deliberation begins. BALLOT polls the members of the simulated jury to determine whether the requisite majority to render a verdict is present. The verdict requirement (Q) is fixed by the experimenter to match the decision rule. If the size of the largest coalition is greater than or equal to the required quorum, then the deliberation cycle ends and the VERDICT subroutine is called. If the requisite majority has not yet been reached, then the jury time limit is checked. If the time limit has been reached, then the DEADLOCK subroutine is called. Otherwise, the voting is simply recorded by the BALLOT routine and deliberation continues by calling the DISCUSSION subroutine.

The BALLOT subroutine serves primarily a bookkeeping function, checking to see if deliberation should be terminated or continued. No attempt is made to simulate the actual rate of formal balloting observed in the mock juries, although the simulation rate can be compared with the empirical balloting frequency. The balloting rate is determined by setting it to maximize the fit of the model to the overall behavior of the juries. In fact, the rate of balloting in the empirical juries is about half the rate of balloting in the model: an average of 23 minutes elapses between ballots for the empirical 12/12 decision condition, as opposed to 10 minutes for model juries. The reason is that in real juries, jurors frequently announce a change of opinion outside a formal vote. In the model, opinion changes can currently be registered only during a BALLOT vote. Therefore, the critical variable on which model and empirical data should match is the frequency of opinion change rather than the frequency of balloting. Future improvements in the model may adjust the role of balloting so that it corresponds to the role of voting in the empirical juries.

The heart of the simulation model is the DISCUSSION routine. JUS does not attempt to model actual discussion. Rather, it represents the products of discussion, namely the changes in individual juror votes that result from the discussion and social influence processes. Changes of an individual juror's opinion are modeled as movement from one verdict preference to another, and the patterns of movement are represented by probabilistic functions (Klevorick & Rothschild, 1979; Suppes & Atkinson, 1960; Criswell, Solomon, & Suppes, 1962; Davis, 1980).

The manner in which movement is characterized reflects the patterns of group change. The strength of the different sources of influence is expected to increase as the number of proponents for a particular position increases; that is, as a coalition advocating a position increases in size, the pressure to conform to it, the informational resources available to it, and its power to reward or punish all increase. Thus the relative coalition sizes within a decision group represent a major, though not an exclusive, determinant of opinion change within that group.

In group decision making, coalition size is related to the likelihood of opinion change. In groups in which the coalitions are roughly equal in size, the larger faction's advantage is slight. As the majority coalition increases in size, it picks up momentum, and the probability that it will continue to grow increases exponentially. In the extreme case, where a substantial majority is opposed by a lone holdout, conformity is almost inevitable (Godwin & Restle, 1974; Davis et al., 1976). In JUS, the effect of coalition size on the movement of individual jurors from verdict to verdict is manifest in two components of the decision to move: WHERE the simulated juror will move if change occurs, and WHETHER the simulated juror will move in the selected direction.

The decision in the WHERE component is controlled by relative faction sizes in the jury according to five rules. The first rule is that jurors will only move to adjacent verdicts. The verdict states of first degree murder, second degree murder, manslaughter, and not guilty are viewed as ordered, and a move from acquittal to first degree murder or other moves between nonadjacent alternatives are not allowed. However, for undecided jurors the categories are considered nonordered, and an undecided juror may move to any of the four remaining verdict states. Furthermore, jurors are not permitted to move to undecided, though such moves do happen at a low rate in empirical juries. Future efforts may bring model performance more in line with actual performance on this point.

The second rule is to treat undecided jurors separately. For undecided jurors the WHERE decision is a direct function of the sizes of the factions voting for each verdict. Thus, if the distribution of votes is 1 undecided, 1 acquittal, 4 manslaughter, 3 second degree murder, and 3 first degree murder, the undecided juror has a 1/11 probability of selecting acquittal, 4/11 probability of selecting manslaughter, 3/11 probability of selecting second degree murder, and 3/11 probability of selecting first degree verdicts during the WHERE component. A random number between 0 and 1 is generated to determine the WHERE decision. Specifically, the range between 0 and 1 is divided into 11 equal segments. If the value of the random number falls in the first segment, between 0 and .0909, then WHERE is set to acquittal. If the random number falls in the next four segments, between .0910 and .4545, then WHERE is set to manslaughter, and so on.

The third rule involves partitioning the jury into two groups lying on either side of the juror under consideration. For jurors already voting for one of the four verdict alternatives, the WHERE decision is a function of the numbers of jurors voting for verdicts in either direction. That factions are partitioned into opposing subsets at the point at which a juror considers changing or staying is suggested by the influence of agendas on social choice (Plott & Levine, 1979). In the absence of an explicit decision agenda, the individual perceives alternate choice subsets. Thus, in the case where the distribution of votes is 1 undecided, 1 acquittal, 4 manslaughter, 3 second degree murder, and 3 first degree murder, the undecided juror is momentarily excluded from consideration and the jury is represented as M1/3, M2/3, MS/4, NG/1.

Conceptually this group is partitioned into three artificial factions relative to the juror who is considering a vote change. Consider the second-degree murder juror considering a move. The group is divided into three factions: F_I, the verdict faction of the juror considering a move (3); F_{A1}, all jurors in verdict states in a one direction from F_I, such as first degree murder (3); and F_{A2}, all jurors in verdict states in the opposite direction from F_{A1}, such as manslaughter and not guilty (5). For the purpose of the WHERE decision, this jury is represented as $F_{A1} = 3$, $F_I = 3$, and $F_{A2} = 5$, which suggests that the second-degree murder faction (F_I) is being pulled from two different directions $(F_{A1}$ and $F_{A2})$. The manslaughter and not guilty groups are viewed as pulling from the same direction. If a manslaughter juror is considering a vote change, the representation is $F_{A1} = 6$, $F_I = 4$, $F_{A2} = 1$, which reflects the pull in one direction from first and second degree murder jurors and in the other direction from the not guilty juror. When there is a pull only from one direction, as in the case of a first-degree murder juror, the situation is represented as $F_{A1} = 0$, $F_I = 3$, and $F_{A2} = 8$.

The fourth rule is to compute probabilities using the partition created in the previous step. A probability is computed for each of the two possible WHERE decisions. If change occurs, the probability that a juror will choose to move in the $A1$ direction is

$$p(\text{WHERE} = A1) = \frac{F_{A1}}{F_{A1} + F_{A2}}$$

and the probability that a juror will choose to move in the A2 direction is

$$p(\text{WHERE} = A2) = \frac{F_{A2}}{F_{A1} + F_{A2}}$$

The WHERE decision determines only the direction of change, given a change. The other four rules do not yield the final, effective probability that a juror will in fact change votes. The WHERE assignment for a particular juror is made by generating a random number and setting WHERE according to the segment in which the number falls, as in the case of undecided jurors.

The fifth rule governs the juror's decision to change votes, WHETHER or not to move to the selected verdict state. The decision is determined by two factors: relative faction sizes within the group and individual juror's resistance to persuasion (R_j). JUS utilizes a simple power function to compute the probability that a particular juror will continue to vote with a current faction and thus not change, given the WHERE decision determined by the fourth rule:

$$p\,(\text{WHETHER} = NO|\text{WHERE} = A) = (.5 + .5|1 - 2s/n|^{2.5})^{1/s} \text{ for } s > n/2$$

$$p\,(\text{WHETHER} = NO|\text{WHERE} = A) = (.5 - .5|1 - 2s/n|^{2.5})^{1/s} \text{ for } s < n/2$$

In these two equations n is the number of jurors in the jury excluding undecided jurors, and s is the faction size of the juror considering a change plus jurors in the direction not selected for change. This function has the following properties. Undecided jurors are excluded from n. Consider the case in which the distribution of votes is 1 undecided, 1 acquittal, 4 manslaughter, 3 second degree murder, and 3 first degree murder. In the previous equation, jury size is represented as $n = 11$ because one of the twelve jurors is undecided and is therefore not counted.

The effective faction size (s) is F_I plus F_A. In the same case, one of the second-degree murder jurors is considering a change of mind. The WHERE routine has been run, and it is now known that if this juror changes, it will be to a verdict of manslaughter. The WHETHER routine now uses the equation to decide if the juror will change positions. To determine s for this second-degree murder juror, since the verdicts are ordered, a decision to let $s = 3$ $(F_I$ alone) does not capture the situation accurately. Five jurors are really pulling in the manslaughter direction, and six jurors are pulling in the second-degree murder direction. Therefore, $s = 6$ in this case, with s defined as the number of members in the juror's own verdict faction (F_I) plus those in verdict factions in the direction not selected $(F_{A1}$ or $F_{A2})$ for change $(3 + 3)$. The remaining jurors are those in the verdict states in the direction selected for change $(4 + 1)$. The effect of this definition of s is to treat the jury as if it were divided into only two opposing groups—one of size s and the other of size $n - s$.

To compute p (WHETHER = NO|WHERE = A), or the probability of an individual not changing, for this case of a second-degree murder juror considering a change to manslaughter, $n = 11$ and $s = 6$. Since $2s = 12$ and $n = 11$, then $2s > n$ and p (WHETHER = NO|WHERE = MS) = .89. Thus once the direction of manslaughter is chosen, there is a .89 probability that this juror will retain the current verdict choice and not move to a manslaughter position on the basis of faction size effects. Later this probability is modified by the resistance to persuasion value assigned to this juror. When the other direction (first degree murder) is chosen, then $s = 8$ and p (WHETHER = NO|WHERE = $M1$) = .92.

The probability that a juror will remain with a current faction is expressed in the previous two equations as a function of the effective faction size s and the jury size n. In this function, the expression $1 - (2s/n)$ is the margin that the faction s has over or under one-half the jury's size. That is, when $s = n/2$ (e.g. $s = 6$ and $n = 12$), this term is zero and p (WHETHER = NO) = $(.5)^{1/s}$. When $s = n$, this term is 1 and p (WHETHER = NO) = $(1)^{1/s}$. The exponent (2.5) reflects the rate of change in staying power as a majority faction grows and determines the probability that an initial majority faction will be reversed.

The effect of coalition sizes on the movement of individual jurors and on a group of jurors in a particular faction is predicted by the WHERE and WHETHER decisions in combination. The probability that a juror in faction size F_I will not change from a current verdict state to either adjacent verdict state is:

$$p = p \text{ (WHERE = A1) } p \text{ (WHETHER = NO|WHERE = A1) +}$$
$$p \text{ (WHERE = A2) } p \text{ (WHETHER = NO|WHERE = A2)}$$

This equation can be expressed as a function of F_{A1}, F_I, and F_{A2}, where F_I is the size of the faction of the juror considering a vote change and F_{A1} and F_{A2} are the number of jurors holding positions in either direction. Graphically, the function p can be represented as a set of points corresponding to each possible ordered triple (F_{A1}, F_I, F_{A2}) for a twelve-person jury $(F_{A1} + F_I + F_{A2} = n = 12)$ (Fig. 9.2). According to the model, a single holdout $(0, 1, 11)$ faced with eleven other jurors pulling from one direction is very unlikely to remain in that state $(p = .1830)$. However, with only one juror pulling in the opposite direction $(1, 1, 10)$ the probability of staying in the current faction of size one jumps considerably $(p = .6023)$. Somewhat counter to intuition, a faction with a single juror flanked by factions of roughly equal size $(5, 1, 6)$ is very unlikely to result in movement for the lone juror $(p = .8983)$.

The function p for individual probabilities of vote changing allows one to compute directly a group function $P = p^{F_I}$, where P represents the probability that none of the F_I members in the faction will change votes. Graphically, the group function P can be represented as a set of points corresponding to each possible ordered triple (F_{A1}, F_I, F_{A2}) for a twelve-person jury (Fig. 9.3). Again, the model predicts that the most stable factions are those surrounded by roughly equivalent factions pulling in opposite directions—$(5, 1, 6)$, $(5, 2, 5)$, and $(1, 10, 1)$—even when the faction size F_I is small (such as $F_I = 1$, in $[5, 1, 6]$). For both the individual functions p and the group function P, the lowermost set of connected points $(F_{A1} = 0)$ represents the case where there are effectively two factions. The plateau in the group function $(0, 5, 7)$, $(0, 6, 6)$, and $(0, 7, 5)$, for which the odds that no one will leave the faction are near 50:50, corresponds to the situation where two groups are equally balanced and movement or nonmovement in either direction is equally likely. On either side, the sharp acceleration illustrates that this function captures the momentum effect of larger factions in unbalanced distributions such that the relative advantage of the larger faction increases dramatically as the factions become unbalanced.

For a single juror, one more calculation determines the final effective probability of remaining in the current verdict state, since in JUS the probability of vote changing is not exclusively determined by faction size. Some group members are more susceptible to group persuasion than are other group members (Padawer-Singer & Barton, 1975; Kerr et al., 1976; McGuire, 1969). Thus, the final step in determining whether a particular

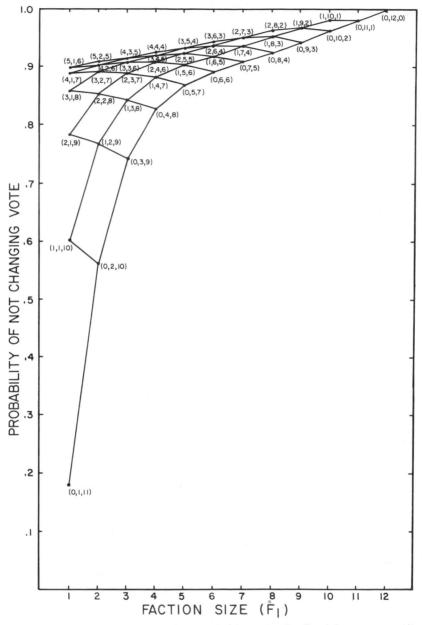

Fig. 9.2 Probability that an individual juror in a faction size F_i will not change votes while a member of a twelve-person jury with a faction balance of F_{A1}, F_i, F_{A2}.

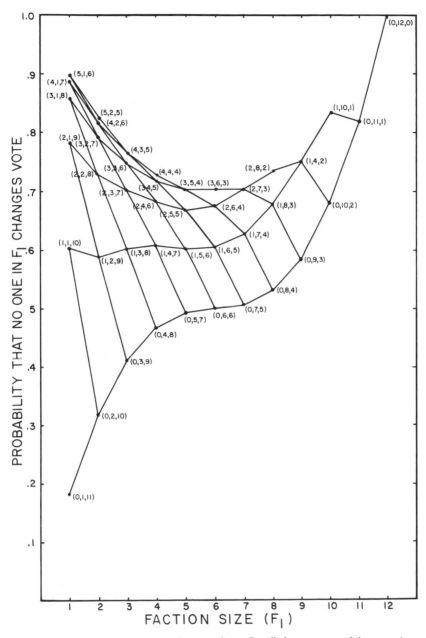

Fig. 9.3 Probability that no juror in a faction of size F_I will change votes while a member of a twelve-person jury with a faction balance of F_{A1}, F_I, F_{A2}.

juror will change votes in the selected direction is to multiply the initial probability of not changing p (WHETHER = NO|WHERE = A) by the particular juror's persuasion resistance coefficient, to produce a final probability of not changing:

$$p \text{ (stay)} = p \text{ (WHETHER} = NO|\text{WHERE} = A) \times R$$

The persuasion resistance coefficient is a likelihood ratio comparing the probability of not changing votes due to internal resistance with the probability of changing votes due to lack of resistance. A juror with a coefficient of 1.0 is equally likely to change or not change, and multiplying p (WHETHER = NO|WHERE = A) by 1.0 does not change the juror's probability of remaining with the original faction. When a juror's coefficient is greater than 1.0, the multiplication rule increases the probability of not changing; if the coefficient is less than 1.0, the probability of not changing is decreased. In other words, the final effective probability of not changing positions is a function of two independent factors multiplied together: the probability p (WHETHER = NO|WHERE = A) of not changing due to faction size effects, and the persuasion resistance score R_j (likelihood ratio) which represents a resistance to change due to a quality of the individual juror.

In order to determine whether a particular juror will change votes at any specific time, a random number between 0.0 and 1.0 is generated and compared to the final effective probability of not changing. If the random number exceeds the effective value, the juror changes to the verdict state determined by the WHERE decision; otherwise the juror remains in the same verdict state. Each simulated juror is given an opportunity to change positions before the model ends DISCUSSION and returns to BALLOT.

The DEADLOCK routine is inoperative until BALLOT determines that the requisite majority has not been attained and the jury time limit has been reached. At this point, if there has been no sign of recent movement toward consensus—that is, no jurors have changed verdict choices in any of the preceding five ballots—the jury declares itself hung and the simulation stops. However, if at least one verdict preference has shifted recently, then deliberation time is extended for additional ballots—that is, the deliberation time is extended 25 percent—and the BALLOT-DISCUSSION cycle continues until either a verdict is reached or the new time limit is exceeded. As long as there is recent movement, the time limit may continue to be extended by DEADLOCK.

At the point where a quorum is reached or the jury is declared hung, the BALLOT-DEADLOCK-DISCUSSION cycle that comprises deliberation is terminated and the VERDICT subroutine is called. VERDICT performs the perfunctory role of announcing a verdict and recording a number of summary statistics to characterize that simulated jury's performance. Typically, between 200 and 1000 juries are run within each experimental condition to produce performance statistics for an experimental condition, such as different decision rules or different jury sizes.

Empirical Evaluation of the Model

JUS can be evaluated by comparing the computer simulation's data on deliberation to the empirical juries' data on specified criteria across variations in decision rule. The six dimensions of the data evaluated are: the distribution of final verdicts, the frequency of vote changes for each verdict category, the distribution of deliberation times, the distribution of initial to final verdict transitions for individual jurors, the growth of the largest faction over time, and the probability of changing verdict position as a function of faction size. All results of the evaluation of these measures are based on $n = 920$ simulated model juries and $n = 23$ empirical juries within each decision rule condition.

For all of the statistical goodness-of-fit tests, the model outputs are considered to be the theoretical population standard. The empirical jury outputs are considered to be a random sample of juries from the population. Each statistical test examines the likelihood that the empirical sample is a sample that could have been drawn from the theoretical population standard represented by the model. In other words, there is always some discrepancy between the empirical and model results. The critical question is whether the discrepancy is sufficiently large to reject the claim that the empirical results represent chance fluctuations within the proposed theoretical distributions.

Initially, JUS was to have exactly the same input to deliberation as did the empirical juries. Since the initial verdict distributions differed empirically for the different decision conditions, the initial verdict distributions for each decision condition were set to match this situation. Thus, the five values defining the multinomial initial verdict distribution (V1-V5) were different for each decision rule (Table 9.1). For example, 57 out of the 276 jurors on 12/12 juries began deliberation with a vote for first degree murder, 67 began with second degree murder votes, 83 for manslaughter, 33 for acquittal, and 36 undecided. The relative frequencies (.21, .24, .30, .12, .13) comprise parameters V1-V5 in the model for the 12/12 condition only. A X^2 goodness-of-fit test indicates that any discrepancies between model and empirical initial verdict distributions may be attributed to chance fluctuation $(p > .975; p > .95$ indicates that the probability of obtaining a more

Table 9.1. Initial verdict distributions.[a]

		M1	M2	MS	NG	UN
12/12	EMPIRICAL FREQUENCY	57	67	83	33	36
	relative frequency model parameters V1-V5 for 12/12	(.2065)	(.2428)	(.3007)	(.1196)	(.1304)
	MODEL FREQUENCY	56.58	68.30	83.62	31.03	36.48

$$X^2_4 = .1638, \; p > .995$$

		M1	M2	MS	NG	UN
10/12	EMPIRICAL FREQUENCY	74	62	78	21	41
	relative frequency model parameters V1-V5 for 10/12	(.2681)	(.2246)	(.2826)	(.0761)	(.1486)
	MODEL FREQUENCY	72.75	63.43	78.50	20.20	41.13

$$X^2_4 = .0890, \; p > .995$$

		M1	M2	MS	NG	UN
8/12	EMPIRICAL FREQUENCY	47	70	92	32	35
	relative frequency model parameters V1-V5 for 8/12	(.1703)	(.2536)	(.3333)	(.1159)	(.1268)
	MODEL FREQUENCY	44.93	71.18	92.20	30.95	36.75

$$X^2_4 = .2344, \; p > .990$$

ALL DECISION CONDITIONS

	M1	M2	MS	NG	UN
EMPIRICAL FREQUENCY	178	199	253	86	112
relative frequency for combined decision rule conditions	(.2150)	(.2403)	(.3056)	(.1039)	(.1353)
MODEL FREQUENCY	174.26	202.91	254.32	82.18	114.36

$$X^2_4 = .3888, \; p > .975$$

a. Within each experimental condition, V1-V5 was set to the relative frequencies shown in parentheses, which resulted in model juries beginning deliberations with the frequencies shown. All model frequencies are based on 11,040 model jurors, but are adjusted for comparison with the 276 empirical jurors in each decision rule condition.

discrepant sample distribution from the proposed theoretical distribution by chance alone is .95). Thus for each decision condition, 920 simulated juries began deliberations with initial verdict distributions that were virtually identical to the empirical juries. Because the initial verdict frequencies for each decision condition were explicitly specified, the data do not constitute a test of the model. The data simply illustrate that the model began deliberations with initial distributions matching the empirical distributions. To improve the match, the number of JUS simulation runs in each condition could have been increased.

Final Verdict Distributions

The final product of both model and empirical jury deliberation is a verdict, although in some cases jurors fail to reach agreement and the jury hangs (Table 9.2). Owing to the low expected frequencies for some of the verdict categories, a X^2 goodness-of-fit test cannot be used in comparing model and empirical distributions. An exact multinomial probability was computed to determine the probability that a more discrepant distribution will occur by chance if the true population frequency is represented by the model frequency.

Model performance under the unanimous decision rule (12/12) fits the empirical data closely ($p = .65$). This is to be expected, since free parameters maximize the fit on this outcome measure for the 12/12 condition. The fit is also close for the 8/12 majority decision rule ($p = .49$). However, the

Table 9.2. Final verdict distributions.[a]

		M1	M2	MS	NG	HUNG
12/12	EMPIRICAL FREQUENCY	0	13	7	0	3
	MODEL FREQUENCY	.78	10.83	8.98	.08	2.35
					Discrepancy index = 1.91, p =.65	
10/12	EMPIRICAL FREQUENCY	5	13	5	0	0
	MODEL FREQUENCY	1.98	12.68	6.13	.03	2.20
					Discrepancy index = 7.05, p =.08	
8/12	EMPIRICAL FREQUENCY	1	13	8	0	1
	MODEL FREQUENCY	.43	10.43	11.33	.13	.70
					Discrepancy index = 2.63, p =.49	

a. Model ouput was adjusted for comparison with 23 empirical juries in each decision condition. The distribution in the 12/12 condition was used to choose free parameter settings.

model verdict distribution and the empirical distribution under the 10/12 majority decision rule are sufficiently different that the discrepancy may be interpreted as indicating that the model results and the empirical results are less likely to represent chance fluctuation within the same theoretical distribution ($p = .08$). The empirical juries in the 10/12 condition began with a higher proportion of first degree murder proponents than did juries in the other two conditions. Empirically, this resulted in a higher proportion of first degree murder final verdicts in the 10/12 condition. Model first degree final verdicts for the 10/12 rule are elevated but not enough relative to other decision rules to match empirical results.

The model mimics one important empirical effect quite well. In both empirical and model data in all three decisions conditions the initial verdict distributions show manslaughter as the modal individual initial verdict choice. Also, the empirical data show that the modal jury final verdict is second degree murder. The computer model mimics this quite well in the 12/12 and 10/12 decision rule conditions and less well in the 8/12 condition.

The model produces the shift in modal verdicts from start to finish of deliberation by the WHETHER routine, whereby a person's faction size (s) is the number of jurors in the juror's current verdict faction plus members of verdict factions in the direction not selected for change, because of the ordered quality of the verdict categories. Using the distribution of 3 first degree, 4 second degree, 5 manslaughter, 0 acquittal, and 0 undecided, consider a manslaughter juror thinking of changing to second degree murder. The juror's faction size is 5 (5 MS and 0 NG), and the opposing faction size is 7 (4 MS and 3 M1). Therefore, even though the modal verdict is manslaughter, there is more pull on the manslaughter jurors to change than on the second-degree murder jurors. This empirical effect is accounted for in part by an implicit ordering of the verdict categories.

However, a flaw in the model performance, suggesting that the ordering explanation is not sufficient, shows up when the initial verdict distributions are collapsed into two opposing groups that ignore the undecideds:

Rule	M1 + M2	MS + NG
12/12	124	116
10/12	136	99
8/12	117	124

Now the final verdict shift from manslaughter to second degree murder can be compared for the model and empirical juries:

	Model		Empirical	
Rule	M2	MS	M2	MS
12/12	10.83	8.98	13	7
10/12	12.68	6.13	13	5
8/12	10.43	11.33	13	8

The model performance for final verdicts follows directly from the collapsed initial verdict distributions. However, the model does not shift to second degree murder quite enough in the 12/12 and 10/12 conditions, and in the 8/12 condition the model slightly favors manslaughter in keeping with the initial verdict distribution. Ordering the verdicts can account for some but not all of this effect. One plausible explanation for the additional empirical shift is an informational influence in favor of a second-degree murder verdict that is above and beyond the informational influence captured by faction size effects. That is, perhaps the arguments in favor of second degree murder or against the other verdicts carry more impact than the simple redundancy modeled by JUS. This possibility cannot be captured by the current model formulation, implying that a complete simulation model of deliberation should include information exchange processes not accounted for simply by the number of people exchanging the information.

Mean Frequencies of Vote Changing

Individual jurors do not alternate repeatedly from one verdict preference to another but display relatively low frequencies of preference changing—usually not more than one or two, rarely three changes of preference during deliberation. Individual vote changing in the model is directly controlled by the transition probability (p) representing the effect of faction size and the persuasion resistance coefficient assigned to each juror. As shown in Fig. 9.2, for the $F_{A1} = 0$ juries the probability of staying with a current vote increases dramatically between faction size equal to one $(p = .1830)$, faction size equal to two $(p = .5644)$, and faction size equal to three $(p = .7439)$. By the time a juror's effective faction size is four, there is only a .17 probability that the juror will leave the faction $(p = .8271)$. In addition, the persuasion resistance coefficient assigned to each juror is drawn from a distribution that has a mean of 1.10 (R) and a standard deviation of .055 (SDR). This implies that about two-thirds of the jurors have persuasion resistance scores between 1.06 and 1.16. The higher the number, the more stubborn the juror, and the effect of multiplying this coefficient with the transition prob-

Table 9.3. Average vote changes per juror.[a]

		M1	M2	MS	NG	HUNG
12/12	EMPIRICAL AVERAGE	--	1.10	1.18	--	1.39
	(standard deviation)	--	(.23)	(.37)	--	(.55)
	MODEL AVERAGE	--	.97	.93	--	1.12

$F_{(3,20)} = .4853$

		M1	M2	MS	NG	HUNG
10/12	EMPIRICAL AVERAGE	1.05	1.01	.68	--	--
	(standard deviation)	(.24)	(.33)	(.37)	--	--
	MODEL AVERAGE	.89	.82	.84	--	--

$F_{(3,20)} = .2802$

		M1	M2	MS	NG	HUNG
8/12	EMPIRICAL AVERAGE	.92	.69	.73	--	.83
	(standard deviation)	(.00)	(.29)	(.33)	--	(.00)
	MODEL AVERAGE	.67	.57	.48	--	.88

$F_{(4,19)} = .3738$

a. Distribution shown in the 12/12 condition was used to choose free parameter settings.

ability is to increase the probability of the juror staying with a current faction.

The distributions of mean number of vote changes per juror for juries reaching each of the five final verdicts within each decision condition were found by using the model distributions as theoretical population values and using a one-sample F-test to contrast the variation between model and empirical means with the variation wthin empirical juries (Table 9.3). All F ratios were less than one, indicating that in all cases the differences between model and empirical distributions are small in comparison with the differences in frequency of vote changing behavior among juries within the empirical sample.

In general, model jurors changed their minds slightly less frequently than did actual jurors, although most of the ordering relations within and between decision rules are captured. For example, within verdict categories there is more vote changing in the 12/12 juries than in the 10/12 juries and still more than in the 8/12 juries. The one exception to this pattern (MS 10/12 and 8/12) is not mimicked by the model. The empirical pattern within decision condition is for harsher verdict categories to reflect more opinion change (M1 > M2 > MS) with hung juries also elevated. This general ordering pattern is also captured by the model performance, and the exception to it (12/12, MS > 12/12, M2) is again not mimicked by the model.

Mean Deliberation Times

Average deliberation time decreases as the required quorum for reaching a verdict decreases. That is, unanimous juries require more time to reach a verdict than do majority decision rule juries. Moreover, juries that hang tend to deliberate substantially longer than do verdict-reaching juries. Empirical and model deliberation time means for juries reaching each verdict within each decision rule condition are shown in Table 9.4. Again, F tests indicate that variability among juries in each condition is greater than differences between model and empirical deliberation times.

Table 9.4. Average deliberation times.[a]

		M1	M2	MS	NG	HUNG
12/12	EMPIRICAL AVERAGE	--	119.15	146.29	--	200.67
	(standard deviation)	--	(54.21)	(65.49)	--	(43.15)
	MODEL AVERAGE	--	123.40	125.80	--	285.20
						$F(3,20) = .7809$
10/12	EMPIRICAL AVERAGE	101.20	100.31	111.60	--	--
	(standard deviation)	(54.60)	(46.32)	(64.88)	--	--
	MODEL AVERAGE	130.90	99.00	112.28	--	--
						$F(3,20) = .1083$
8/12	EMPIRICAL AVERAGE	61.00	71.77	63.50	--	231.00
	(standard deviation)	(0.00)	(53.75)	(31.37)	--	(0.00)
	MODEL AVERAGE	100.60	62.20	54.00	--	263.90
						$F(4,19) = .3238$

a. Distribution shown in the 12/12 condition was used to choose free parameter settings.

The model clearly captures the decision rule effect; that is within each verdict category 12/12 juries deliberate longer than 10/12 juries, which deliberate longer than 8/12 juries. In addition to the proper ordering, the actual deliberation time values fit quite well for the second-degree murder juries, for which there is the most empirical data. For the manslaughter juries, the fit is also quite good except in the 12/12 condition, where the empirical deliberation time average is oddly elevated.

For the verdict-reaching juries, the worst fit is obtained for the first-degree murder juries. The model needed to deliberate considerably longer to reach a first-degree murder verdict than did actual juries. First, as there are few empirical observations of first degree murder (5 juries for 10/12; 1 jury for 8/12), this may be random error. If it is not random error, the difference is a matter of speculation. That the model takes a long time to reach a first-degree murder verdict is expected, because the modal individual verdict is manslaughter, the model has relatively low rates of opinion change, and jurors are allowed to move only one position at a time. But it is surprising that the empirical juries took such a short time. These six juries have been discussed earlier (Chapter 8), and it was noted that they may have reached agreement through errors rather than through real resolution of differences. The model performance suggests that the actual resolution of differences should take much longer in reaching a first-degree murder verdict. This suggestion is also consistent with the inability of the model to mimic the high proportion of first-degree murder verdicts in the 10/12 decision condition even when initial verdict distributions were matched.

Model juries that fail to reach consensus on a verdict and are declared hung deliberate considerably longer than verdict-reaching juries. Hung model juries appear to deliberate longer than actual hung juries, and the order between conditions (8/12 > 12/12) is not preserved. These differences match the empirical results but are difficult to evaluate because hung juries were infrequent in the mock jury study (4 juries total).

Initial to Final Verdict Transitions

Further detail about the relation between initial and final verdict distributions is available from data on individual juror movements from initial vote to final vote within each decision condition (Table 9.5). These verdict transition matrices show that the general transition pattern for the empirical data has been mimicked by the model. The Spearman product-moment correlation coefficients (r) for each decision condition, ranging between .93 and .98, indicate the extent to which empirical transition patterns are matched by model patterns.

However, the most theoretically important aspect of the model and em-

Table 9.5. Model and empirical verdict transition frequencies for initial to final vote.[a]

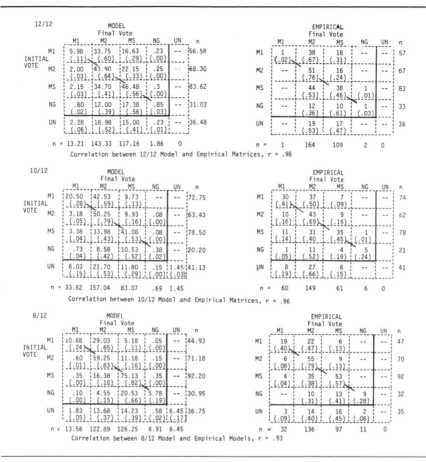

a. For each matrix cell the row proportion is shown in parentheses. All frequencies are based on 11,040 jurors in each decision rule but are adjusted for comparison with the 276 empirical jurors in each rule.

pirical transition matrices are the ways in which the patterns do not match. The first kind of mismatch between model and empirical matrices concerns those jurors who do not change verdict positions from initial to final vote. These jurors form the upper-left to lower-right diagonal on each matrix (Table 9.5). The model formulation is quite simple in its predicted effects for each decision rule condition: as decision quorum decreases, with fewer jurors needing to agree in order to reach a verdict, the proportion of jurors who stay, retaining their original verdict preference, increases. In other words, for 8/12 and 10/12 juries fewer jurors than in 12/12 juries need to

Table 9.6. Transition from initial to final votes (undecided jurors not included) (%).

Decision rule	Jurors	Model	Empirical
12/12	Staying (not changing vote)	40.59	37.92
	Moving down (to more lenient position)	28.82	30.42
	Moving up (to harsher position)	30.61	31.67
	Moving down out of those who moved	51.51	48.99
10/12	Staying	47.76	48.09
	Moving down	25.71	22.98
	Moving up	26.55	28.94
	Moving down out of those who moved	50.82	44.26
8/12	Staying	63.04	56.43
	Moving down	17.77	15.35
	Moving up	19.20	28.22
	Moving down out of those who moved	51.94	35.24

change their votes in order to reach the requisite consensus; the faction size effects operate for a shorter period of time, resulting on the average in fewer vote changes and therefore in increasing proportions of jurors who retain their original votes (Table 9.6). For the decision conditions 12/12, 10/12, and 8/12, the percentages of model jurors who stay are 41 percent, 48 percent, and 63 percent respectively. This effect holds for the empirical juries where 12/12, 10/12, and 8/12 decision rules result in 37 percent, 47 percent, and 55 percent respectively of empirical jurors who stay. The model juries tend to stay too much; that is, empirical jurors change votes somewhat more often, particularly in the 8/12 condition. Returning to the marked diagonals in Table 9.5, this observation can be elaborated. The overall increase in the proportion of jurors who stay in empirical juries is accounted for entirely by increases in staying jurors in the extreme verdict categories only, that is, first-degree murder jurors and not guilty. In contrast, more model jurors in all verdict states stay as decision quorum decreases. The model cannot capture this effect, and it cannot be explained on the basis of faction size effects.

A second effect that the model does not fully mimic is the movement from an initial individual juror modal verdict of manslaughter to the final individual and group modal verdict of second degree murder. Comparing the column totals for model and empirical matrices, the model does not show enough movement from manslaughter to second degree murder in any of the decision conditions. Within the matrices this is the result of too many MS jurors who stay and not enough movement from manslaughter to second degree murder and from self defense to second degree murder (Table 9.5). The model has an excess of jurors who stay and not enough movement into harsher verdict categories (Table 9.6).

Growth of the Largest Faction

The growth of the winning faction over time is central to the outcomes of the persuasive process in both model and empirical juries. The empirical jury data suggest that larger factions are likely to form and pick up momentum sooner under the nonunanimous decision rules (Fig. 9.4). For example, after ninety minutes of deliberation, the probability that a 12/12 jury has a faction of eight or larger is .48, for 10/12 the probability is .70, and for 8/12 the probability is .83.

No explicit theoretical provision in the model predicts the differential growth rate for the winning faction phenomenon. Therefore, if the model mimics any part of the empirical effect, it requires explanation. The growth of a faction in the model depends only on the relative sizes of the factions and individual juror resistance. However, a by-product of the decision rules may account for part of the effect that should be mimicked by the model. In the 8/12 decision rule in the model a verdict is rendered when a faction size of eight is reached and deliberation stops. Since the probabilities are cumulative, the verdict rendering jury counts as having reached eight from that point on. For example, if an 8/12 jury reaches a faction size of eight at 40 minutes, it is counted as having reached eight at 40, 50, 60 minutes and so on. However, in the 10/12 and 12/12 conditions, when a faction reaches size eight at 40 minutes, deliberation continues and the possibility exists of the faction losing a member and returning to size seven at, say, 50 minutes, and this in fact happens in the empirical juries. Meanwhile other juries may be reaching faction sizes of eight, so that the total cumulative probability that a faction of size eight has been reached may continue to rise, but for 10/12 and 12/12 conditions it may not rise as fast because of the backsliding possible after a faction of eight has been reached.

According to the empirical data, backsliding does not account for all of the differential rate of growth effect, and thus the model should display only some portion of the effect. To test the model on this dimension, a special experiment was run. All previous model data had been based on simulation runs for which the model's initial verdict preference distribution (V1-V5) was set to match the empirical juries distribution for each decision rule. In this special experiment, initial verdict distributions were set to be the same values for all three decision rules. The values chosen were the average ini-

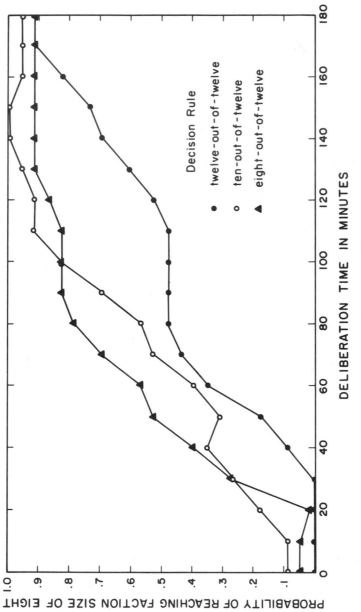

Fig. 9.4 Probability that the winning faction has at least eight members as a function of time for empirical juries in each decision rule condition.

tial verdict frequencies across decision rules for the empirical juries. Any differences between decision conditions in model jury performance may be attributed to the model's theoretical representation of decision rule effects alone, since other initial differences between conditions have been eliminated. The model shows a small effect of decision rule on the growth of the winning faction (Fig. 9.5). The separation of the 8/12 and 10/12 curves at about 50 minutes indicates that more 8/12 juries begin to reach verdicts at that time than in the other conditions. The 10/12 and 12/12 curves barely separate at about 60 minutes, indicating point when 10/12 juries begin ending deliberation at a higher rate.

The extreme result of a current majority faction losing members, or backsliding, is that another faction starts growing and a reversal results; that is, a minority faction succeeds in reversing the trend and becomes the verdict-reaching faction. In the case of reversals, the initial majority faction and the eventual winning faction are different. An indicator of reversals is the difference between the average time it takes an initial majority faction to reach sizes of six and eight, when the initial majority is defined as the first faction to reach six or eight, and the average time it takes the winning faction to reach sizes of six or eight. In cases where the initial majority factions are identical to the winning factions, the average times are identical. The average times empirical and model juries take for the first faction, or initial majority, to reach six and eight were compared with the average times for the same juries' winning factions (Table 9.7). The initial verdict frequencies (V1-V5) were equated across decision rules to produce model data shown in the first panel of Table 9.7. For initial majority factions of six, reversals take place at about the same rate across decision conditions. However, initial majorities of size eight do not reverse at the same rate across decision rules. For the model, in the 8/12 condition, the first faction to reach eight is always the winner. Thus the average times to reach eight are equal for the initial majority faction and for the winning faction. However, for the 10/12 and 12/12 conditions, reversals of initial majorities do occur. Thus the faster rate of growth of the winning faction for the 8/12 condition can be attributed to the backsliding-reversal effect that cannot occur in the model for majority factions of size eight in the 8/12 decision rule. However, comparison of empirical juries and the model simulation shows that the backsliding explanation accounts for only a part of the rate of growth effect.

It is possible that the differences in initial verdict distributions between the decision rules contribute to the differences in rate of growth. In the original simulation runs, where model and empirical initial distributions match, if the empirical differences in the growth of the largest faction are due to initial discrepancies in verdict distributions, then the model data should mimic the empirical data (Fig. 9.6). Comparison of the two model

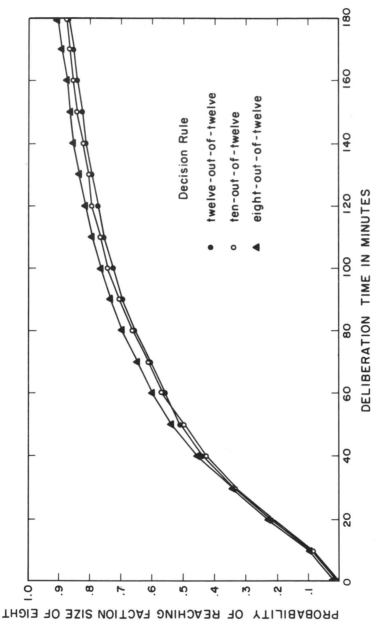

Fig. 9.5 Probability that the winning faction has at least eight members as a function of time for JUS juries when initial verdict preference distributions are equated across decision rule conditions. (Each decision rule condition begins with the average distribution across conditions for empirical juries.)

Table 9.7. Average time, in minutes, of initial majority vs. winning faction reaching sizes of six and eight.

	Model times with same average initial verdict distributions across decision rules		Model times with initial verdict distributions matching empirical distributions for each decision rule		Empirical jury times	
12/12	Size 6	Size 8	Size 6	Size 8	Size 6	Size 8
Initial majority	21.37	69.28	22.70	60.30	51.96	87.61
Winning faction	30.40	71.19	30.70	70.70	66.87	100.09
10/12						
Initial majority	22.32	68.27	24.55	70.48	41.13	62.65
Winning faction	29.49	69.74	32.47	72.27	51.83	63.09
8/12						
Initial majority	21.60	69.37	18.80	59.19	24.83	57.83
Winning faction	28.50	69.37	23.66	59.19	39.35	60.04

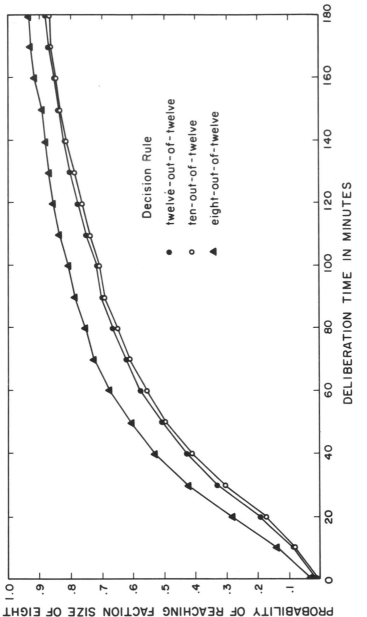

Fig. 9.6 Probability that the winning faction has a least eight members as a function of time for JUS juries when model initial verdict preference distributions are set to match the empirical initial verdict distribution within each decision rule condition.

simulation experiments shows that the 10/12 and 12/12 decision condition curves match in the two graphs except for a slight shift down for the 10/12 juries (Fig. 9.6 versus Fig. 9.5). However, the 8/12 curve is elevated. The difference between the 8/12 curves is an effect of the initial verdict distribution in the 8/12 condition. This effect is also seen by comparing factions of size eight, where the 12/12 and 10/12 average times are virtually identical in both model experiments (Table 9.7). The 10/12 condition has a slightly larger reversal effect than 12/12 and a slightly lower rate of growth, accounting for the 10/12 and 12/12 curve positions (Fig. 9.6). The important comparison is the 8/12 average minute for reaching a faction size of 8. This difference can be attributed to an initial verdict distribution effect in the 8/12 juries, set to match the empirical distribution, and it results in the elevated 8/12 curve (Fig. 9.6).

Comparison of the second model simulation and empirical juries shows that the combined backsliding-reversal effect and the slight initial verdict distribution effect still do not account for the substantial rate of growth difference in the empirical juries (Fig. 9.4). However, at least part of the extreme depression of the 12/12 growth curve can be accounted for by a high rate of 12/12 empirical jury reversals. Comparison of initial majority versus winning faction times for the empirical juries shows that for 12/12 juries the first faction to reach a size of eight took 88 minutes on the average, but the winning faction took an average of 100 minutes, or a 12 minute difference. Yet reversals in the other two conditions resulted in average differences of less than three minutes. The reason is shown by the percentage of reversals according to decision rule (Table 9.8). Over 17 percent of the unanimous juries reversed initial majorities of size eight. Only four percent of the 10/12 and 8/12 empirical juries did so. This accounts for at least some of the depression of the 12/12 growth curve (Fig. 9.4). The extent to which other factors contribute to this effect awaits further explanation.

In terms of actual time taken to reach a faction size of six, the model is much quicker than the real juries (Table 9.7). However, by size eight, the model times are closer to the empirical times, and by sizes ten and twelve, the model and empirical times are virtually identical. In other words, the empirical juries are slower to start moving than are the model juries. Videotapes of the deliberating juries suggest that the empirical juries often engage in summarizing and organizing activities at the beginning of deliberation. In contrast, the model maintains a rate of opinion change that is constant throughout.

The model also captured reversals for initial factions of size six but did not reverse enough for initial factions of size eight (Table 9.7). The model reversed only 1.3 percent of factions reaching size eight in the 12/12 deci-

Table 9.8. Reversal rates for initial factions of six and eight (%).[a]

Juries	12/12	10/12	8/12
	Reversing an initial majority of six		
Empirical	26.09	21.74	21.74
	(6)	(5)	(5)
Model	15.11	14.67	12.50
	(139)	(135)	(115)
	Reversing an initial majority of eight		
Empirical	17.39	4.35	4.35
	(4)	(1)	(1)
Model	1.30	1.30	0.00
	(12)	(12)	(0)

a. Based on 23 empirical juries in each decision rule and 920 model juries per rule. Actual number of juries reversing initial factions of six and eight are shown in parentheses.

sion rule condition, versus 17.4 percent reversals for the empirical juries in the same condition (Table 9.8). In the empirical juries that reversed initial factions of size eight, informational effects beyond those captured by faction size were apparently at work. Many of the empirical reversals appear to be due to simultaneous shifts of four to eight people. In one case a 12/12 empirical jury had reached a split of eight for second degree murder and four for manslaughter. The manslaughter jurors maintained that the second-degree murder advocates were interpreting the trial judge's instructions about the meaning of the two verdict categories incorrectly. After requesting a rereading of the relevant instructions, all eight second-degree murder jurors switched to manslaughter in a single vote, and a unanimous decision resulted. JUS has no provision for this kind of information intervention, and the probability, on the basis of faction size and stubbornness effects, that all eight jurors would leave a faction of eight and join a faction of four is tiny. The frequency of "simultaneous" shifts, those in which more than one person changes votes in a single poll, over all the juries followed a pattern: for both model and empirical juries, 62 percent of all vote changes involved only one person changing at a time; for model juries, 27 percent of shifts involved two persons, 8 percent involved three persons, and 3 percent involved four or five persons; and for empirical juries, 8 percent involved two persons, 9 percent involved three, 9 percent involved four, and 10 percent involved five to eight. In other words, for the model juries 3 percent of all shifts involved more than three persons, in contrast to 19 percent for empirical juries.

Probabilities of Changing Factions

The network of transition probabilities that characterized faction size effects in JUS (Figs. 9.2–9.3) cannot be compared directly with the empirical transition data because the effects of the actual persuasion resistance coefficients unique to each juror were not included. Therefore, model performance is compared directly with the empirical transition data to evaluate the model's fit. The probability that a juror in a faction of size F_I would leave that faction to join another faction differed for jurors under the different decision rules in the empirical juries (Fig. 9.7).

The model should mimic two characteristics of the empirical jury behavior. First, for all decision conditions, jurors are most likely to leave small factions of sizes one, two, and three. As faction size increases, the probability that a juror will leave decreases. Model distributions show this general pattern, although the model rates of leaving decelerate much more quickly than empirical distributions; that is, real jurors are less likely to leave small factions and more likely to leave medium size factions than the model predicted (Fig. 9.8). The major discrepancies are for factions of size one, where model predictions are too high, and for factions ranging from four to six, where model predictions are too low. Second, decision rule affects the probabilities that jurors will leave factions of different sizes. For faction sizes one and two, empirical results show that jurors in 12/12 juries are more likely to leave their faction than are jurors in 10/12 juries. Jurors in 10/12 juries are in turn more likely to leave factions of one, two, and three than are jurors in 8/12 juries. The model results mimic the 12/12 > 10/12 phenomenon but not the 10/12 > 8/12 (Fig. 9.8). The model results are easier to explain than the empirical results. In the 12/12 condition jurors have to persuade everyone, so that remaining in factions of one and two is not allowed for verdict-reaching juries unless those jurors can persuade others to join them. In 10/12 and 8/12 conditions, factions of one and two may still be in existence and a verdict rendered. This is no more true for 10/12 than for 8/12 conditions, which the model performance reflects. The model distributions then diverge in the 8/12 condition, for factions of three and four reflecting the reduced quorum required. From faction size six and greater, the discrepancies reflect the reversal phenomenon that elevates probabilities of leaving larger factions in the 12/12 condition.

The transition probabilities do not depend solely on the size of the juror's own faction but also depend on the numbers of jurors voting for verdicts in either direction from the juror considering a move. Some predictions follow from the model's characterization of movement probabilities. For example, a juror in the situation $F_{A1} = 0$, $F_I = 1$, $F_{A2} = 11$ is among the least likely to

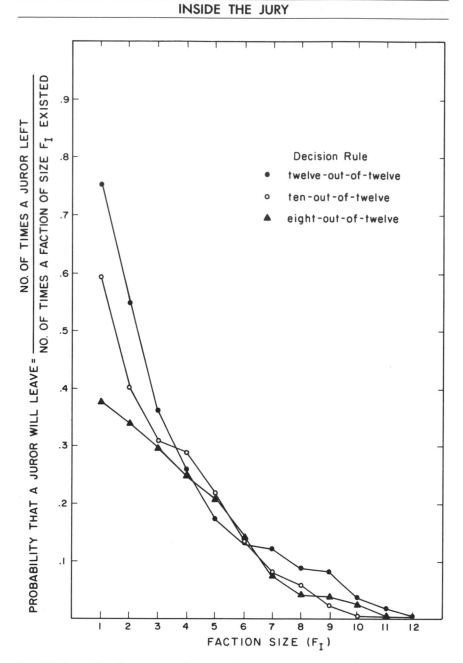

Fig. 9.7 Probability that a juror will leave a faction of size $F_I = 1,2 \ldots 12$ for empirical juries.

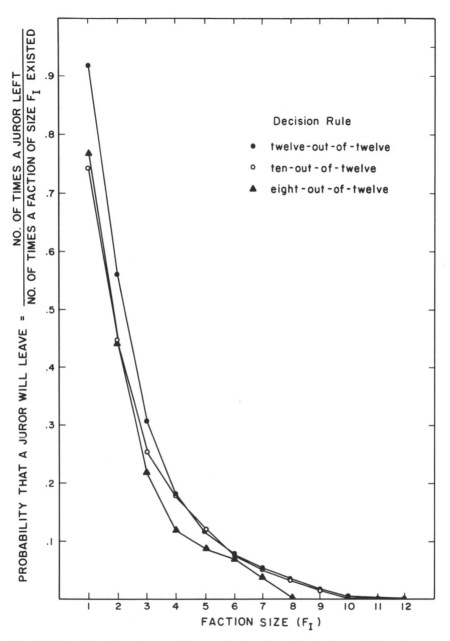

Fig. 9.8 Probability that a juror will leave a faction of size $F_i = 1,2 \ldots 12$ for JUS juries.

stay in a faction, while a juror in the situation $F_{A1} = 5$, $F_I = 1$, $F_{A2} = 6$ is among the most likely to stay in a faction, although in both cases the juror is alone in holding a particular verdict preference.

Model transition probabilities based on actual model performance combining the three decision rules are shown in Figure 9.9. These probabilities include the effect of the persuasion resistance coefficient assigned to each model juror, and they are based on simulated model trials rather than on theoretical computations. The transition probabilities for the empirical juries are shown in Figure 9.10. In both cases the probability that a juror will stay with a faction is a function of the juror's own faction size and the faction size in either direction. These faction sizes are noted next to each point by the ordered triple (F_{A1}, F_I, F_{A2}). Points that are out of place according to theoretical model predictions are marked with an "x" and are connected within the network by dotted lines. The result of persuasion resistance is both to elevate all probabilities of staying and to exaggerate differences between $F_{A1} = 0$ points and $F_{A1} > 0$ points (Fig. 9.2 vs. Fig. 9.9). However, we are mostly concerned with a comparison between model and empirical transition probabilities (Fig. 9.9 vs. Fig. 9.10).

A number of the empirical probabilities are based on low frequencies in the sample, and therefore many of the discrepancies may be accounted for by sampling error. In general, the model and empirical networks resemble each other. For points in which $F_{A1} = 0$, such as (0, 1, 11) and (0, 2, 10) mismatches are apparent, namely the model jurors leave smaller factions (0, 1, 11) and (0, 2, 10) more frequently than the empirical jurors, and they leave medium size factions (3-9) less frequently. Predictions about what constitute the least likely factions for someone to leave are in part confirmed by the empirical data: (5, 1, 6), (4, 1, 7), (3, 1, 8), (4, 4, 4), (3, 6, 3), (2, 7, 3), (1, 9, 2), (1, 10, 1), (0, 11, 1), and (0, 12, 0). The most striking regular departure between model predictions and empirical data are the parabolic tails on the $F_{A1} = 1, 3, 4, 5$ curves, for which there is no obvious explanation. In general, the model jurors do not leave factions as much as empirical jurors do, a fact supported by the rates of vote changing (Table 9.3).

Other Empirical Evaluations

JUS has also been evaluated by comparing model performance to empirical jury performance reported in other jury research. The empirical data used for this purpose include a study with six- and twelve-person juries considering two verdict alternatives, acquittal and conviction, for a murder case under unanimous and nonunanimous decision rules, and a study with six-person juries using a nonunanimous decision rule considering two decision

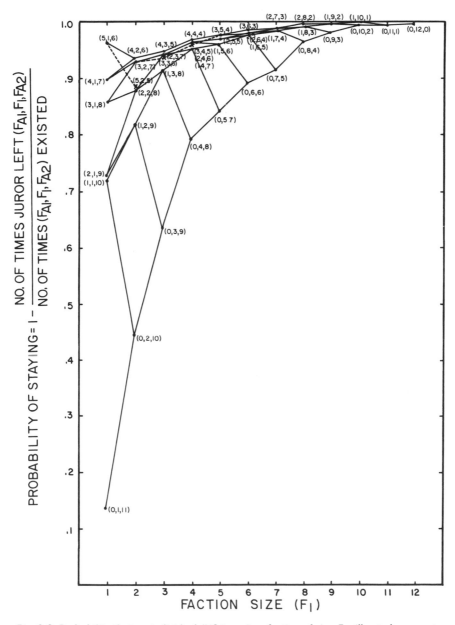

Fig. 9.9 Probability that an individual JUS juror in a faction of size F_I will not change votes while a member of a twelve-person jury with a faction balance of F_{A1}, F_I, F_{A2}.

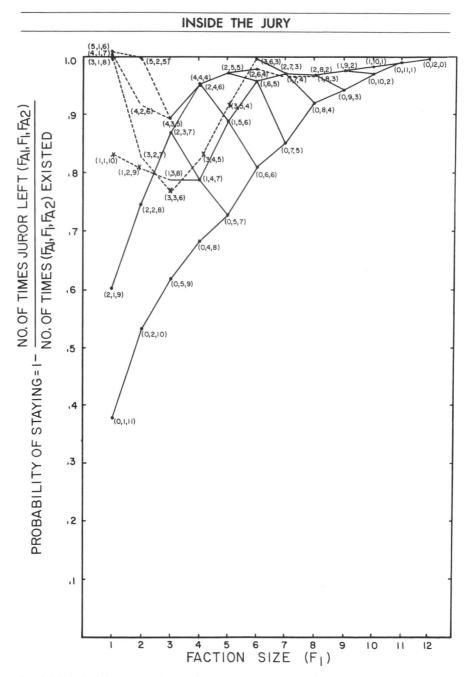

Fig. 9.10 Probability that an individual empirical juror in a faction of size F_I will not change votes while a member of a twelve-person jury with a faction balance of F_{A1}, F_I, F_{A2}.

alternatives, conviction and acquittal, for a rape case (Padawer-Singer & Barton, 1975; Davis, Kerr, Stasser, Meek, & Holt, 1977).

In general, results of these evaluations on measures of final verdict distribution, numbers of reversals of initial majorities, deliberation times, and frequencies of vote changing indicate that JUS can successfully model jury performance across variations in jury size (six and twelve), decision rule (unanimous, 2/3 majority, 5/6 majority), number of decision alternatives (two and four), and case type (murder and rape). In addition to relatively close fits between model and empirical jury performance, the four free parameters for the model—rate of balloting, deliberation time limit, individual persuasion resistance score mean, and standard deviation—which must be estimated anew for each model application, are very close in value for two of the three applications. For example, persuasion resistance means varied between 1.10 for the current application and 1.14 for the other two applications with the standard deviation remaining constant at .055. Rates of balloting varied between 10 and 13 minutes, and mean deliberation time limits varied between 240 and 310 minutes.

Model Projections

In order to maximize and evaluate the fit between JUS's simulated products and empirical jury results, initial verdict preferences for each decision condition in JUS matched the empirical distribution of initial verdicts by decision rule, but in some cases this obscured the relatively simple, systematic nature of JUS's outputs and decision rule predictions. One example of such model-only effects is the model-predicted decision effects on growth of largest faction (Fig. 9.5) holding initial verdict distributions constant. In addition to clarifying the model's behavior, these effects exhibit the model's capacity to project to jury behavior under conditions we have not yet studied (Table 9.9). The theoretical predictions derived from the model are straightforward. As a decision quorum increases, juries are less likely to reach a verdict and therefore more likely to hang. For the mock-jury stimulus case, final verdict distributions are virtually identical across decision conditions. As the decision quorum increases, jurors are more likely to change verdict preferences rather than retaining initial verdict choices. As decision quorum increases, juries are also more likely to deliberate longer, and hung juries deliberate substantially longer in all conditions.

There were not strong decision rule effects on final verdict for an initial verdict preference distribution like the one obtained empirically for the stimulus murder case. However, JUS predicts decision rule effects for three other types of initial verdict distribution, all of which are likely to occur: a

Table 9.9. Decision rule effects predicted by JUS for *Commonwealth v. Johnson*.[a]

		Initial Vote Distributions Using Empirical Average Relative Frequency				
		M1	M2	MS	NG	UN
A.	12/12	59.88	66.77	84.45	28.18	36.73
	10/12	60.50	67.20	83.68	27.70	36.93
	8/12	57.83	66.90	85.73	28.90	36.65

		Final Verdicts				
		M1	M2	MS	NG	HUNG
B.	12/12	.90	10.98	8.63	.03	2.48
	10/12	1.05	11.60	8.33	.08	1.95
	8/12	.78	11.45	9.85	.13	.80

		Average Number of Vote Changes per Juror				
		M1	M2	MS	NG	HUNG
C.	12/12	1.15	.96	.95	1.58	1.11
	10/12	.92	.82	.79	1.06	1.08
	8/12	.67	.62	.54	.77	.98

		Average Deliberation Times				
		M1	M2	MS	NG	HUNG
D.	12/12	158.60	126.20	128.80	150.00	282.80
	10/12	138.30	105.80	105.70	203.30	280.90
	8/12	87.10	72.40	63.80	124.00	276.60

Table 9.9. (*continued*)

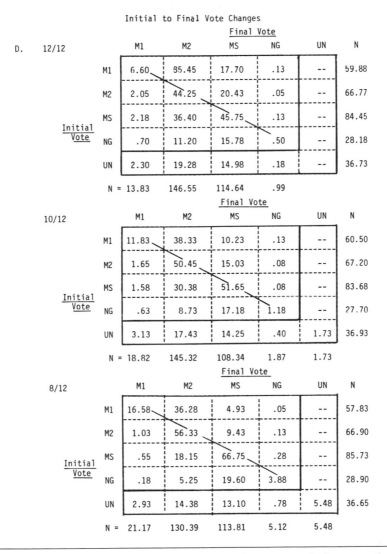

Initial to Final Vote Changes

D. 12/12

Final Vote

Initial Vote	M1	M2	MS	NG	UN	N
M1	6.60	85.45	17.70	.13	--	59.88
M2	2.05	44.25	20.43	.05	--	66.77
MS	2.18	36.40	45.75	.13	--	84.45
NG	.70	11.20	15.78	.50	--	28.18
UN	2.30	19.28	14.98	.18	--	36.73
N =	13.83	146.55	114.64	.99		

10/12

Final Vote

Initial Vote	M1	M2	MS	NG	UN	N
M1	11.83	38.33	10.23	.13	--	60.50
M2	1.65	50.45	15.03	.08	--	67.20
MS	1.58	30.38	51.65	.08	--	83.68
NG	.63	8.73	17.18	1.18	--	27.70
UN	3.13	17.43	14.25	.40	1.73	36.93
N =	18.82	145.32	108.34	1.87	1.73	

8/12

Final Vote

Initial Vote	M1	M2	MS	NG	UN	N
M1	16.58	36.28	4.93	.05	--	57.83
M2	1.03	56.33	9.43	.13	--	66.90
MS	.55	18.15	66.75	.28	--	85.73
NG	.18	5.25	19.60	3.88	--	28.90
UN	2.93	14.38	13.10	.78	5.48	36.65
N =	21.17	130.39	113.81	5.12	5.48	

a. All figures are based on 920 simulated model juries in each decision rule but are adjusted to 23 for comparison with other tables. Any differences in initial vote distributions are due to chance fluctuations, since each set of decision condition runs received the same initial vote relative frequencies.

bimodal distribution in which the initial verdict relative frequencies are M1 = .40, MS = .05, MS = .05, NG = .40, UN = .10; a second-degree murder skew in which the initial verdict relative frequencies are M1 = .05, M2 = .50, MS = .25, NG = .10, UN = .10; and a not guilty skew in which the initial verdict relative frequencies are M1 = .05, M2 = .10, MS = .25, NG = .50, UN = .10.

The initial juror verdict preference distributions and final jury distribution are shown as percentages (Table 9.10). The major decision rule effect on jury verdict for each of these initial distributions (bimodal, M2 skew, NG skew) is the increasing proportion of hung juries predicted as decision quorum increases. For the bimodal distribution, the model predicts 31 percent hung juries for the unanimous decision rule and 12 percent for the 8/12 rule. The important result for an innocent defendant (40 percent of initial individual verdicts) is that 19 percent of the juries in the 8/12 condition do not hang because of the relaxed decision quorum requirement and are distributed so that 14 percent go into the guilty verdict categories and 5 percent into the not guilty category. A more subtle version of the same effect is present for the two skewed initial distributions.

Model jury size (J) can be set equal to other sizes besides twelve-person juries. JUS was set for a jury size equal to six: and quorum size equal to four, five, and six, with everything else exactly as it was for the twelve-person model. The resulting model predictions are shown in Table 9.11. The initial verdict distributions are different for each decision rule, and the distributions reflect the same relative frequency as the initial verdict distributions from the empirical jury sample. In comparison to the equivalent twelve-person juries, nearly twice as many final verdicts of first degree murder (6.03 vs. 3.19) are predicted for the six-person juries and six times as many not guilty verdicts (1.46 vs. .24), although the not guilty verdict has a low frequency in both samples. Thus, JUS predicts an increase in extreme verdicts for six-person juries. The amount of vote changing is predicted to be equivalent for twelve- and six-person juries, while deliberation times are substantially shorter for six-person juries.

Precise predictions about transition probabilities in six-person juries can be made from JUS and compared to twelve-person jury predictions. For example, JUS predicts that jurors in six-person juries are more likely to leave their factions than are jurors in twelve-person juries with the same balance of power, by comparing splits (0, 4, 2) with (0, 8, 2). Predictions such as these concerning the behavior of juries under a wide range of conditions are useful both practically and theoretically. They can be used to anticipate policy implications and they can be submitted to empirical test.

Table 9.10. Decision rule effects predicted by JUS for other initial verdict distributions.[a]

% Initial Vote Distributions
Using Bimodal Relative Frequencies

BIMODAL		M1	M2	MS	NG	UN
A.	12/12	40.29	5.13	5.24	39.32	10.03
	10/12	39.69	4.81	4.95	40.26	10.29
	8/12	39.67	4.74	4.95	39.99	10.66

% Final Verdicts

		M1	M2	MS	NG	HUNG
B.	12/12	18.17	16.00	15.87	18.61	31.43
	10/12	19.57	17.52	16.43	20.13	26.43
	8/12	23.83	21.96	19.26	22.83	12.17

% Initial Vote Distributions
Using M2 Skewed Relative Frequencies

M2 SKEW		M1	M2	MS	NG	HUNG
A.	12/12	4.83	50.16	25.09	9.94	9.99
	10/12	5.05	49.78	24.64	10.63	9.92
	8/12	4.54	49.64	25.33	10.36	10.14

% Final Verdicts

		M1	M2	MS	NG	HUNG
B.	12/12	0.00	68.70	22.30	0.00	9.04
	10/12	0.00	71.00	23.61	.13	5.35
	8/12	0.00	70.43	26.87	.65	2.09

Table 9.10. (*Continued*)

		% Initial Vote Distributions Using NG Skewed Relative Frequencies				
NG SKEW		M1	M2	MS	NG	UN
A.	12/12	4.80	10.08	25.26	50.14	9.71
	10/12	5.14	9.20	25.16	50.45	10.05
	8/12	5.01	10.14	24.89	49.92	10.05

		% Final Verdicts				
		M1	M2	MS	NG	HUNG
B.	12/12	0.00	.87	34.26	57.17	7.74
	10/12	0.00	.87	35.57	55.78	7.83
	8/12	0.00	1.43	37.83	58.61	.02

a. All entries are expressed in percentages and so cannot be compared directly to other tables.

In summary, our computer simulation model JUS provides a realistic and psychologically plausible theory of jury decision making, and the performance of the model closely resembles the outputs produced by juries over a range of conditions. First, the final jury verdict outcome is not random but is related to the distribution of the jurors' initial verdict preferences. JUS mimics the major empirical relation between initial individual votes and final jury verdict and the shift from a modal initial individual verdict preference of manslaughter to a modal final jury verdict of second degree murder (Table 9.2). In addition, model individual juror transition patterns from initial to final verdict choices show a .97 correlation with empirical juror transitions (Table 9.5). However, JUS's performance is not perfect. JUS jurors do not shift enough to the second degree murder category. Informational impact for some verdict categories in addition to that represented by the size of the faction advocating the particular verdict is not currently provided for in JUS.

Second, we suggested earlier that initial majority persuasion characterizes jury decision making in many cases. In a small proportion of cases, initial majorities are reversed or the jury fails to reach a verdict and hangs. With respect to majority persuasion, JUS relies on the effects of coalition size as a major component in controlling juror movement from verdict state

Table 9.11. Decision rule effects predicted by JUS for six-person juries.[a]

		M1	M2	MS	NG	UN
		Initial Vote Distributions Using Relative Frequencies Matching Empirical for Each Decision Condition				
A.	6/6	28.33	34.00	40.63	16.65	18.40
	5/6	35.68	31.83	39.38	10.03	21.10
	4/6	22.45	34.85	46.03	16.68	18.00

		M1	M2	MS	NG	UN
		Final Verdicts				
B.	6/6	1.85	11.15	9.40	.58	.03
	5/6	3.00	12.78	7.00	.23	--
	4/6	1.18	9.70	11.48	.65	--

		M1	M2	MS	NG	UN
		Average Vote Changes per Juror				
C.	6/6	1.09	1.05	1.04	1.51	3.50
	5/6	.83	.92	.87	1.35	--
	4/6	.67	.56	.46	.76	--

		M1	M2	MS	NG	UN
		Average Deliberation Times				
D.	6/6	72.20	65.20	66.00	101.30	270.00
	5/6	48.50	53.10	48.10	88.90	--
	4/6	39.40	28.10	22.50	40.00	--

a. All figures are based on 920 simulated juries in each condition but are adjusted for comparison with 23 empirical juries. Initial verdict distributions are set to match empirical (12-person jury) distributions in each decision rule.

to verdict state. JUS juries hang about as often as actual juries (Table 9.2). In addition, they deliberate longer than verdict-reaching juries, as do empirical hung juries (Table 9.4). JUS reverses initial factions reaching six about as often as empirical juries but fails to reverse majorities of eight as frequently as empirical juries (Table 9.7). This may be due to JUS's lack of simultaneous shifts in which four or more people change votes at once. Again, the influence of information intervention, such as hearing only a portion of the trial judge's instructions, and the influence of particular agenda structures or other kinds of information exchange not captured by faction size may be at work in real juries but not in JUS model juries.

Third, the growth of the winning factions in JUS juries mimics some but not all of the characteristics of empirical juries (Figs. 9.4–9.6; Tables 9.7–9.8). Some of the decision rule effect on the growth of the largest faction in empirical juries is accounted for in the model by the backsliding-reversal phenomenon. Another small portion is accounted for by different initial verdict distributions for the different decision rules. The remaining differences between decision rules cannot be accounted for by the theoretical provisions embodied in JUS.

Finally, empirical jurors do not change their minds repeatedly, and individual jurors differ in the extent to which they are susceptible to persuasion. The low empirical rate of vote changing is matched by JUS, and most of the orderings within verdict and within decision rule are preserved (Table 9.3). If anything, JUS jurors need to change votes slightly more often to approach a better match to empirical data. JUS includes a parameter for an individual difference dimension that affects the jurors' likelihood of changing votes when combined with the effect of faction sizes in the jury (Figs. 9.2, 9.9–9.10).

JUS presents precise projections for six-person juries viewing the stimulus murder trial and for twelve-person juries viewing a criminal trial that is similar to the stimulus case except for initial verdict distribution. Evaluation of the validity of these projections would require additional empirical research.

Several failures of the model to fit empirical data have also been identified which suggest directions for future research, most notably the need to examine further the information exchange processes in jury deliberation and the cognitions of individual jurors contributing to that exchange.

10

Implications for Law and Social Science

At the most elementary level the products of the present mock jury study are facts about the behavior and ideation of jurors. It is a truism of science and philosophy that facts must be connected to a conceptual context to become meaningful or useful. The study's findings have significance in three conceptual domains: legal policy concerning the right to trial by jury, psychological theories of group decision making, and principles to guide attorneys in winning cases at trial.

Legal Policy

The research addresses two questions that interest legal professionals and policy makers concerning the effect of changing the decision rule requirement on jury performance and the factors that facilitate or hinder proper jury decision-making. Both questions relate to standards of performance that underlie the legal conceptualization of the right to trial by jury.

At an abstract level, the Supreme Court has defined the function of the jury as to create an effective deliberation process. We translated this general function into five empirically measurable characteristics of effective jury performance: representing a cross-section of the community, expressing a variety of viewpoints, performing accurate and thorough factfinding, remembering and properly applying the judge's instructions on the law, and rendering accurate or proper verdicts. The present study addresses each of

By Hastie

227

these aspects of jury performance except for composition and representation. However, the individual differences found in deliberation behavior are relevant to jury composition and thus to any consideration of which classes or types of individuals ought to be included on (at least not excluded from) juries.

Decision rule affects each of the remaining characteristics of effective deliberation. Decision rule affects the counterbalancing of viewpoints during deliberation, because dissenting viewpoints, or views favored by relatively small numbers of jurors within a jury, are at a relative disadvantage in nonunanimous juries as compared to unanimous juries. Members of very small dissenting factions participate at lower rates in majority rule juries and are less satisfied with the jury verdict when compared to small-faction members in unanimous juries.

Decision rule also affects the thoroughness of the jury's consideration of evidence and the law during deliberation, although measures of accuracy on facts and the law per se are not affected by decision rule. Nonunanimous juries discuss both evidence and law during deliberation far less thoroughly than do unanimous rule juries. However, there is no indication that juries are biased in favor of either prosecution or defense as a function of decision rule.

The effect of decision rule on verdict accuracy is not dramatic. However, because even subtle signs of a decision rule effect on verdicts are important to a policy maker, it is significant that in the study the first degree murder verdict was rendered only by nonunanimous juries. We argued that a first degree murder verdict could be treated as an error because it required a truly exceptional interpretation of the evidence presented at trial. The relationship obtained between first degree murder verdicts and nonunanimous rule juries should be viewed with caution because of the sampling variability in the study, which produced an uneven distribution of large first degree murder factions across juries. However, an examination of juries with equivalent starting points supports the conclusion that juries in majority decision rule conditions as compared to the unanimous rule are more likely to reach improper, first degree murder verdicts for the stimulus case. For example, five of the unanimous rule juries started deliberation with four or more jurors favoring first degree murder verdicts, but none of these juries rendered such verdicts. Under majority rules, eleven juries started with four or more jurors favoring first degree murder, and four of these juries rendered that verdict. Furthermore, the moderating influence of the longer, more thorough deliberations under the unanimous rule might have damped the sampling effects that occurred in the study and that can also occur in actual juries. A systematic pattern of errors on the law, not the evidence, is also associated with first degree murder verdicts. Again, the evidence suggests that longer, more thorough deliberation might eradicate these errors, as in the unanimous rule juries.

Two other findings on the thoroughness of deliberation, and by implication on the jury's accuracy on the evidence and the law, favor the unanimous decision rule. First, in unanimous juries, a substantial number of important events occur during deliberation after the largest faction has reached a size of eight members. For example, a large proportion of discussion occurs during the interval between the largest faction reaching ten and the verdict being rendered. This discussion usually includes several error corrections and references to the standard of proof. Typically this is also the interval during which requests for additional instructions from the trial judge occur. Second, in juries under the unanimous decision rule, majority factions with eight members, a sufficient number to render a verdict under the eight-out-of-twelve rule, do not always prevail in the final jury verdict; these juries also hang and reverse themselves. In effect, the jury decision task is not completed even when the majority faction is quite large.

Decision rules also affect conditions at the end of deliberation. Majority rule juries finish more quickly than unanimous rule juries. Typically in majority rule juries there are small factions of holdouts, jurors who do not subscribe to the majority-rendered verdict. These holdouts express negative views of the quality of deliberation, and jurors from both majority and holdout factions have lower respect for their fellow jurors' open-mindedness and persuasiveness under the nonunanimous decision rules. These findings favor the unanimous rule.

Other findings emphasize the positive characteristics of majority rule juries. Deliberation time is shorter on the average in majority rule juries. The distribution of final verdicts does not shift dramatically from decision rule to decision rule. Deadlocked juries are also less likely to result under majority rules, and deliberation is more direct, unequivocal, and fierce.

It is up to policy makers and perhaps the voting public to assign appropriate weight to these empirical results. In our view, the unanimous rule appears preferable to majority rules because of the importance of deliberation thoroughness, expression of individual viewpoints, and protection against sampling variability effects of initial verdict preference. Furthermore, because respect for the institution of the jury is a critical condition for public acceptance of jury decisions, the lower postdeliberation evaluations of the quality of their decision by jurors in nonunanimous juries and the larger number of holdouts who reject the jury's verdict under these rules greatly diminish the usefulness of the majority rule jury as a mechanism for resolving legal disputes.

Other factors affect the quality of the jury's performance of deliberative functions. One is the counterbalancing of biases. This counterbalancing has two aspects: inclusion of a variety of viewpoints on the jury panel and expression of all viewpoints during deliberation. The issue of inclusion of viewpoints lies outside of the present study because it depends on the composition of the jury pool and the particular impanelment and selection procedures implemented at trial. But the study's focus on the contents of deliberation yields findings about the expression of views. Members of small factions express themselves less fully under majority decision rules as compared to unanimous rules. Juries that deliberate with an evidence-driven style, starting deliberation with a discussion of evidence rather than law and deferring formal voting until later in deliberation, also tend to discuss more fully and equitably. However, this latter trend is not statistically significant and deserves further study.

In their task of factfinding, juries perform efficiently and accurately. The reconstruction of the testimony and the construction of plausible narrative schemes to order, complete, and condense the trial evidence occur with thoroughness and precision. These accomplishments in jury deliberation are especially impressive when compared to the performance of even the most competent individual jurors. The view of the evidence produced by deliberation processes is invariably more complete and more accurate than the typical individual juror's rendition of the same material. This conclusion is supported by postdeliberation measurement of jurors' memory for trial evidence. Not only do erroneous statements about evidence occur roughly half as frequently as errors on the law, but evidence errors are also more likely to be corrected during deliberation.

Because jury performance of the factfinding task is so remarkably competent, few innovations are needed to improve performance. An evidence-driven deliberation style produces more thorough and impartial assessment and integration of the evidence. Thus, an instruction to the jury to begin deliberation with a review of the evidence and to avoid early or frequent vote-taking might facilitate performance.

In general, on the question of competency at the factfinding task: good attorneys make good jurors. The case used in the present study was tried by two exceptionally skillful attorneys, to whose competence can be partly credited the juries' strong performance of the factfinding task. In lengthier trials where especially heavy demands are to be placed on the jurors' comprehension and memory capacity, various devices may alleviate these problems, such as extensive, well-indexed evidence books and other visual or mechanical exhibits that organize and summarize important evidentiary materials. Jurors' errors frequently involve confusion over which witness contributed which portions of testimony. A simple directory of witnesses, including a photograph and identifying information for each witness, could be useful, particularly when many witnesses testify. Even with only seven witnesses as in the *Commonwealth v. Johnson* stimulus trial confusion still occurs.

As for accuracy on the law, jury decision processes do not falter when confronted by abstract legal concepts, such as the beyond reasonable doubt standard, reasonable inference, and the presumption of innocence. Perhaps juries should balk at these conceptual hurdles, but on the whole they manage with an impressive display of common sense. By their actions, jurors acknowledge the impossibility of perfect conceptual clarity and accept crude, but serviceable, approximations.

The major conceptual obstacles to reaching a proper verdict arise from jurors' inability to keep the verdict categories and their elements in order. These conceptual errors do not occur because the judge's instructions are jumbled or overly complex. In fact, the contents of the instructions in the stimulus case are unusually succinct, clear, and crisp. Nonetheless, comprehension, memory, and application of the law are major problems for juries.

To avoid these failures of jury decision making, improvements are needed in the manner in which the trial judge communicates the law to the jury. Many, if not all, of these verdict errors can be avoided if the jury accurately comprehends and retains the judge's substantive instructions concerning the crime categories. Providing the jury with a written transcript, written summary, or audiotaped recording of the final charge can effectively remedy these confusions. The repetition or elaboration of specific instructions by the judge will help when the jury appears to be blocked or requests further instructions. Of course, the judge must exercise care to avoid a misleading or biasing emphasis and must not encourage the jury to depend on the Court rather than its own resources for solutions to the factfinding task. Yet concise, responsive additional instructions can facilitate error correction and productive discussion by the jury.

In the course of judge-jury communication, the judge's instructions to disregard inadmissible testimony appear to be strictly followed during deliberation. In the present study, efforts by jurors to introduce testimony that had been stricken from the trial record were blocked by other jurors. However, it would be unwise to generalize from these observations to actual jury behavior, for experimental juries may be abnormally well-behaved when dealing with the inadmissibility issue while under observation by social scientists. Furthermore, research has repeatedly shown that jurors do not or cannot disregard biasing extralegal testimony. The direct observation method is less sensitive to factors such as attractiveness, social class, or race that influence an individual juror than the experimental techniques that have demonstrated these biasing effects.

In defense of the realism of mock juries, however, it is plausible to assume that actual juries are as well-behaved as experimental juries in obeying a judge's instruction to disregard testimony. Stricken testimony may tend to be rejected in open discussion but have an impact, perhaps even an unconscious one, on the individual juror's judgment. In fact, interviews with jurors following actual jury trials support the conclusion that stricken testimony is rarely discussed openly during deliberation.

The modal second degree verdict is the most defensibly proper verdict for the stimulus case. However, almost one-half of the mock juries did not finish deliberation with a second degree murder verdict. Initial large factions favoring other verdicts are the major cause of deviations from the modal verdict. However, faction size alone cannot explain all of the jury's movement down the road to consensus. Frequently an improper verdict is reached because a misunderstanding of the trial judge's instructions on the law is maintained throughout deliberation. Errors in the discussion of the judge's charge appear repeatedly and often are not corrected in deliberation. Misunderstandings, frequently involving a reordering of verdict category elements, are common for all of the verdicts studied.

The appearance of deadlocked juries also marks a practical failure of the jury, although we believe that the presence of some hung juries is a desirable property of the jury institution. Hung juries often end deliberation with sizable factions voting for opposing verdicts. In some juries a repetition of the judge's instructions would probably result in verdicts. In others, alternate views of the credibility of defense and prosecution witnesses underlie the disagreement. Or a lone holdout may resist the arguments of eleven jurors. Once the holdout is identified, efforts are made to persuade him to change. Often these messages concern extralegal issues, such as the proper function of the jury or possible subjects for discussion, and pay surprisingly little attention to decision-relevant case material. Under this onslaught of communication the holdout can become completely unresponsive. Attempts by the foreman to move to a final verdict by calling for written ballots may prove fruitless, and the dynamite charge from the trial judge, though it has a constructive influence can ultimately prove ineffective. The holdout may respond to the charge by attempting to present his position to the rest of the jury, but hostile reactions send him back into his protective shroud of silence. The majority faction finally abandons its efforts and, after perhaps directing a few punishing remarks to the holdout, declares the jury deadlocked.

Deadlocked juries can be avoided in a number of ways. The special instruction for deadlocked juries is a useful device. Juries that receive this charge often then move to a verdict. These verdicts are predictable from the most preferred verdict in the jury before the charge is given, and juries do not shift toward either harsher or more lenient verdicts following the charge. Early and frequent voting during deliberation is also obstructive of reaching a verdict. High rates of voting are associated with the appearance of tight-knit, defensive factions that do not devote all of their energies to an open-minded search for truth in the evidence. Jury instructions should caution the jury to avoid early or frequent polling during deliberation.

Social Science Theory

Social science theories of small group behavior, even those that are explicitly designated as relevant to jury decision making, are skeletal and incomplete. For example, none of the models that relate initial juror verdict preferences to jury verdicts attempts to account for information pooling during deliberation. At the same time, most hypotheses about social influence processes do not include considerations of group structure or group dynamics. Chapter 9 was an introduction to the JUS computer program, which provides an empirically validated theoretical account of many of the characteristics of jury behavior. The computer model synthesizes theoretical principles from social choice theory, the psychology of small group performance, and attitude change theories. In the model, individual differences in resistance to persuasion, the sizes of extant factions in the jury, and an agenda-like partitioning rule combine to predict accurately the movement of jurors from verdict faction to verdict faction. In addition, the model predicts the effects of variations in jury composition, jury impanelment procedures, jury size, and jury decision rule on the behavior of jurors during deliberation.

Given the economy of assumptions concerning individual and group decision making, the model provides an impressive match to the data from mock juries. In some cases the model predicts behavior that confounds expectations. For example, the model predicts shifts from a modal individual predeliberation verdict of manslaughter to a modal postdeliberation jury verdict of second degree murder, although none of the principles on which the model is founded explicitly prescribe such shifts. The model also identifies phenomena that can not be accounted for with existing theoretical principles. For example, factions grow at different rates under differing decision rules; however, this phenomenon was not predicted by the model.

A class of phenomena that is currently outside the model concerns the contents of discussion during deliberation. First, there is considerable inequality among jurors in the amount of participation in deliberation. This finding is consistent with the dramatic differences between the most and the least talkative participants in almost any group discussion. Higher status occupations, more education, male gender, and foreman status are associated with higher rates of participation. Moreover, the size of the faction in which a juror is aligned has a subtle impact on the amount of talking. The smaller the faction, the greater the participation rate for an individual juror. There are three plausible explanations for this effect of faction size on speaking rate: the convention of polite discussion that gives all sides in a debate approximately equal discussion time, the wish to avoid repeating arguments already generated by other members of a person's faction, and the possibility that more talkative individuals tend to adhere to unpopular points of view. In addition, verdict preference has a small effect on speaking rate. Jurors advocating self defense and first degree murder are more talkative than other jurors. Jurors who declare themselves undecided are distinctly less talkative than jurors aligned in verdict-favoring factions.

The sequence of discussion in the jury follows the prescriptions of a cognitive model, called the Story Model, which characterizes the major subtasks in the individual juror's larger decision task. In a typical jury the start of deliberation is dominated by discussions of testimony and other evidentiary issues as well as by frequent references to the judge's instructions concerning the credibility of witnesses. This discussion represents the jury's efforts to converge on a credible story of the events described by testimony. Later portions of deliberation are dominated by a discussion of verdict categories, verdict elements, and classification rules such as the beyond reasonable doubt standard of proof. This phase of discussion reflects the jury's efforts to establish verdict categories and classify the story into a verdict category as postulated by the general Story Model. The errors that occur in deliberation mostly concern matters of law, particularly definitions of verdict categories and their elements. There is also a rather low citation of the beyond reasonable doubt standard of proof, although no particular level of citation can be claimed to be minimally sufficient.

Two styles of deliberation are distinguishable, verdict-driven versus evidence-driven. Evidence-driven juries follow the three-stage sequence of story construction, verdict categorization, and classification suggested by the Story Model. Verdict-driven juries have high rates of voting at the start of deliberation and emphasize verdict categories early in discussion. In a sense, these juries start with classification and work backward to determine which story is most coherent. The evidence-driven style is associated with desirable characteristics of deliberation, such as thoroughness and positive postdeliberation evaluations of each other by jurors.

The development of an adequate theory tying dynamics of individual opinion change to patterns of information exchange in deliberation remains a major challenge for research on jury decision making. One traditional theory classifies the bases of social influence into normative and informational messages. However, our observations of deliberation yield a more complex typology of jurors' motives for maintaining or changing verdict-relevant beliefs. The list includes seven types of incentive: to find the truth, to follow the judge's instructions on the jury's task, to protect the defendant from a disagreeable law, to promote or hinder the wishes of reference individuals or groups, to attack or protect members of social groups represented by the defendant, to escape deliberation, and to win deliberation.

An alternate theoretical approach is a valence model that relies on simple counts of the number of arguments for and against a position. This approach does not predict jury verdicts accurately. Our descriptive analysis of deliberation phases (applying the Story Model for juror decisions to jury deliberation) helps explain why simple valence models fail. Furthermore, we find that initial faction sizes can both explain discussion valence and predict final verdict better than the simple valence model itself.

Three phenomena are associated with variations in the jury decision rule, which are important targets for future conceptual and empirical analysis. First, the decision rule does not simply cut off deliberation at the point at which the required quorum to render a verdict is reached. Rather, various types of events are distributed proportionally across deliberation. However, the social mechanism that adjusts discussion to reflect a typical pattern of content, regardless of duration, is a mystery. Second, the largest faction grows more quickly during deliberation under majority rules as compared to the unanimous rule. At least four factors may account for these differences in growth. Jurors may take their task less seriously in the nonunanimous decision rules as contrasted with the unanimous decision rules. Jurors may want to avoid membership in the holdout faction in verdict-rendering nonunanimous juries and so defect from factions that are likely to lose in the race to render a verdict. Jurors may also be motivated to shift to join the largest faction and put the jury over the top of the quorum requirement. Finally, the suppression of discussion by small faction members in nonunanimous juries may produce an imbalance in participation rates that gives larger factions an advantage in information pressure to persuade other jurors to join their faction. The third phenomenon is the differential participation rates for members of small factions in unanimous and majority decision rule juries. This phenomenon may be accounted for by motivational factors affecting the small faction members' probability of speaking or the large faction members' probability of cutting off argument by the small faction members.

One view of the individual in jury deliberation is provided by jurors' perceptions of each other. An egocentric bias characterizes jurors such that each juror sees himself or herself as exceptionally persuasive and exceptionally open-minded. This bias generalizes, so that other members of the juror's own faction are seen as more persuasive and more open-minded than members of opposing factions. Since this finding holds across all jurors, regardless of faction membership, it seems to be a general bias of social perception that transcends the specifics of a particular view of the case.

Comparison of individual and group memory for information from the testimony and from the judge's instructions replicates the common finding that groups outperform individuals on such memory tests. The group memory advantage over the typical or even the exceptional individual is one of the major determinants of the superiority of the jury as a legal decision mechanism.

Trial Tactics

The mock-jury procedure is not just a research tool. It can be used to preview and evaluate an attorney's presentation at trial. In this application a case is pretried before one or more mock juries, and the reactions of the juries are used to plan trial tactics. A variation on this method is to place a shadow jury in the courtroom during a trial and, at the end of each day's trial presentation, to use the reactions of the shadow jurors as a guide to subsequent case presentation.

Jurors and juries do indeed try to construct a story, based on credible evidence, that summarizes events testified about, and the number of plausible stories that jurors consider in this construction process is limited. Specific items of evidence play a critical role both in the construction process and in the subsequent decision to select one story as superior to another. Furthermore, subtle variations in the trial judge's instructions can produce dramatic differences in jurors' classifications when the story is compared with the verdict categories. Mock jury or shadow jury methods can provide clear pictures of the alternate stories, identify critical pieces of evidence in determining which story is selected or the form of the story constructed, and point out contents in the judge's instructions that are bases of jurors' verdict classification judgments. This information can be put to direct use by an attorney in presenting evidence, designing closing arguments, or making motions to request jury instructions.

Deliberation is a critical element of the mock-jury method. The legal practitioner needs to know both what individual jurors will contribute at the start of deliberation as well as which of those contributions will be important determinants of the outcome of the group consensus process. The shift from an initial verdict preference of manslaughter to a final jury verdict of second degree murder observed in the present study is clear evidence that jurors' initial verdicts do not directly predict the outcome of the jury decision process.

Mock jury and shadow jury methods are powerful tools to aid attorneys preparing for trial. In fact, we believe that these methods are far more powerful aids to winning cases than the systematic jury selection methods that have received more publicity.

Systematic jury selection methods can alter the composition of the jury panel and influence the jury's verdict. There are systematic relationships between individual differences of demography or assigned role and individual behavior. For example, education, occupation, income, and gender have clear and predictable correlations with participation during discussion. Similarly, foreman status, persuasiveness, and open-mindedness are all related to speaking. Political ideology, occupation, education, age, and rated persuasiveness are related to memory for testimony and the judge's instructions. Initial verdict preference and holdout status also affect jurors' sense of pressure, thoroughness, and seriousness of deliberation.

In the present study there was no simple relationship between individual differences and initial verdict preferences. The literature on juror personology available to practicing attorneys is rich in predictions of individual bias in verdict preference which were not borne out in the present results for the *Commonwealth v. Johnson* case materials. We conclude that the systematic methods used to advise attorneys concerning juror selection strategies are only marginally useful in typical felony cases. As yet, there is no scientific evaluation of the systematic selection methods for any other type of case. These limits are acknowledged in handbooks for jury selection that emphasize the need to combine the systematic survey and modeling methods with other selection methods. Because selection strategies are heavily dependent on the particulars of a case, such as the charge, the evidence, and the character of the defendant and witnesses, we would caution against overgeneralization of selection strategies across all legal applications.

Underlying the expectation that demography, personality, and attitude govern initial verdict preference is an implicit model for juror decision making. This model assumes that jurors are characterized by enduring traits, attitudes, or prejudices that manifest themselves in behavior in different situations. These underlying traits, attitudes, or prejudices are linked to identifiable demographic characteristics of the jurors. They also condition the jurors' responses to general classes of defendants or to defendants charged with certain crimes. Finally, jurors' reactions to the trial evidence are simple projections from these attributes onto a single continuum of perceived guiltiness. However, similar models relating personality and attitudinal variables to behavior have not fared well in field or laboratory research in social psychology. The low utility of personality traits to predict behavior is well-documented.

The present study emphasizes cognitive aspects of the juror's performance, such as world knowledge, and comprehension of testimony and legal instructions. The failure of simple social, personality, and attitudinal variables to predict verdict preference is not surprising given that case circumstances are relevant to a great diversity of real world domains. Personality, attitudes, and social background typically have low correlations with individual world knowledge. Thus, we would expect there to be few general principles relating demographic, personality, and attitudinal differences to verdict preferences.

The attempt to predict a juror's decision based on the trial evidence cannot sidestep the complex information processing aspects of the task that confronts a juror who accepts the instruction to seek the truth. Any adequate model for predicting a juror's initial predeliberation verdict preference must be based on an analysis of the cognitive requirements of the juror's task. The Story Model generalized to apply to deliberation provides the framework for such predictions. Furthermore, the power of selection techniques, though limited, can be enhanced if they are combined with a model of jury decision processes. Such a model has the power to evaluate selection strategies, to sharpen the specific guidelines in a single strategy, and to aid the legal practitioner in anticipating the effect of variations in jury pool composition or other local conditions on the impact of a selection strategy.

In summary, although differences in the frequency of verdicts rendered by juries under the three decision rules are not large, the final verdict patterns are important. First, only majority rule juries return first degree murder verdicts. Some of these verdicts occur because of predeliberation sampling variability in the assignment of jurors to experimental conditions. However, there is convincing evidence that a part of this result is due to decision rule influence on performance. Even quantitatively small effects such as those observed are of great significance in the context of the legal commitment to a trial process that is not biased against the defendant. Second, hung juries are less likely under majority decision rules, and majority rule juries reach verdicts more quickly than unanimous juries. Furthermore, deliberation quality with respect to thoroughness or seriousness is diminished, minority or small faction viewpoints are suppressed, and overall juror satisfaction is lowered in majority rule as compared to unanimous juries. The proper decision rule is thus the unanimous rule.

The major obstacle to proper jury decision making is also the difficulty of correctly comprehending, remembering, and applying the trial judge's substantive instructions on the law. Procedures or devices should be adopted to aid the trial judge in communicating the law to the jury. Two specific procedures are written transcripts or summaries of the instructions and audiotaped recordings to go into the jury room.

The use of computer simulation models of jury decision making such as JUS is the best way both to arrive at a scientific theory of group processes and to aid legal policy makers in predicting the effects of changes in jury procedures. Computer simulations also permit the analysis of group processes using simple variables such as faction size, individual differences in biases to favor one side in a case, and differences in confidence or stubbornness. The most important problems for future theoretical analysis concern the relationship between the content and patterning of information exchange and opinion change within the jury.

For those whose goal is to win cases and who have the resources, the use of mock jury or shadow jury methods is an aid in the preparation for trial. Systematic jury selection methods, involving survey-based modeling, are currently limited in their power to control verdicts in common criminal trials. The usefulness of these techniques can be increased if the resulting model of the relationship between individual differences and verdict preferences is combined with a model of the trial process. This allows the legal practitioner to evaluate selection strategies in a theoretical context that includes the composition of the jury pool, competing selection strategies, and group process effects.

Legal institutions are conservative. They exhibit great resistance to new findings and new procedures. Resistance is greatest when new concepts challenge traditional assumptions or methods. Modern behavioral science creates many such threats to fundamental assumptions. New conceptions of motivation and preference replace the concept of free will; new empirical methods for determining truth challenge traditional rational analysis and trial procedures; and new trial tactics extend the adversarial competition to jury selection and beyond. However, the conservativism of legal institutions is sensible. The foundations of behavioral science are uneven. For example, scientists know much more than the man-in-the-street or the philosopher-in-an-armchair about attention, perception, memory, and decision making, but they know little more than nonscientists about human motivation or altered states of consciousness. Uncritical acceptance of social science findings and theories is a mistake. Even when a scientific result is clearly established, the question of generalization to new conditions must be addressed.

Behavioral science is starting to exert a small influence on some judicial decisions and policies. Acknowledgment by some jurists that empirical data may sharpen and advance legal arguments and even resolve disputes is relatively recent. The use of research findings and methods to guide policy decisions is increasing. The employment of social scientists to assist attorneys in their preparation for trial is new and increasingly popular. One avenue for the introduction of scientific results into the literature of legal precedents is the presentation of evidence by expert witnesses. Such witnesses from the field of psychology include clinicians who testify when a case involves insanity or other questions of mental condition, experts who comment on other witnesses' ability to observe, remember, or accurately report on events, and experts who present research results that are relevant to a practice challenged on constitutional grounds.

In many instances the adversarial system shields the legal process of determining truth from the influence of equivocal or weak scientific procedures, such as clinical analysis of insanity or polygraphic lie detection. However, the acceptance of unequivocal, valid scientific results is also frustratingly slow. Although the institutional safeguards, such as adversarial testing in court, should not be removed, legal scholars, practitioners, and policy makers should be more open to the findings of behavioral science. Just as with the laws of society, those who ignore the laws of science will be controlled by those who understand them.

APPENDIX

BIBLIOGRAPHY

COURT CASES

INDEX

Appendix
The Statistical Analysis

Two types of statistics are used in drawing conclusions from data (Dixon & Massey, 1969; Snedecor & Cochran, 1980; Winer, 1971; Morrison & Henkel, 1970). The first class of statistics, often labeled "descriptive," includes values such as frequencies, proportions, percentages, means, standard deviations, and correlations. The primary function of these quantities is to describe precisely and economically the major characteristics and patterns in the data. As a rule, in the present volume the most common descriptive statistics are reported. In many cases more "robust" statistics were also calculated but not included in this report because they are in complete agreement with the more familiar statistics.

The other class of statistics, labeled "inferential," is used to discriminate between empirical relationships that are reliable or systematic and those that are probably spurious or haphazard. These inferential statistics, such as the F-test, t-test, and chi-squared test, are based on assumptions about the relationships between the sample of subjects observed in the study and the potential population of subjects who might be sampled if the experimental program was repeated under essentially the same conditions. The sampling procedures employed in the present research provide an explicit definition of sample-population relationships that satisfies the restrictive assumptions for the significance tests applied. Furthermore, statutes governing jury service provide a definition of the population, juries in Massachusetts Superior Courts, to which conclusions should generalize. Some results obtained in the present experiment are systematic or reliable and should be observed in any representative sample of juries subjected to a similar experimental treatment. If an inferential statistic is deemed significant, it means that, based on assumptions about the sample-population relationship, the observed result would be obtained again if the experimental procedures were repeated.

By Hastie

243

The *F*-test is the most common inferential statistical procedure used in the present study. We will provide an example analysis of variance, including the calculation of several *F*-statistics, for the dependent variable measure of jury deliberation time. The average deliberation times in minutes for juries from each decision rule are ordered according to the strictness of the decision rule requirement from twelve-out-of-twelve to eight-out-of-twelve with times of 138, 103, and 75 minutes respectively (Table 4.1). To determine whether these differences among the means in the sample should be labeled significant and treated as reliable and worthy of theoretical or practical interpretation, it is necessary first to determine whether the mean values provide an acceptable descriptive summary by examining the distributions of the raw deliberation time data, separated into the three decision rule treatment groups. In the case of deliberation times, the distributions by experimental condition are reasonably well-behaved, or symmetric. For example, median values clearly match the respective mean values: 136 versus 138, 98 versus 103, and 61 versus 75 minutes. Furthermore, no distinctive subgroups of deliberation time values stand out from the others within any condition, with the possible exception of the relatively long times produced by hung juries. However, even the values for hung juries are "not off the scale", and they are obviously relevant to a general summary of jury behavior in terms of the deliberation time statistics.

Once the means are accepted as adequate descriptive statistics, inferential statistics can be calculated to evaluate differences between the treatment groups. In one type of significance test, an analysis of variance is performed on the deliberation time data from the sixty-nine experimental juries. A summary inferential statistic called a *F* is calculated to answer the question of whether the means from the three decision rule treatment groups, each including twenty-three juries, are reliably different. The larger the F-statistic, the more likely that the three means are reliably different.

It is a convention in scientific research to assign threshold significance levels to the F-statistics. If the assessed reliability of a difference exceeds the threshold, the difference is deemed significant and treated as supporting conclusions that assume the difference is true or repeatable. Again by convention, these significance levels are associated with probabilities rather than with the raw *F*-statistic, to allow comparisons across different types of test statistics. A common threshold value in psychological research is the $p < .05$ level of significance. Loosely speaking, the $p < .05$ label indicates, under the assumptions of the significance test, that the obtained differences would have appeared for unsystematic or haphazard reasons with a probability of less than 0.05. That is, if the jury study was repeated one hundred times and there was no true difference among the three means, statistical analysis would obtain a significance test value or F-statistic at least as extreme as the one obtained in only about five of the replications. All of this is a convoluted but precise way of saying that the lower the $p <$ value, the more reliable the result, namely a difference among means in the example analysis of deliberation time data.

In the present mock jury research dozens of inferential statistics were calculated to evaluate the reliability of results from many different types of data. The repeated calculation of inferential statistics from data in a single, albeit very large study can degrade the significance level threshold. In fact, when repeated test statistics are calculated, the probability of labeling some spurious differences reliable becomes quite large. The problem posed by these inflated rates of spurious differences, technically labeled Type I errors, is serious in research such as the present jury study in which many inferential statistics are reviewed and practical limits on funds and time preclude replication experiments. Several procedures were adopted in the present research to safeguard against unwarranted interpretation of spurious differences or relationships. First, the threshold significance level for acceptance of a difference as reliable is set at $p < .01$. This is a somewhat more stringent level than the usual $p < .05$ value, and it reduces the chances of Type I errors, although it increases the chances of not identifying a true difference, the so-called Type II error. Second, inferential statistics and associated error terms are displayed with most descriptive statistics. These values allow the reader to evaluate relationships of interest. Third, many relationships can be evaluated by checking for convergence across different measures available in the experiment itself or in other research. To the extent that a common pattern appears across related measures or similar conclusions are reached in related research, the reliability of the observed difference increases.

An analysis of variance was applied to many dependent variables in the present research (Table A). The general form of this analysis is illustrated by the deliberation time dependent variable with one observation provided by each of the sixty-

Table A. Analysis of deliberation time data (number of juries on which each mean is based is shown in parentheses).

Summary of means

	12/12	10/12	8/12	Mean	
Bill	150.4 (11)	101.6 (13)	62.9 (14)	101.5 (38)	$F(1,63) = 0.08$
					$p < 0.70$, $MS_e = 3096$
Joan	126.8 (13)	104.7 (10)	94.8 (9)	110.4 (31)	
Total	138.1 (23)	102.9 (23)	75.4 (23)		

Decision rule: $F(2,63) = 6.56$, $p < .003$, $MS_e = 3096$

Analysis of variance summary table

Source	Sum of squares	df	Mean square	F-statistic	p-value
Grand mean	770018.4	1	770018.4	248.74	0.0000
Decision rule	40593.0	2	20296.5	6.56	0.003
Coder	243.1	1	243.1	0.08	0.780
Decision rule X Coder interaction	8644.6	2	4322.3	1.40	0.255
Error term	195025.8	63	3095.6		

nine experimental juries. Each jury was classified according to two independent variables: decision rule, which had three levels, (twelve-out-of-twelve [23 juries], ten-out-of-twelve [23 juries], and eight-out-of-twelve [23 juries]); and coder (the researchers who converted the videotaped records of deliberation to the numerical codes), which had two levels (one person coding 38 juries and the other coding 31 juries). Wherever appropriate, the effect of the coder was included in statistical analyses. There were occasional main effects of the coder factor but virtually no interactions between coder and any other factors.

The mean values show one apparent relationship between decision rule and deliberation time, with longer times under stricter decision rules, but no other notable patterns. The analysis of variance supports this summary. The significance level associated with the main effect of decision rule is $F(2, 63) = 6.56$, $p < .003$, which is beyond the $p < .01$ threshold and establishes this empirical difference as reliable. In contrast, the main effect of the coder factor is $F(1, 63) = .08$, $p < .78$, which is not significant. Reports of the study's mean results generally include the important figures from the analysis of variance, usually in the righthand margin of the appropriate table.

Degrees of freedom in the analysis of variance will vary when certain values are not calculable, such as in analyses of dependent variables where there is missing data (e.g., jurors' reports of family income). The unequal n's for the coder independent variable also introduce complications in the numerical calculations underlying the reported figures. The error terms are based on a model that uses the interaction of the jury (replications factor treated as a random effect) with the highest order grouping of relevant fixed effects factors. Most statistics were calculated using the BMDP Biomedical Computer Programs 1977 software package (Dixon & Brown, 1977).

Bibliography

Abelson, R. P. Concepts for representing mundane reality in plans. In D. Bobrow & A. Collins, eds. *Representation and understanding: Studies in cognitive science.* New York: Academic Press, 1975.

Adkins, J. C. An art? A science? Or luck? *Trial,* Dec./Jan. 1968–1969, pp. 37–39.

Adler, F. Socioeconomic factors influencing jury verdicts. *N.Y.U. Review of Law and Social Change,* Winter 1973, pp. 1–10.

Adorno, T., Frenkel-Brunswik, E., Levinson, D., & Sanford, N. *The authoritarian personality.* New York: Harper, 1950.

American Bar Association. New Jersey experiments with six-man juries. *Bulletin of the Section of Judicial Administration of the ABA.* American Bar Association, May 1966.

Amsterdam, A. G., Segal, B. L., & Miller, M. K. *Trial manual for defense of criminal cases, III,* Student ed. Philadelphia: American Law Institute, 1974.

Anderson, J. R. *Cognitive psychology and its implications.* San Francisco: Freeman, 1980.

——— & Bower, G. H. *Human associative memory.* Washington, D.C.: Winston, 1973.

Anderson, N. H. Test of a model for opinion change. *Journal of Abnormal and Social Psychology,* 1959, 59, 371–381.

———. Information integration theory: A brief survey. In D. H. Krantz, R. C. Atkinson, R. D. Luce, & P. Suppes, eds. *Contemporary developments in mathematical psychology,* vol. 2. San Francisco: Freeman, 1974.

——— & Graesser, C. C. An information integration analysis of attitude change in group discussion. *Journal of Personality and Social Psychology,* 1976, 34 (2), 210–222.

Appleman, J. A. *Successful jury trials: A symposium.* Indianapolis: Bobbs-Merrill, 1952.

Arrow, K. J. *Social choice and individual values,* 2nd ed. New Haven: Yale University Press, 1963.

Asch, S. E. Studies of independence and conformity: I. A minority of one against a unanimous majority. *Psychological Monographs,* 1956, 70 (9), no. 416.

Austin, J. L. *How to do things with words.* Oxford: Oxford University Press, 1962.

Bailey, F. L., & Rothblatt, H. B. *Fundamentals of criminal advocacy.* New York: The Lawyers Co-operative, 1974.

Baldus, D. C., & Coles, J. W. L. Quantitative proof of intentional discrimination. *Evaluation Quarterly,* 1977, 1, 53–86.

Baldwin, J., & McConville, M. *Jury trials.* Oxford: Clarendon Press, 1979.

Bales, R. F. *Interaction process analysis: A method for the study of small groups.* Cambridge: Addison-Wesley, 1950.

―――. *Personality and interpersonal behavior.* New York: Holt, Rinehart, & Winston, 1970.

――― & Cohen, S. P. *Systematic multiple level observation of groups.* New York: Free Press, 1979.

Bandura, A., Ross, D., & Ross, S. Transmission of aggression through imitation of aggressive models. *Journal of Abnormal and Social Psychology,* 1961, *63,* 575–582.

Barksdale, H. C. *The use of survey research findings as legal evidence.* Pleasantville, N.Y.: Printers' Ink Books, 1957.

Barnlund, D. C. A comparative study of individual, majority, and group judgment. *Journal of Abnormal and Social Psychology,* 1959, *58,* 55–60.

Bartlett, F. C. *Remembering: A study in experimental and social psychology.* Cambridge: Cambridge University Press, 1932.

Begam, R. G. The attorneys. *Judicature,* 1977, *61,* 71, 76–78.

Beiser, E., & Varrin, R. Six-member juries in the federal courts. *Judicature,* 1975, *58,* 425–433.

Belli, M. M. *Modern trials.* Indianapolis: Bobbs-Merrill, 1954 (*Supplement,* 1966).

Bennett, W. L. Storytelling in criminal trials: A model of social judgment. *Quarterly Journal of Speech,* 1978, *64,* 1–22.

―――. Rhetorical transformation of evidence in criminal trials: Creating grounds for legal judgment. *The Quarterly Journal of Speech,* 1979, *65,* 311–323.

――― & Feldman, M. S. Justice and judgment in American culture. Paper, University of Washington, 1980.

Berg, K., & Vidmar, N. Authoritarianism and recall of evidence about criminal behavior. *Journal of Research in Personality,* 1975, *9,* 147–157.

Berk, R. A., Hennessy, M., & Swan, J. The vagaries and vulgarities of scientific jury selection: A methodological evaluation. *Evaluation Quarterly,* 1977, *1,* 143–158.

Berman, J., & Sales, B. D. A critical evaluation of the systematic approach to jury selection. *Criminal Justice and Behavior,* 1977, *4,* 219–240.

Bermant, G., & Coppock, R. Outcomes of six- and twelve-member jury trials: An analysis of 128 civil cases in the state of Washington. *Washington Law Review,* 1973, *48,* 593–596.

―――, McGuire, W., McKinley, W., & Salo, C. The logic of simulation in jury research. *Criminal Justice and Behavior,* 1974, *1,* 224–233.

Biskind, E. L. *How to prepare a case for trial.* New York: Prentice-Hall, 1954.

Black, D. *The theory of committees and elections.* Cambridge: Cambridge University Press, 1958.

Blackstone, W. Commentaries on the Laws of England of Public Wrongs. Boston: Beacon, 1962 (originally published in 1769).

Blalock, H. M. *Social statistics,* 2nd ed. rev. New York: McGraw-Hill, 1979.

Bodin, H. S. *Selecting a jury.* New York: Practicing Law Institute, 1954.

Boehm, V. Mr. Prejudice, Miss Sympathy and the authoritarian personality: An application of psychological measurement to the problem of jury bias. *Wisconsin Law Review*, 1968, pp. 734–750.

Bonora, B., & Krauss, E. *Jury work: Systematic techniques.* National Jury Project, 1979.

Borda, J-C. de. Memoire sur les elections au scrutin. *Histoire de l'Academie Royal des Sciences.* Paris, 1781.

Brams, S. J. *Game theory and politics.* New York: Free Press, 1975.

———— & Davis, M. D. Optimal jury selection: A game-theoretic model for the exercise of peremptory challenges. *Operations Research*, 1978, *26*, 966–991.

Bransford, J. B. *Human cognition.* Belmont, Cal.: Wadsworth, 1979.

Bray, R. M. *Decision rules, attitude similarity, and jury decision making.* Unpublished doctoral dissertation, University of Illinois, 1974.

———— & Kerr, N. L. Methodological considerations in the study of the psychology of the courtroom. In N. L. Kerr & R. M. Bray, eds. *The psychology of the courtroom.* New York: Academic Press, 1982.

———— & Noble, A. M. Authoritarianism and decisions of mock juries: Evidence of jury bias and group polarization. *Journal of Personality and Social Psychology*, 1978, *36*, 1424–1430.

———— & Struckman-Johnson, C. Effects of juror population, assigned decision rule, and insurance option on decisions of simulated juries. Paper presented at American Psychological Association meeting, San Francisco, Aug. 1977.

————, Struckman-Johnson, C., Osborne, M. D., McFarlane, J. B., & Scott, J. The effects of defendant status on the decisions of student and community juries. *Social Psychology*, 1978, *41*, 256–260.

Broadbent, D. E. *In defense of empirical psychology.* London: Methuen, 1973.

Broeder, D. W. The University of Chicago jury project. *Nebraska Law Review*, 1958, *38*, 744–761.

————. Previous jury trial service affecting juror behavior. *Insurance Law Journal*, Mar. 1965, pp. 138–143.

Bronson, E. J. On the conviction proneness and representativeness of the death-qualified jury: An empirical study of Colorado veniremen. *University of Colorado Law Review*, 1970, *42*, 1–32.

————. Does the exclusion of scrupled jurors in capital cases make the jury more likely to convict? Some evidence from California. *Woodrow Wilson Journal of Law*, 1980, *3*, 11–34.

Brown, R. D. Emotional expression, interpersonal attraction, and rejection of a deviate. *Dissertation Abstracts International*, 1970, *31*, 3365-A. University Microfilms No. 70-26, 849.

Buckhout, R. *Jury without peers* (CR-2). Brooklyn: Center for Responsive Psychology, 1973.

————, Licker, J., Alexander, M., Gambardella, J., Eugenio, P., & Kakoullis, B. Discretion in jury selection. In L. E. Abt & I. R. Stuart, eds. *Social psychology and discretionary law.* New York: Van Nostrand Reinhold, 1979.

————, Weg, S., Reilly, F., & Frohboese, R. Jury verdicts: Comparison of 6- vs. 12-person juries and unanimous vs. majority decision rule in a murder trial. *Bulletin of the Psychonomic Society*, 1977, *10*, 175–178.

Bullock, H. Significance of the racial factor in the length of prison sentences. *Journal of Criminal Law, Crimonology and Police Science*, 1961, *52*, 411–417.

Burnstein, E. Persuasion as argument processing. In H. Brandstatter, J. H. Davis, and G. Stocker-Kreichgauer, eds. *Group decision making.* New York: Academic Press, 1982.

———— & Vinokur, A. Persuasive argumentation and social comparison as determinants of attitude polarization. *Journal of Experimental Social Psychology*, 1977, *13*, 315–332.

Calhoun, L. G., Selby, J. W., & Warring, L. J. Social perception of the victim's causal role in rape: An exploratory examination of four factors. *Human Relations*, 1976, *29*, 517–526.

Campbell, D. T., & Stanley, J. C. *Experimental and quasi-experimental designs for research.* Chicago: Rand McNally, 1963.

Campbell, S. The multiple function of the criminal defense voir dire in Texas. *American Journal of Criminal Law*, 1972, *1*, 255–282.

Cartwright, D. Risk taking by individuals and groups: An assessment of research employing choice dilemmas. *Journal of Personality and Social Psychology*, 1971, *20*, 361–378.

Center for Jury Studies. Short terms vs. the seasoned juror. *Center for Jury Studies Newsletter*, 1981a, *3* (3), 2–4.

————. Nonunanimous verdicts by states. *Center for Jury Studies Newsletter*, 1981b, *3* (6), 7.

Chaberski, G. Inside the New York Panther trial. *Civil Liberties Review*, 1973, *1*, 111–155.

Clark, R. D., III. Group-induced shift toward risk: A critical appraisal. *Psychological Bulletin*, 1971, *76*, 251–270.

Cohen, J. Factors of resistance to the resources of the behavioral sciences. *Journal of Legal Education*, 1959, *12*, 67–70.

————. A coefficient of agreement for nominal scales. *Educational and Psychological Measurement*, 1960, *20*, 37–46.

————. Weighted kappa: Nominal scale agreement with provision for scaled disagreement or partial credit. *Psychological Bulletin*, 1968, *70*, 213–220.

———— & Cohen, P. *Applied multiple regression/correlation analysis for the behavioral sciences.* New York: Wiley, 1975.

Cohen, L. J. *The probable and the provable.* Oxford: Clarendon Press, 1977.

Cohen, M. R., & Nagel, E. *An introduction to logic and scientific method.* New York: Harcourt Brace, 1934.

Colasanto, D., & Sanders, J. From laboratory to jury room: A review of experiments on jury decision-making. Paper, University of Michigan, 1976.

————. Methodological issues in simulated jury research. Paper, University of Michigan, 1978.

Collingwood, R. G. *An essay on metaphysics.* Oxford: Clarendon Press, 1940.

Condorcet, M. de. *Essai sur l'application de l'analyse à la probabilité des decisions rendues à la pluralité des voix.* Paris, 1785.

Cook, S. W. Social science and school desegregation: Did we mislead the Supreme Court? *Personality and Social Psychology Bulletin*, 1979, *5*, 420–437.

Cook, T. D., & Campbell, D. T. *Quasi-experimentation: Design and analysis issues for field research.* New York: Houghton-Mifflin, 1979.

Coombs, C. H. Thurstone's measurement of social values revisited forty years later. *Journal of Abnormal and Social Psychology,* 1967, *6,* 85–91.

Cornelius, A. L. *Trial Tactics.* New York: Bender, 1932.

Criswell, J., Solomon, H., & Suppes, P. *Mathematical methods in small group processes.* Stanford: Stanford University Press, 1962.

Cronback, L. J., Gleser, G. C., Nanda, H., & Rajaratnam, N. *The dependability of behavioral measurements.* New York: Wiley, 1972.

Cronin, P. M. Six-member juries in district courts. *Boston Bar Journal,* 1958, p. 27.

Crowder, R. G. *Principles of learning and memory.* Hillsdale, N.J.: Erlbaum, 1976.

Darrow, C. Attorney for the defense. *Esquire Magazine,* May 1936. Reprinted in *California Trial Lawyers Journal,* 1974–1975.

Davis, B. E., & Wiley, R. E. Thoughts on jury selection. *Journal of the Bar Association of the District of Columbia,* 1967, *34,* 15–20.

Davis, J. H. *Group performance.* New York: Addison-Wesley, 1969a.

————. Individual-group problem solving, subject preference, and problem type. *Journal of Personality and Social Psychology,* 1969b, *13* (4), 362–374.

————. Group decision and social interaction: A theory of social decision schemes. *Psychological Review,* 1973, *80,* 97–125.

————. Group decision and procedural justice. In M. Fishbein, ed. *Progress in Social Psychology,* vol. 1. Hillsdale, N.J.: Erlbaum, 1980.

————, Bray, R. M., & Holt, R. W. The empirical study of social decision processes in juries. In J. Tapp, & F. Levine, eds. *Law, justice, and the individual in society: Psychological and legal issues.* New York: Holt, Rinehart, & Winston, 1977.

————, Kerr, N. L., Atkin, R. S., Holt, R., & Meek, D. The decision processes of 6- and 12-person mock juries assigned unanimous and two-thirds majority rules. *Journal of Personality and Social Psychology,* 1975, *32,* 1–14.

————, Kerr, N. L., Stasser, G., Meek, D., & Holt, R. Victim consequences, sentence severity, and the decision processes in mock juries. *Organizational Behavior and Human Performance,* 1977, *18,* 346–365.

———— & Restle, F. The analysis of problems and prediction of group problem solving. *Journal of Abnormal and Social Psychology,* 1963, *66,* 103–116.

————, Stasser, G., Spitzer, C. E., & Holt, R. W. Changes in group members' decision preferences during discussion: An illustration with mock juries. *Journal of Personality and Social Psychology,* 1976, *34,* 1177–1187.

Dawes, R. M. The mind, the model, and the task. In F. Restle, R. M. Shiffrin, N. J. Castellan, H. R. Lindman, & D. B. Pisoni, eds. *Cognitive Theory,* vol. 1. Hillsdale, N.J.: Erlbaum, 1975.

Deutsch, M., & Gerard, H. B. A study of normative and informational social influences upon individual judgment. *Journal of Abnormal and Social Psychology,* 1955, *51,* 621–636.

Diamond, S. S. A jury experiment reanalyzed. *University of Michigan Journal of Law Reform,* 1974, *7,* 520–535.

DiMona, J. The real surprise of the Mitchell-Stans trial. *New York,* July 8, 1974, pp. 31–37.

Dixon, W. J., & Brown, M. B. *Biomedical computer programs, P-series.* Berkeley: University of California Press, 1977.

——— & Massey, F. J. *Introduction to statistical analysis.* New York: McGraw-Hill, 1969.

Donovan, J. *Modern jury trials and advocates.* 1887.

Duncan, O. D. A socioeconomic index for all occupations. In A. J. Reiss, ed. *Occupations and social status.* New York: The Free Press, 1961.

Efran, M. G. The effect of physical appearance on the judgment of guilt, interpersonal attraction, and severity of recommended punishment in a simulated jury task. *Journal of Research in Personality,* 1974, *8,* 45–54.

Einhorn, H. J., Hogarth, R. M., & Klempner, E. Quality of group judgment. *Psychological Bulletin,* 1977, *84,* 158–172.

Eisen, S. V., & McArthur, L. Z. Evaluating and sentencing a defendant as a function of his salience and the perceiver's set. *Personality and Social Psychology Bulletin,* 1979, *5,* 48–52.

Ellsworth, P. C. From abstract ideas to concrete instances: Some guidelines for choosing natural research settings. *American Psychologist,* 1977, *32,* 304–309.

——— & Fitzgerald, R. Due process vs. crime control: The impact of death qualification on jury attitudes. *Law and Human Behavior,* 1983, in press.

——— & Getman, J. G. Social science in legal decision making. In L. Lipson & S. Wheeler, eds. *Handbook of law and social science.* New York: Russell Sage Foundation, in press.

———, Thompson, W., & Cowan, C. Juror attitudes and conviction proneness: The relationship between attitudes towards the death penalty and predisposition to convict. *Law and Human Behavior,* 1983, in press.

Eron, L. D. Parent-child interaction, television violence, and aggression in children. *American Psychologist,* 1982, *37,* 197–211.

Estes, W. K. *Learning theory and mental development.* New York: Academic Press, 1970.

———. The information-processing approach to cognition: A confluence of metaphors and methods. In W. K. Estes, ed. *Handbook of learning and cognitive processes,* vol. 5. Hillsdale, N.J.: Erlbaum, 1978.

Etzioni, A. Creating an imbalance. *Trial,* Nov./Dec. 1974, pp. 28, 30.

Fairley, W. B., & Mosteller, F. *Statistics and public policy.* Reading, Mass.: Addison-Wesley, 1977.

Farmer, L. C., Williams, G. R., Cundick, B. P., Howell, R. J., Lee, R. E., & Rooker, C. K. Juror perceptions of trial testimony as a function of the method of presentation. In G. Bermant, C. Nemeth, & N. Vidmar, eds. *Psychology and the law.* Lexington, Mass.: Lexington Books, 1975.

———. The effect of the method of presenting trial testimony on juror decisional processes. In B. D. Sales, ed. *Psychology in the legal process.* New York: Spectrum, 1977.

Farquharson, R. *Theory of voting.* New Haven: Yale University Press, 1969.

Faust, W. L. Group versus individual problem-solving. *Journal of Abnormal and Social Psychology*, 1959, *59*, 68–72.

Feild, H. S. Juror background characteristics and attitudes toward rape. *Law and Human Behavior*, 1978, *2*, 73–93.

Fishburn, P. C. Voter concordance, simple majorities, and group decision methods. *Behavioral Science*, 1973, *19* (3), 166–176.

Forsyth, W. *History of trial by jury*. London, 1852.

Foss, R. D. Group decision processes in the simulated trial jury. *Sociometry*, 1976, *39*, 305–316.

———. Structural effects in simulated jury decision making. *Journal of Personality and Social Psychology*, 1981, *40*, 1055–1062.

Friedman, H. Trial by jury: Criteria for convictions, jury size, and Type I and Type II errors. *American Statistician*, 1972, *26*, 21–23.

——— & Shaver, K. The effect of jury deliberations and decisions in mock criminal cases of six- and twelve-member juries and of unanimous and non-unanimous verdict requirements. Paper, College of William and Mary, 1975.

Garner, W. R., Hake, H. W., & Eriksen, C. W. Operationism and the concept of perception. *Psychological Review*, 1956, *63*, 149–159.

Gelfand, A. E., & Solomon, H. A study of Poisson's models for jury verdicts in criminal and civil trials. *Journal of the American Statistical Association*, 1973, *68*, 241–278.

———. Modeling jury verdicts in the American legal system. *Journal of the American Statistical Association*, 1974, *69*, 32–37.

———. Analyzing the decision-making process of the American jury. *Journal of the American Statistical Association*, 1975, *70*, 305–309.

Gerbasi, K. C., Zuckerman, M., & Reis, H. T. Justice needs a new blindfold: A review of mock jury research. *Psychological Bulletin*, 1977, *84*, 323–345.

Ginger, A. F. *Jury Selection in Criminal Trials*. Tiburon, Cal.: Lawpress, 1975.

Glass, G. V. Analysis of data on the Connecticut speeding crackdown as a time-series quasi-experiment. *Law and Society Review*, 1968, *3*, 55–76.

Godwin, W. F., & Restle, F. The road to agreement: Subgroup pressures in small group consensus processes. *Journal of Personality and Social Psychology*, 1974, *30*, 500–509.

Goldberg, F. Toward expansion of Witherspoon: Capital scruples, jury bias, and the use of psychological data to raise presumption in the law. *Harvard Civil Rights and Civil Liberties Law Review*, 1970, *5*, 53–69.

Goldstein, I. *Trial technique*. Chicago: Callaghan, 1935.

Goodman, N. *Fact, fiction, and forecast*, 2nd ed. Indianapolis: Bobbs-Merrill, 1965.

Gray, D. B., & Ashmore, R. D. Biasing influence of defendants' characteristics on simulated sentencing. *Psychological Reports*, 1976, *38*, 727–738.

Green, E. Inter- and intra-racial crime relative to sentencing. *Journal of Criminal Law, Criminology, and Police Science*, 1964, *55*, 348–358.

———. The reasonable man: Legal fiction or psychosocial reality? *Law and Society Review*, 1967, *2*, 241–257.

Green, S. G., & Taber, T. D. The effects of three social decision schemes on decision group process. *Organizational Behavior and Human Performance*, 1980, 25, 97–106.

Grice, H. P. Utterance meaning, sentence meaning, and word meaning. *Foundations of Language*, 1968, 4, 225–242.

———. Logic and conversation. In P. Cole & J. L. Morgan, eds. *Syntax and semantics*, vol. 3. New York: Academic Press, 1975.

Griffit, W., & Jackson, T. Simulated jury decisions: The influence of jury-defendant attitude similarity-dissimilarity. *Social Behavior and Personality*, 1973, 1, 1–7.

Grofman, B. Not necessarily twelve and not necessarily unanimous. In G. Bermant & N. Vidmar, eds. *Psychology and the law*. Lexington, Mass.: Heath, 1976.

———. The slippery slope: Jury size and jury verdict requirements—legal and social science approaches. *Law and Policy Quarterly*, 1980, 2, 285–304.

———. Mathematical models of juror and jury decision making: The state of the art. *Perspectives on law and psychology, Vol. 2: The judicial process*. New York: Pergammon Press, 1981.

Gurnee, H. A comparison of collective and individual judgments of facts. *Journal of Experimental Psychology*, 1937a, 21, 106–112.

———. Maze learning in the collective situation. *Journal of Psychology*, 1937b, 3, 437–443.

Hacking, I. *Logic of statistical inference*. Cambridge: Cambridge University Press, 1965.

Hackman, J. R., & Morris, C. G. Group tasks, group interaction process, and group performance effectiveness: A review and proposed integration. In L. Berkowitz, ed. *Advances in experimental social psychology*, vol. 8. New York: Academic Press, 1975.

Hagan, J. Extra-legal attributes and criminal sentencing: An assessment from a sociological viewpoint. *Law and Society Review*, 1974, 8, 357–383.

Hamilton, V. L. Obedience and responsibility: A jury simulation. *Journal of Personality and Social Psychology*, 1978, 36, 126–146.

Hans, V. P. The effects of the unanimity requirement on group decision processes in simulated juries. Doctoral dissertation, University of Toronto, 1978.

——— & Doob, A. N. S.12 of the Canada evidence act and the deliberation of simulated juries. *Criminal Law Quarterly*, 1976, 18, 235–253.

Hare, A. P. *Handbook of small group research*, 2nd ed. New York: The Free Press, 1976.

Harrington, D. C., & Dempsey, J. Psychological factors in jury selection. *Tennessee Law Review*, 1969, 37, 173–178.

Harris, Louis, & Associates. *Report of 1971 national survey*. New York: Louis Harris and Associates, 1971.

Hartwick, J., Sheppard, B. H., & Davis, J. H. Group remembering: Research and implications. In R. Guzzo, ed. *Improving group decision making in organizations: Working from theory*. New York: Academic Press, 1982.

Hastie, R. An empirical evaluation of five methods of instructing the jury. Paper, Northwestern University, 1982.

Hawkins, C. H. Interaction and coalition realignments in consensus-seeking groups: A study of experimental jury deliberations. Doctoral dissertation, The University of Chicago, 1960.

———. Interaction rates of jurors aligned in factions. *American Sociological Review*, 1962, *27*, 689–691.

Hensley, V., & Duval, S. Some perceptual determinants of perceived similarity, liking, and correctness. *Journal of Personality and Social Psychology*, 1976, *34*, 159–168.

Herbsleb, J. D., Sales, B. D., & Berman, J. J. When psychologists aid in voir dire: Legal and ethical considerations. In L. E. Abt & I. R. Stuart, eds. *The social psychology of discretionary law*. New York: Van Nostrand Reinhold, 1978.

Hermann, P. J. Occupations of jurors as an influence on their verdict. *Forum*, 1969–1970, *5*, 150–155.

Heyl, C. W. Selection of the jury. *Illinois Bar Journal*, 1952, *40*, 328–341.

Hoffman, L. R. Group problem solving. In L. Berkowitz, ed. *Advances in experimental social psychology*, vol. 2. New York: Academic Press, 1965.

———, ed. *The group problem solving process: Studies of a valence model*. New York: Praeger, 1979.

——— & Maier, N. R. F. Valence in the adoption of solutions by problem-solving groups: Concept, method, and results. *Journal of Abnormal and Social Psychology*, 1964, *69*, 264–271.

———. Valence in the adoption of solutions by problem-solving groups: II. Quality and acceptance as goals of leaders and members. *Journal of Personality and Social Psychology*, 1967, *6* (2), 175–182.

Hogarth, R. M. A note on aggregating opinions. *Organizational Behavior and Human Performance*, 1978, *21*, 40–46.

———. *Judgement and choice*. New York: Wiley, 1980.

Hoiberg, B., & Stires, L. The effect of several types of pre-trial publicity on the guilt attributions of simulated jurors. *Journal of Applied Social Psychology*, 1973, *3*, 267–275.

Holdsworth, W. S. *A history of the English law*. London: Methuen, 1956.

Institute for Judicial Administration (IJA). *A comparison of six- and twelve-member juries in New Jersey superior and county courts*. New York: IJA, 1972.

James, R. Status and competence of jurors. *American Journal of Sociology*, 1959, *64*, 563–570.

Janis, I. L., & Mann, L. *Decision making*. New York: Free Press, 1977.

Jones, C., & Aronson, E. Attribution of fault to a rape victim as a function of respectability of the victim. *Journal of Personality and Social Psychology*, 1973, *26*, 415–419.

Jurow, G. L. New data on the effect of a "death qualified" jury on the guilt determination process. *Harvard Law Review*, 1971, *84*, 567–611.

Kadane, J. B., Kairys, D. Fair numbers of peremptory challenges in jury trials. *Journal of the American Statistical Association*, 1979, *74*, 747–753.

——— & Lewis, G. H. The distribution of participation in group discussions: An empirical and theoretical reappraisal. *American Sociological Review*, 1969, *34* (5), 710–723.

Kairys, D., Schulman, J., & Harring, S., eds. *The jury system: New methods for reducing prejudice.* Philadelphia: National Jury Project and National Lawyers Guild, 1975.

Kalven, H. The quest for the middle range: Empirical inquiry and legal policy. In G. Hazard, ed. *Law in a changing America.* Englewood Cliffs, N.J.: Prentice-Hall, 1968.

―――. Memorandum regarding jury system. *Hearings on the recordings of jury deliberations before the Subcommittee on Internal Security of Senate Judiciary Committee,* 84th Congress, vol. 48, pp. 63–81.

――― & Zeisel, H. *The American jury.* Boston: Little, Brown, 1966.

Kaplan, J. *Criminal justice: Introductory cases and materials.* Mineola, N.Y.: Foundation Press, 1978.

Kaplan, M. F. Information integration in social judgment: Interaction of judge and informational components. In M. F. Kaplan & S. Schwartz, eds. *Human judgment and decision processes.* New York: Academic Press, 1975.

―――. Judgment by juries. In M. F. Kaplan & S. Schwartz, eds. *Human judgment and decision processes in applied settings.* New York: Academic Press, 1977.

――― & Kemmerick, G. D. Juror judgment as information integration: Combining evidential and nonevidential information. *Journal of Personality and Social Psychology,* 1974, *30,* 493–499.

――― & Miller, L. E. Reducing the effects of juror bias. *Journal of Personality and Social Psychology,* 1978, *36,* 1443–1455.

――― & Schersching, C. Reducing juror bias: An experimental approach. In M. Lipsitt & B. D. Sales, eds. *New directions in psycholegal research.* New York: Van Nostrand Reinhold, 1980.

―――, Steindorf, J., & Iervolino, A. Courtrooms, politics, and morality: Toward a theoretical integration. *Personality and Social Psychology Bulletin,* 1978, *4,* 155–160.

Karcher, J. T. The importance of the voir dire. *Practical Lawyer,* 1969, *15,* 59–66.

Katz, J. *Experimentation with human beings.* New York: Russell Sage, 1972.

Katz, J. J. *Propositional structure and illocutionary force.* New York: Crowell, 1977.

Katz, L. S. The twelve man jury. *Trial,* Dec./Jan. 1968–1969, pp. 39–40, 42.

Kauffman, R. A., & Ryckman, R. M. Effects of locus-of-control, outcome severity, and attitudinal similarity of defendant on attributions of criminal responsibility. *Personality and Social Psychology Bulletin,* 1979, *5,* 340–343.

Keeton, R. E. *Trial tactics and methods.* Boston: Little, Brown, 1973.

Kennebeck, E. *Juror number four.* New York: Norton, 1973.

Kenny, D. A. *Correlation and causality.* New York: Wiley, 1979.

Kerlinger, F. N., & Pedhazur, E. J. *Multiple regression in behavioral research.* New York: Holt, Rinehart, & Winston, 1973.

Kerr, N. L. Severity of prescribed penalty and mock jurors' verdicts. *Journal of Personality and Social Psychology,* 1978, *36,* 1431–1442.

―――. Effects of prior juror experience on juror behavior. Paper presented at Annual Meeting of the Law and Society Association, Madison, Wis., June 1980.

————. Social transition schemes: Charting the group's road to agreement. *Journal of Personality and Social Psychology*, 1981, *41*, 684–702.

————, Atkin, R., Stasser, G., Meek, D., Holt, R., & Davis, J. Guilt beyond a reasonable doubt: Effects of concept definition and assigned rule on the judgments of mock jurors. *Journal of Personality and Social Psychology*, 1976, *34*, 282–294.

————, Nerenz, D. R., & Herrick, D. Role playing and the study of jury behavior. *Sociological Methods & Research*, 1979, *7*, 337–355.

————, Stasser, G., & Davis, J. H. Model-testing, model-fitting, and social decision schemes. *Organizational Behavior and Human Performance*, 1979, *23*, 399–410.

Kessler, J. An empirical study of six- and twelve-member jury decision-making processes. *University of Michigan Journal of Law Reform*, 1973, *6*, 712–734.

Kiesler, D. J. *The process of psychotherapy: Empirical foundations and systems of analysis.* Chicago: Aldine, 1973.

Kintsch, W. *The representation of meaning in memory.* Hillsdale, N.J.: Erlbaum, 1974.

Klevorick, A. K., & Rothschild, M. A model of the jury decision process. *Journal of Legal Studies*, 1979 (8), 141–164.

Klugman, S. F. Group and individual judgments for anticipated events. *Journal of Social Psychology*, 1947, *26*, 21–33.

Kolmogoroff, A. *Grundbegriffe der Wahrscheinlichkeitsrechnung.* Berlin: Springer, 1933. Trans. in N. Morrison. *Foundations of the theory of probability.* New York: Chelsea, 1956.

Kosslyn, S. M. *Image and mind.* Cambridge: Harvard University Press, 1980.

Krantz, D. H., Luce, R. D., Suppes, P., & Tversky, A. *Foundations of measurement*, vol. 1. New York: Academic Press, 1971.

Kuhn, D., Pennington, N., & Leadbeater, B. Adult thinking in developmental perspective. In P. Baltes & O. Brim, eds. *Life-span development and behavior*, vol. 5. New York: Academic Press, 1983.

Latane, B. The psychology of social impact. *American Psychologist*, 1981, *36*, 343–356.

———— & Wolf, S. The social impact of majorities and minorities. *Psychological Review*, 1981, *88*, 438–453.

Laughlin, P. R., McGlynn, R. P., Anderson, J. A., & Jacobson, E. S. Concept attainment by individuals versus cooperative pairs as a function of memory, sex, and concept rule. *Journal of Personality and Social Psychology*, 1968, *8*, 410–417.

Lempert, R. O. Uncovering "nondiscernible" differences: Empirical research and the jury-size cases. *Michigan Law Review*, 1975, *73*, 643–708.

Levine, J. M. Reaction to opinion deviance in small groups. In P. B. Paulus, ed. *Psychology of group influence.* Hillsdale, N.J.: Erlbaum, 1980.

———— & Ranelli, C. J. Majority reaction to shifting and stable attitudinal deviates. *European Journal of Social Psychology*, 1978, *8*, 55–70.

Levine, M. E., & Plott, C. R. Agenda influence and its implications. *Virginia Law Review*, 1977, *63*, 561–604.

Loftus, E. F. *Eyewitness testimony.* Cambridge: Harvard University Press, 1979.

───── & Monahan, J. Trial by data: Psychological research as legal evidence. *American Psychologist*, 1980, *35*, 270–283.

Lorge, I., Fox, D., Davitz, Z., & Brenner, M. A survey of studies contrasting the quality of group performance and individual performance, 1920–1957. *Psychological Bulletin*, 1958, *55*, 337–372.

Maier, N. R. F., & Solem, A. R. The contribution of a discussion leader to the quality of group thinking: The effective use of minority opinions. *Human Relations*, 1952, *5*, 277–288.

Marshall, C. R., & Wise, J. A. Juror decisions and the determination of guilt in capital punishment cases: A Bayesian perspective. In D. Wendt & C. Vlek, eds. *Utility, probability, and human decision making*. Dordrecht, Holland: Reidel, 1975.

Marvell, T. B. Appellate courts and the adversary system: Information gathering and appellate decision making. Doctoral dissertation, University of Michigan, 1976.

McConahay, J. B., Mullin, C. J., & Frederick, J. The uses of social science in trials with political overtones: The trial of Joan Little. *Law and Contemporary Problems*, 1977, *41*, 205–229.

McCready, J. C. Challenging jurors. *Dickinson Law Review*, 1954, *58*, 384–386.

McCurdy, H. G., & Lambert, W. E. The efficiency of small human groups in the solution problems requiring genuine cooperation. *Journal of Personality*, 1952, *20*, 478–494.

McGuire, W. J. The nature of attitudes and attitude change. In G. Lindzey & E. Aronson, eds. *The handbook of social psychology*, vol. 3, 2nd ed. Reading, Mass.: Addison-Wesley, 1969.

Meehl, P. E. Law and the fireside inductions: Some reflections of a clinical psychologist. *Journal of Social Issues*, 1971, *27*, 65–100.

───── & Rosen, A. Antecedent probability and the efficiency of psychometric signs, patterns, or cutting scores. *Psychological Bulletin*, 1955, *52*, 194–216.

Miller, G. R. Juror's responses to videotaped trial materials: Some recent findings. *Personality and Social Psychology Bulletin*, 1975, *1*, 561–564.

─────, Bender, D. C., Foster, F., Florence, B. T., Fontes, N., Hocking, J., & Nicholson, H. The effects of videotape testimony in jury trials. *Brigham Young University Law Review*, 1975, pp. 331–373.

───── & Fontes, N. E. *Videotape on trial: A view from the jury box*. Beverly Hills: Sage Publications, 1979.

Miller, M., & Hewitt, J. Conviction of a defendant as a function of juror-victim racial similarity. *Journal of Social Psychology*, 1978, *105*, 159–160.

Mills, L. R. Six- and twelve-member juries: An empirical study of trial results. *University of Michigan Journal of Law Reform*, 1973, *6*, 671–711.

Minsky, M. A framework for representing knowledge. In P. H. Winston, ed. *The psychology of computer vision*. New York: McGraw-Hill, 1975.

Mischel, W. *Personality and assessment*. New York: Wiley, 1968.

Mitchell, H. E., & Byrne, D. The defendant's dilemma: Effects of jurors' attitudes and authoritarianism. *Journal of Personality and Social Psychology*, 1973, *25*, 123–129.

Mitchell, S. K. Interobserver agreement, reliability, and generalizability of data collected in observational studies. *Psychological Bulletin,* 1979, *86,* 376–390.

Morrison, D. E., & Henkel, R. E. *The significance test controversy.* Chicago: Aldine, 1970.

Moscovici, S. *Social influence and social change.* London: Academic Press, 1976.

Mosteller, F., & Tukey, J. W. *Data analysis and regression.* Reading, Mass.: Addison-Wesley, 1977.

Myers, D. G. Polarizing effects of social interaction. In H. Brandstatter, J. H. Davis, and G. Stocker-Kreichgauer, eds. *Group decision making.* New York: Academic Press, 1982.

—————— & Kaplan, M. F. Group-induced polarization in simulated juries. Paper presented at American Psychological Association annual convention, 1976.

—————— & Lamm, H. The group polarization phenomenon. *Psychological Bulletin,* 1976, *83,* 602–627.

Nagao, D. H., & Davis, J. H. The effects of prior experience on mock juror case judgments. *Social Psychology Quarterly,* 1980a, *43,* 190–199.

——————. The implications of temporal drift in social parameters. *Journal of Experimental Social Psychology,* 1980b, *16,* 479–498.

Nagel, S. S., & Neef, M. Deductive modeling to determine an optimum jury size and fraction required to convict. *Washington University Law Quarterly,* 1975, *58,* 933–978.

Nemeth, C. Rules governing jury deliberations: A consideration of recent changes. In G. Bermant & N. Vidmar, eds. *Psychology and the law: Recent frontiers.* Lexington, Mass.: Heath, 1976.

——————. Interactions between jurors as a function of majority vs. unanimity decision rules. *Journal of Applied Psychology,* 1977, *7,* 38–56.

——————. Jury trials: Psychology and law. In L. Berkowitz, ed. *Advances in experimental social psychology,* vol. 14. New York: Academic Press, 1981.

——————, Endicott, J., & Wachtler, J. From the '50's to the '70's: Women in jury deliberations. *Sociometry,* 1977, *39,* 292–304.

—————— & Sosis, R. A simulated jury study: Characteristics of the defendants and the jurors. *Journal of Social Psychology,* 1973, *90,* 221–229.

Newell, A., & Simon, H. A. *Human problem solving.* Englewood Cliffs, N.J.: Prentice-Hall, 1972.

Note. Six-member juries tried in Massachusetts District Court. *Journal of the American Judicial Society,* 1958, *42,* 136.

Olson, P., & Davis, J. H. Divisible tasks and pooling performance in groups. *Psychological Reports,* 1964, *15,* 511–517.

Ostrom, T. M., Werner, C., & Saks, M. J. An integration theory analysis of jurors' presumptions of guilt or innocence. *Journal of Personality and Social Psychology,* 1978, *36,* 436–450.

Padawer-Singer, A. M. Justice or judgments. In *The American jury system* (Final Report of the Annual Chief Justice Earl Warren Conference on Advocacy in the United States). Cambridge: The Roscoe Pound-American Trial Lawyers Foundation, 1977.

—————— & Barton, A. H. *Interim report: Experimental study of decision making in*

the 12- versus 6-man jury under unanimous versus non-unanimous decisions.
New York: Columbia University, Bureau of Applied Social Research, 1975.

———, Singer, A. N., & Singer, R. L. J. An experimental study of twelve vs. six member juries under unanimous vs. nonunanimous decisions. In B. D. Sales, ed. *Psychology in the legal process.* New York: Spectrum, 1977.

Pennington, N. Causal reasoning and decision making: The case of juror decisions. Doctoral dissertation, Harvard University, 1981.

——— & Hastie, R. Representation and inference in juror reasoning: Two illustrative analyses. Paper presented at meeting of the Cognitive Science Society, New Haven, June 1980.

———. Juror decision-making models: The generalization gap. *Psychological Bulletin,* 1981a, *89,* 246–287.

———. Juror decision making: Story structure and verdict choice. Paper presented at meeting of the American Psychological Association, Los Angeles, 1981b.

Penrod, S. D. Study of attorney and "scientific" jury selection models. Doctoral dissertation, Harvard University, 1979.

——— & Hastie, R. Models of jury decision making: A critical review. *Psychological Bulletin,* 1979, *86,* 462–492.

——— & Hastie, R. A computer simulation of jury decision making. *Psychological Review,* 1980, *87,* 133–159.

———, Rosenblum, S., Stefek, D., & Hastie, R. Optimal jury selection. Paper, Harvard University, 1979.

Phillips, J. A jury of six in all cases. *Connecticut Bar Journal,* 1956, *30,* 354–365.

Plott, C. R., & Levine, M. E. A model of agenda influence on committee decisions. *The American Economic Review,* 1978, *68,* 146–160.

Plutchik, R., & Schwartz, A. K. Jury selection: Folklore or science? *Criminal Law Bulletin,* 1965, *1,* (4), 3–10.

Pollock, R., & Maitland, F. *History of English law before the reign of Edward I.* Cambridge: Cambridge University Press, 1895.

Pruitt, D. G. Choice shifts in group discussion: An introductory review. *Journal of Personality and Social Psychology,* 1971a, *20,* 339–360.

———. Conclusions: Toward an understanding of choice shifts in group discussion. *Journal of Personality and Social Psychology,* 1971b, *20,* 495–510.

Reed, J. Jury deliberation, voting and verdict trends. *Southwest Social Science Quarterly,* 1965, *45,* 361–370.

Richey, M. H., & Fichter, J. J. Sex differences in moralism and punitiveness. *Psychonomic Science,* 1969, *16,* 185–186.

Rose, A., & Prell, A. Does the punishment fit the crime? A study in social valuation. *American Journal of Sociology,* 1955, *61,* 247–259.

Rosen, P. *The Supreme Court and Social Science.* Urbana: University of Illinois Press, 1972.

Rosenblum, V. G. Report on the uses of social science in judicial decision making. Paper, Northwestern University, 1979.

Roth, A., Kadane, J. B., & DeGroot, M. H. Optimal peremptory challenges in trials by juries: A bilaterial sequential process. *Operations Research*, 1977, *25*, 901–919.

Rumsey, M. G., & Rumsey, J. M. A case of rape: Sentencing judgments of males and females. *Psychological Reports*, 1977, *41*, 459–465.

Russell, R. L., & Stiles, W. B. Categories for classifying language in psychotherapy. *Psychological Bulletin*, 1979, *86*, 404–419.

Sage, W. Psychology and the Angela Davis jury. *Human Behavior*, Jan. 1973, pp. 56–61.

Saks, M. J. Jury decision-making as a function of group size and social decision rule. Doctoral dissertation, Ohio State University, 1975.

———. The limits of scientific jury selection. *Jurimetrics Journal*, 1976, *17*, 3–22.

———. *Jury verdicts*. Lexington, Mass.: Heath, 1977.

——— & Hastie, R. *Social psychology in court*. New York: Van Nostrand Reinhold, 1978.

Sampson, E. E., & Brandon, A. C. The effects of role and opinion deviation on small group behavior. *Sociometry*, 1964, *27*, 261–281.

Schank, R. C. The structure of episodes in memory. In D. G. Bobrow & A. Collins, eds. *Representation and understanding: Studies in cognitive science*. New York: Academic Press, 1975.

——— & Abelson, R. *Scripts, plans, goals, and understanding*. Hillsdale, N.J.: Erlbaum, 1977.

Schulman, J., Shaver, P., Colman, R., Emrich, B., & Christie, R. Recipe for a jury. *Psychology Today*, May 1973, pp. 37–83.

Schum, D. A. The weighing of testimony in judicial proceedings from sources having reduced credibility. *Human Factors*, 1975, *17*, 172–182.

———. The behavioral richness of cascaded inference models: Examples in jurisprudence. In N. J. Castellan, D. B. Pisoni, & G. R. Potts, eds. *Cognitive theory*, vol. 2. Hillsdale, N.J.: Erlbaum, 1977.

———. A review of the case against Blaise Pascal and his heirs. *Michigan Law Review*, 1979, *77*, 446–483.

Schutz, W. C. *FIRO: A three dimensional theory of interpersonal behavior*. New York: Rinehart, 1958.

Scroggs, J. R. Penalties for rape as a function of victim provocativeness, damage, and resistance. *Journal of Applied Social Psychology*, 1976, *6*, 360–368.

Sealy, A. P., & Cornish, W. R. Jurors and their verdicts. *Modern Law Review*, 1973a, *36*, 496–508.

——— & Cornish, W. R. Juries and the rules of evidence. *Criminal Law Review*, April 1973b, pp. 208–223.

Searle, J. R. Human communication theory and the philosophy of language: Some remarks. In F. X. Dance, ed. *Human communication theory*. New York: Holt, Rinehart, & Winston, 1967.

———. *Speech acts*. Cambridge: Cambridge University Press, 1969.

———. A taxonomy of illocutionary acts. In K. Gunderson, ed. *Language, mind, and knowledge*. Minneapolis: University of Minnesota Press, 1975.

Shaw, M. & Wright, J. *Scales for the measurement of attitudes*. New York: McGraw-Hill, 1967.

Sherif, M. A. A study of some social factors in perception. *Archives of Psychology,* 1935, *187,* 60.

Silver, D. A case against the use of public opinion polls as an aid in jury selection. *Journal of Computers and Law,* 1978, *6,* 177–195.

Simon, R. J. *The jury and the defense of insanity.* Boston: Little, Brown, 1967.

———. Beyond a reasonable doubt: An experimental attempt at quantification. *Journal of Applied Behavioral Science,* 1970, *6,* 203–209.

——— & Mahan, L. Quantifying burdens of proof. *Law and Society Review,* 1971, *5,* 319–330.

Smoke, W. H., & Zajonc, R. B. On the reliability of group judgments and decisions. In J. J. Criswell, H. Solomon, & P. Suppes, eds. *Mathematical methods in small group processes.* Stanford: Stanford University Press, 1962.

Snedecor, G. W., & Cochran, W. G. *Statistical methods.* Ames: Iowa State University Press, 1980.

Sonquist, J. A. *Multivariate model building: The validation of a search strategy.* Ann Arbor: Survey Research Center, University of Michigan, 1970.

———, Baker, E., & Morgan, J. *Searching for structure.* Ann Arbor: Institute for Social Research, 1973.

Sosis, R. Internal-external control and the perception of responsibility of another for an accident. *Journal of Personality and Social Psychology,* 1974, *30,* 393–399.

Sperlich, P. W. Scientific methods for the selection of trial jurors: Practical and ethical considerations. Paper presented at Western Political Science Association Meeting, Phoenix, 1977.

———. Trial by jury: It may have a future. In P. B. Kurland & G. Casper, eds. *Supreme Court review, 1978.* Chicago: University of Chicago Press, 1979.

———. The case for preserving the jury trial in complex civil litigation. *Judicature,* 1982, *65,* 394–419.

Stasser, G., & Davis, J. H. Opinion change during group discussion. *Personality and Social Psychology Bulletin,* 1977, *3,* 232–256.

———. Group decision making and social influence: A social interaction sequence model. *Psychological Review,* 1981, *88,* 523–551.

———, Kerr, N. L., & Bray, R. N. The social psychology of jury deliberation: Structure, process, and product. In N. L. Kerr & R. M. Bray, eds. *The psychology of the courtroom.* New York: Academic Press, 1982.

Steiner, I. D. *Group process and productivity.* New York: Academic Press, 1972.

Stephan, C. Sex prejudice in jury simulation. *Journal of Psychology,* 1974, *88,* 305–312.

——— & Tully, J. C. The influence of physical attractiveness of a plaintiff on the decisions of simulated jurors. *Journal of Social Psychology,* 1977, *101,* 149–150.

Stephan, F. F., & Mishler, E. G. The distribution of participation in small groups: An exponential approximation. *American Sociological Review,* 1952, *17,* 598–608.

Stoner, J. A. F. A comparison of individual and group decision involving risk. Master's thesis, Massachusetts Institute of Technology, 1961.

Strodtbeck, F. L., & Hook, L. H. The social dimensions of a twelve man jury table. *Sociometry*, 1961, *24*, 397–415.

————, James, R. M., & Hawkins, C. Social status in jury deliberations. *American Sociological Review*, 1957, *22*, 713–718.

———— & Mann, R. D. Sex role differentiation in jury deliberations. *Sociometry*, 1956, *19*, 3–11.

Sue, S., Smith, R., & Caldwell, C. Effects of inadmissible evidence on the decisions of simulated jurors: A moral dilemma. *Journal of Applied Social Psychology*, 1973, *3*, 344–353.

Suggs, D., & Sales, B. D. Using communication cues to evaluate prospective jurors in the voir dire. *Arizona Law Review*, 1978, *20*, 629–642.

Suppes, P. *A probabilistic theory of causality*. Amsterdam: North-Holland, 1970.

———— & Atkinson, R. C. *Markov learning models for multi-person interactions*. Stanford: Stanford University Press, 1960.

Thomas, E. A., & Hogue, A. Apparent weight of evidence, decision criteria, and confidence ratings in juror decision making. *Psychological Review*, 1976, *83*, 442–465.

Thurstone, L. L. The method of paired comparison for social values. *Journal of Abnormal and Social Psychology*, 1927, *21*, 384–400.

Timothy, M. *Jury woman*. Palo Alto: Emty Press, 1974.

Tivnan, E. Jury by trial. *New York Times Magazine*, Nov. 16, 1975, pp. 30–31, 54, 56, 58, 60, 64, 68, 70.

Tukey, J. W. *Exploratory data analysis*. Reading, Mass.: Addison-Wesley, 1977.

Tulving, E. Cue-dependent forgetting. *American Scientist*, 1974, *62* (1), 74–82.

Tversky, A. Assessing uncertainty. *Journal of the Royal Statistical Society-Series B*, 1974, *36*, 148–159.

———— & Kahneman, D. Judgment under uncertainty: Heuristics and biases. *Science*, 1974, *185*, 1124–1131.

Ungar, S. J. The Pentagon papers trial. *Atlantic Monthly*, Nov. 1972, pp. 22–23, 26–28, 30, 32, 34.

Valenti, A. C., & Downing, L. L. Differential effects of jury size on verdicts following deliberation as a function of apparent guilt of the defendant. *Journal of Personality and Social Psychology*, 1975, *32*, 655–663.

Vinokur, A., & Burnstein, E. Depolarization of attitudes in groups. *Journal of Personality and Social Psychology*, 1978, *36*, 872–885.

Vollrath, D. A., & Davis, J. H. Evaluating proposals for social change with minimal data. *Law and Human Behavior*, 1979, *3*, 121–134.

Walker, L., Thibaut, J., & Andreoli, V. Order of presentation at trial. *Yale Law Journal*, 1972, *82*, 216–226.

Webb, E. J., Campbell, D. T., Schwartz, R. D., & Sechrest, L. *Unobtrusive measures: Nonreactive research in the social sciences*. Chicago: Rand McNally, 1966.

Weinreb, L. L. *Criminal process: Cases, comments, questions*. Mineola, N.Y.: Foundation Press, 1978.

Weld, H. P., & Danzig, E. R. A study of the way in which a verdict is reached by a jury. *Journal of American Psychology,* 1940, *53,* 518–536.

——— & Roff, M. A study in the formation of opinion based upon legal evidence. *The American Journal of Psychology,* 1938, *51,* 609–628.

White, A. J., Jr. Selecting the jury. In J. A. Appleman, ed. *Successful jury trials: A symposium.* Indianapolis: Bobbs-Merrill, 1952.

Wiehl, L. L. The six-man jury. *Gonzaga Law Review,* 1968, *4,* 35–44.

Wigmore, J. H. *A student's textbook of the law of evidence.* Mineola, N.Y.: Foundation Press, 1935.

———. *The science of judicial proof.* Boston: Little, Brown, 1937.

Wilson, D. W., & Donnerstein, E. Guilty or not guilty? A look at the "simulated" jury paradigm. *Journal of Applied Social Psychology,* 1977, *2,* 175–190.

Winer, B. J. *Statistical principles in experimental design.* New York: McGraw-Hill, 1971.

Winkler, R. L., & Murphy, A. H. On the generalizability of experimental results. In C-A. Stael Von Holstein, ed. *The concept of probability in psychological experiments.* Dordrecht, Holl.: Reidel, 1974.

Wish, M., D'Andrade, R. G., & Goodnow, J. E. Dimensions of interpersonal communication: Correspondence between structures for speech acts and bipolar scales. *Journal of Personality and Social Psychology,* 1980, *39,* 848–860.

Wolf, S., & Montgomery, D. A. Effects of inadmissible evidence and level of judicial admonishment to disregard on the judgments of mock jurors. *Journal of Applied Social Psychology,* 1977, *7,* 205–219.

Woocher, F. D. Did your eyes deceive you? Expert psychological testimony on the unreliability of eyewitness identification. *Stanford Law Review,* 1977, *29,* 969–1030.

Yale Law Journal. Notes and comments: On instructing deadlocked juries. *Yale Law Journal,* 1968, *78,* 100–142.

Yankelovich, C. Who gets ahead in America? *Psychology Today,* 1979, July, pp. 28; 31; 33–34; 40; 43; 90–91.

Zeisel, H. What determines the amount of argument per juror? *American Sociological Review,* 1963, *28,* 279.

———. Some data on juror attitudes towards capital punishment. Technical Report, Center for Studies in Criminal Justice, University of Chicago Law School, 1968.

———. . . . And then there were none: The diminution of the federal jury. *University of Chicago Law Review,* 1971, *38,* 710–724.

———. The waning of the American jury. *American Bar Association Journal,* 1972, *58,* 367–370.

——— & Diamond, S. S. Convincing empirical evidence on the six-member jury. *University of Chicago Law Review,* 1974, *41,* 281–295.

———. The jury selection in the Mitchell-Stans conspiracy trial. *American Bar Foundation Research Journal,* 1976, *1,* 151–174.

———. The effect of peremptory challenges on jury and verdict: An experiment in a federal district court. *Stanford Law Review,* 1978, *30,* 491–531.

Ziskin, J. *Coping with psychiatric and psychological testimony.* Beverly Hills: Law and Psychology Press, 1975.

Addendum

Mosteller, F., Rourke, R. E. K. *Sturdy statistics.* Reading, Mass.: Addison-Wesley, 1973

Saks, M. J., & Ostrom, T. M. Jury size and consensus requirements: The laws of probability vs. the laws of the land. *Journal of Contemporary Law,* 1975, *1,* 163–173.

Schum, D. A., & Martin, A. W. Formal and empirical research on cascaded inference in judgment. *Law and Society Review,* 1982, *17,* 105–152.

Walbert, D. F. The effect of jury size on the probability of conviction: An evaluation of *Williams v. Florida. Case Western Reserve Law Review,* 1971, *22,* 529–554.

Court Cases

Allen v. United States, 164 U.S. 492 (1896).

Apodaca, Cooper, and Madden, v. Oregon, 406 U.S. 404 (1972).

Baldwin v. New York, 399 U.S. 66 (1970).

Ballew v. Georgia, 435 U.S. 223 (1978).

Beacon Theatres, Inc., v. Westover, 359 U.S. 500 (1959).

Brown v. Board of Education of Topeka, Kansas, 347 U.S. 483 (1954).

Burch v. Louisiana, 99 S.Ct. 1623 (1979).

Capitol Traction Co. v. Hof, 174 U.S. 1 (1899).

Colgrove v. Battin, 413 U.S. 149 (1973).

Commonwealth v. Rodriguez, Mass 300 N.E. 2nd 192 (1973).

Commonwealth v. Tuey, 62 Mass. (8 Cush.) 1 (1851).

Dairy Queen, Inc., v. Wood, 369 U.S. 469 (1962).

Duncan v. Louisiana, 391 U.S. 145 (1968).

Estelle v. Williams, 425 U.S. 501 (1976).

Grigsby v. Mabry, 483 F.Supp. 1372 (E.D., Ark., 1980).

Hovey v. Superior Court of Alameda County, Cal., 616 Pac 2d 1301 (1980).

In re Winship, 397 U.S. 358 (1970).

Johnson v. Louisiana, 406 U.S. 356 (1972).

Kentucky v. Whorton, 444 U.S. 887 (1979).

Maxwell v. Dow, 176 U.S. 581 (1900).

Muller v. Oregon, 208 U.S. 412 (1908).

Ristaino v. Ross, 424 U.S. 589 (1976).

Ross v. Bernard, 396 U.S. 531 (1970).

Swain v. Alabama, 380 U.S. 202 (1965).

Thompson v. Utah, 170 U.S. 343 (1898).

Williams v. Florida, 399 U.S. 78 (1970).

Witherspoon v. Illinois, 391 U.S. 510 (1968).

Name Index

Subject Index